# FINANCIAL PLANNING BASICS *for* DOCTORS

## THE PERSONAL FINANCE COURSE NOT TAUGHT IN MEDICAL SCHOOL

### MARSHALL WEINTRAUB
#### MICHAEL MERRILL | COLE KIMBALL

ARCHWAY
PUBLISHING

Archway Publishing books may be ordered through booksellers or by contacting:

Archway Publishing
1663 Liberty Drive
Bloomington, IN 47403
www.archwaypublishing.com
1 (888) 242-5904

ISBN: 978-1-4808-7211-0 (sc)
ISBN: 978-1-4808-7212-7 (hc)
ISBN: 978-1-4808-7213-4 (e)

Library of Congress Control Number: 2018914115

Print information available on the last page.

Archway Publishing rev. date: 01/24/2019

To our clients, who allow us to share their journey.

And to our families, who support us along the way.

# CONTENTS

# FINITY GROUP STORY

Finity Group, LLC was established in 2011 by twenty individuals with a vision of building a world-class, comprehensive financial-services firm. The happenstance of their paths crossing and them merging into a dynamic group with a common goal is amazing in itself. However, the thousands of families that have benefited from their financial guidance is the most significant outcome of all.

The journey began in 2004, when two of Finity Group's founding members began their careers with a large financial-services firm and formed a joint practice catering to medical professionals in training. The purpose behind partnering was simple: combine strengths to more efficiently market, manage day-to-day operations, and, above all, provide clients with the highest level of service possible. This approach proved to be successful, to the degree that growth outpaced their capacity to handle the volume of clients. For most financial advisors new to the business, this is a problem you dream of having. That was the moment the seeds of Finity Group were planted. The critical need at that time was adding like-minded, service-oriented advisors and staff members with the utmost integrity and professionalism to our team. Over the following few years, we did just that.

As the fall of 2011 approached, it became apparent that our current employer could not support the growth or team model our practice had created. Recognizing this was simultaneously disappointing and exhilarating. We realized we could run a financial firm better than the one we worked for. We could reach and help more of those in need, provide better service and more products, and increase overall client satisfaction. It was the dawn of a new beginning, and Finity (short for "Financial Clarity") Group opened for business.

The lessons learned from that experience and, more importantly, from listening to our clients were clear. Doctors want an advisor knowledgeable in comprehensive financial planning, specifically one who is acutely aware of the unique challenges they face in building a long-term financial plan. Furthermore, they want a relationship with a truly independent advisor, one who will put the client's interest first.

As of 2018, Finity Group's advisors are registered in all fifty states with more than five thousand doctor clients across the country. Our team has over doubled in size since 2011, comprised of the finest men and women you will find in our industry. Finity continues to grow, but one thing will never change: our clients will always come first.

# INTRODUCTION

Welcome to *Financial Planning Basics for Doctors*. As the subtitle references, many doctors do not receive a formal course in planning their finances throughout their medical education. Because of this, they will turn to outside sources to learn about constructing their financial plans. Some of these are excellent, while others may not be geared toward doctors in training or the initial years that follow. This is an important period in the lives of new doctors and their families, as planning in the years leading up to your transition and immediately afterward is instrumental in establishing good habits for long-term financial success. With this in mind, we set out to create a holistic financial planning reference that speaks to the men and women of our medical community.

This book is written with the goal of saving doctors the most precious resource we possess—time. We will examine the purpose of financial planning, the nature of a doctor's financial situation, typical pitfalls, risks doctors face, behavioral finance, and much more. To begin, we must set a baseline understanding of three important questions: What is financial planning? Why is it important? What makes a doctor's financial plan different?

## What is financial planning?

On a basic level, financial planning is the process of using your current and future resources to maintain your desired lifestyle through your career and retirement, as well as prepare for any surprises along the way. This includes decisions that may be difficult to come to, including when you would like the ability to retire and how much you wish to provide for your family if something were to happen to you. The planning process begins with assessing the current state of your assets, debts, income, expenses, spending habits, risk exposures, dependents' needs, economic factors, employment, concerns, and goals.

The last one mentioned—goals—can be thought of as your purpose, financially speaking. What is the purpose behind your monetary decisions? Some readers may have a hard time answering this. Many doctors are not practicing medicine for the money and, if it were up to them, would prefer to work as long as possible, professing their love for the job and helping patients. Others may find it difficult to visualize what impact their financial decisions today will have on their future, and since the future is not here today, planning for later in life is dismissed until another time. In many cases, doctors would like the option to fully retire or scale down to part-time, perhaps staying active in medicine through donating their time to underserved populations. Whatever your goals may be, they will not be accomplished accidentally. Achieving them requires a well-designed outline and intentional effort.

After reviewing your current situation and future goals, you will need to understand the various strategies available to further develop your financial plan. It is easy to wander between options during this stage, potentially losing motivation to fully commit to any one course of action. If you find yourself in this rut, recognize it and take a moment to pause. Pick a strategy that shows the greatest promise to fulfill your goals in a manner consistent with your values. Taking even a small step is better than not moving forward at all. After selecting a strategy, you can now implement, monitor, and periodically revise your plan over time.

Building a comprehensive financial plan is broad in its scope. The most common thought that comes to mind with the term "financial planning" is saving for retirement. This is similar to saying a healthy lifestyle requires exercise, which is true but would be an incomplete description. Financial planning is far more dynamic than just saving for retirement. We will cover retirement planning in depth but will also address many other areas that affect your financial well-being.

These include risk management and debt management strategies, with student loans receiving plenty of attention. This book will also examine tax challenges, home ownership and financing strategies, and college funding for your children, among other subjects.

## Why is financial planning important?

In the past, older generations could rely on employer pensions for a decent amount of their retirement income. Social security was better funded, further providing a source of income for a retirement that often lasted five to fifteen years. These factors, combined with a less complicated financial landscape, resulted in a lower need to plan one's finances ahead of retirement.

Many of these elements have changed since the middle of the last century. Only a small fraction of employers now offer a pension. Of those that do, many of these plans are not adequately funded to pay the promised benefits. Social security, which was never intended to be the primary source of retirement income, is increasingly uncertain for the generations to come. The demographics of what retirement will look like are also changing, with people living much longer than in the past. It will not be uncommon for doctors today, especially those early in their careers, to have at least a twenty-year retirement. With less employer and governmental support, Americans are now increasingly responsible for providing for themselves in retirement. Many will face the very real possibility of outliving their savings if adequate planning is not started well in advance.

In addition to a delayed start to retirement saving, doctors face a number of other factors that complicate their financial plans. Balancing large student loan payments with a home purchase is one example. Unlike other important skills, like how to drive a car, how to effectively manage your finances is usually not something parents teach their children. It is rare for children to have an accurate sense of their parents' incomes, expenses, liabilities, and investments and how these function within their lifestyle. Without much financial background, if any, many doctors begin their student loan balance at age eighteen without a plan to manage this or the large six-figure income they will earn ten to fifteen years later. If we combine these with the lack of financial education most doctors receive in training, we understand why financial planning is not only important, but also why there is such a large need for comprehensive education in the medical community.

**What makes a doctor's financial plan different?**

Remember, for a moment, back to that fateful spring day of your high school senior year. The procession of gown-clad teens followed by an eruption of caps tossed in the air marked a turning point. Until then, you and your cohort took similar classes and shared extracurricular interests. Your lives then began to diverge as some joined the labor force at eighteen, others at twenty-two. Only a few who walked alongside you back then may be wearing white coats with you today. With your educational and occupational life vastly different from the average American, we would not expect your financial life to fall in line with everyone else's either. This is indeed what we find. Longer workweeks and more stressful environments are not the only themes that separate you from non-doctors. Financial differences extend to your training time, student loan balances, and incomes, to name a few.

According to the 2017 US Census Bureau, only 11.4 percent of the population held a graduate or professional degree, with doctors being a subset of this select group. Doctors commonly delay saving for retirement by a decade or more due to their training, yet many would like to retire near the same age as the average American who retires today at sixty-two. This creates a catch-up aspect not required of other careers. In addition to devoting considerable resources for later in life, doctors bear larger student loan burdens and the hefty payments that come with them. The average student loan balance of a graduating doctor is $190,000, which can translate into monthly payments of $2,000 or more. Fortunately, this can be absorbed within the median doctor salaries of $217,000 (primary care) and $316,000 (specialists), representing the top 5 percent of households and nearly four to six times the national average. Higher incomes cause larger tax bills, given the progressive nature of our income tax system. As this sinks in, we realize the financial profile of a doctor could not look further from that of an average household.

**Why write this book?**

Our team is part of the financial planning industry and collectively represents a specialized practice with a clientele of doctors and their families. We understand financial planning is more complicated than ever, and the abundance of literature can cause confusion, particularly if sources take conflicting views or are not geared toward doctors. For these reasons, we feel a responsibility to the medical community to provide this book as an educational resource.

The material that follows is not intended to be specific recommendations but rather serve as a framework you can use to make informed decisions about building your plan. For financial planning enthusiasts, this title may join several others on your crowded bookshelf. Other readers may be taking up this book as their first foray into the financial world. We will not assume you have any background knowledge about planning and will begin each topic with the basics before getting to more advanced details. Regardless of how financially literate you are, we hope all readers are able to take a few ideas away from these pages.

While we aim to provide a thorough summary of many financial planning subjects, we acknowledge there is always more we can include. We welcome questions and appreciate any feedback you have by emailing us at info@thefinitygroup.com.

Without further ado, let's dive in!

# CHAPTER 1

# PERSONAL FINANCE BASICS

ADRIENNE WAS IN her final year of radiology residency when we met to begin planning. Like many of her colleagues, she was eager to prove herself in her post-training position. However, her confidence quickly faded when the discussion turned to her finances.

"I know images inside and out, but I feel overwhelmed when I try to organize my expenses. Honestly, the last thing I want to do after a long shift is see whether I overspent this month. I haven't worked through a budget in years," Adrienne admitted. "How am I expected to be a full-time doctor and know exactly where each part of my paycheck is supposed to go?"

"It can definitely be a lot to handle. If it's any comfort, know that this isn't the first time we've heard this—and it certainly won't be the last. Some doctors in training have described managing their finances like treading water. They can do just enough to stay afloat, but it can be difficult to make any forward progress, especially if you haven't been taught the basics."

"Exactly! And at times if feels like I'm treading water with weights on …"

Some of you may have been able to relate to Adrienne at one point or another. With night shifts, call, and board exams, the demanding lifestyle of a doctor leaves little time and energy to worry about financial chores that can easily be put off until tomorrow. Unfortunately, these chores can become large problems if neglected for too long. This chapter will cover four fundamental areas of financial planning. We will begin by reviewing two primary financial documents, your net worth statement and monthly spending analysis, before reviewing the concepts behind establishing a proper emergency reserve and concluding with how to responsibly use credit cards.

## Building Your Net Worth Statement

It is difficult to know whether you are making financial progress over time without a reliable way to track this. To do this, we use the net worth statement, which lists your assets (what you own) and subtracts your liabilities (what you owe); the difference is your net worth. Yes, for many physicians in training, or shortly out of it, your net worth can be a large negative number. This is normal, and the most common culprit is a line labeled "student loans." This should not be cause for concern, and we prefer to view student loans as proof of the investment you have made in yourself. This document often categorizes assets by their liquidity (how quickly they can be converted to cash) and may divide debts into groups as well, as seen in the following examples.

## Net Worth Statement

| Assets | |
|---|---|

Fixed Assets:
   Checking                                     _____
   Saving                                         _____
                         Total Fixed Assets    _____

Variable Assets:
   Non-Retirement Accounts:
      Mutual Fund Account                   _____
   Retirement Accounts:
      Roth IRA                                 _____
      403(b)                                    _____
                       Total Variable Assets   _____

Personal Assets:
   Home                                      _____
   Auto                                        _____
   Personal Property                      _____
                       Total Personal Assets   _____

                                Total Assets   _____

| Liabilities | |
|---|---|

   Credit Cards                             _____
   Student Loans                         _____
   Mortgage                               _____
   Auto Loan                              _____
                       Total Liabilities   _____

| Net Worth (Assets - Liabilities) | |
|---|---|

You can download a copy of this spreadsheet at
www.TheFinityGroup.com/Net-Worth-Statement.

Your net worth statement can be as simple or as detailed as you would like. Here is Adrienne's net worth statement.

## Net Worth Statement

| Assets | | |
|---|---|---|

**Fixed Assets:**

| | | |
|---|---|---|
| Checking | | $500 |
| Saving | | $6,000 |
| | Total Fixed Assets | $6,500 |

**Variable Assets:**

| | | |
|---|---|---|
| Non-Retirement Accounts: | | |
| Mutual Fund Account | | |
| Retirement Accounts: | | |
| Roth IRA | | $2,000 |
| 403(b) | | $15,000 |
| | Total Variable Assets | $17,000 |

**Personal Assets:**

| | | |
|---|---|---|
| Home | | |
| Auto | | $5,000 |
| Personal Property | | $5,000 |
| | Total Personal Assets | $10,000 |
| | Total Assets | $33,500 |

| Liabilities | | |
|---|---|---|

| | | |
|---|---|---|
| Credit Cards (10% - 20%) | | $8,000 |
| Student Loans (6.80%) | | $200,000 |
| Mortgage | | |
| Auto Loan | | |
| | Total Liabilities | $208,000 |

| Net Worth (Assets - Liabilities) | -$174,500 |
|---|---|

We suggest revisiting your assets and liabilities once a year, at a minimum, to update your financial position. This provides an objective way to quantify your progress over time, as opposed to eyeballing how much your finances are improving by the size of your house or the type of car you drive. Not much change is expected throughout training, but you should begin to see your net worth trend upward in the months and years afterward. At this time, one of the first goals for newly graduated doctors is to pay off credit card balances and build cash in their savings account as an emergency reserve, which is determined by the level of monthly expenses you need to cover in the event of a financial hardship.

## Maintaining a Balanced Monthly Spending Analysis

One of the most important parts of a financial plan is developing a personal cash flow statement, otherwise referred to as a budget. The word "budget" is boring enough to put any well-intentioned doctor to sleep, so we prefer to call this a "monthly spending analysis" instead. This projects the cash flow that will be available for expected activities, support, and maintenance of the household. It will also show how income is allocated among various activities in the past and will serve as a guide to plan for the future.

A prerequisite to completing a monthly spending analysis consists of setting goals and priorities. Goals are what you are trying to achieve financially, which will include some that are of greater importance than others. This is where prioritizing comes into play. After listing goals, you will carefully rank them in order of importance. You might find that your current resources prevent you from achieving all of them. By prioritizing goals, you will gain focus and increase the likelihood of achieving what is most important to you.

There are dozens of software programs designed to help track your spending. Our suggestion is to have this be as simple or as detailed as you would like. If you prefer simple over detailed, then here is an example of what a monthly spending analysis could look like.

## Monthly Spending Analysis

Monthly Take Home

_____

Fixed Expenses
    Mortgage / Rent
    Utilities / Phone / Internet       _____
    Student Loans                   _____
    Auto Loan                       _____
    Gas / Maintenance            _____
    Auto / Home / Umbrella Insurance   _____
    Disability / Life Insurance        _____
    Groceries / Personal Items       _____
    Child Care Expenses           _____
    Other Fixed Expenses          _____

    Total Fixed Expenses

_____

Flexible Expenses
    Entertainment / Dining Out
    Travel / Vacations            _____
    Miscellaneous                 _____

    Total Flexible Expenses

_____

    Total Monthly Expenses (Fixed + Flexible Expenses)

_____

    Disposable Income After All Expenses

_____

You can download a copy of this spreadsheet at
www.TheFinityGroup.com/Monthly-Spending-Analysis.

The first line, monthly take home, is the net cash inflow after contributions to employer pretax retirement plans, taxes withheld, and other expenses taken out of your pay before settling in your bank account, such as health insurance premiums. An easy way to find this number is to look at your paystubs and see what the bottom line is, which is commonly titled "net pay" or some variation of this. If you are paid twice a month, then multiply this number by two to estimate your monthly take home.

The next step is to list all fixed expenses that cannot easily be eliminated or reduced. An example is the cost of your primary residence, which will likely be one of your largest expenses and can potentially consume over half of your take-home income in training. Student loan payments are often another major cost, depending on your balance and repayment method. It is important to have a clear idea of your total fixed expenses because this number will determine the target range of your emergency reserve account.

Your flexible expenses include discretionary spending that is variable from one month to the next or can be easily eliminated or reduced. Some of the more common flexible expenses are entertainment, dining out, and travel. With large flexible costs that are paid in a short period, such as vacations, you can divide the estimated annual cost of this by twelve to get an idea of how much to allocate to your spending on a monthly basis. Adding these to your fixed expenses will result in your total monthly expenses, which is then compared to your monthly take home to determine whether you have a positive or negative cash flow in an average month.

We acknowledge this example does not include costs for future planning, such as contributions to investment accounts in addition to employer retirement plans. We will spend plenty of time on long-term savings in later chapters, but first we want you to get in the habit of tracking your expenses.

Here is Adrienne's spending analysis after going through this exercise.

## Monthly Spending Analysis

| | |
|---|---:|
| Monthly Take Home | $3,500 |
| **Fixed Expenses** | |
| Mortgage / Rent | $1,500 |
| Utilities / Phone / Internet | $200 |
| Student Loans | $400 |
| Auto Loan | $0 |
| Gas / Maintenance | $50 |
| Auto / Home / Umbrella Insurance | $100 |
| Disability / Life Insurance | $100 |
| Groceries / Personal Items | $400 |
| Child Care Expenses | $0 |
| Other Fixed Expenses | $0 |
| Total Fixed Expenses | $2,750 |
| **Flexible Expenses** | |
| Entertainment / Dining Out | $100 |
| Travel / Vacations | $0 |
| Miscellaneous | $100 |
| Total Flexible Expenses | $200 |
| Total Monthly Expenses (Fixed + Flexible Expenses) | $2,950 |
| Disposable Income After All Expenses | $550 |

As we can see, Adrienne does not have much room after her monthly expenses. This is common in training and leaves only a small cushion for unexpected costs. Upon the transition to an attending role, many doctors' incomes will increase between two to ten times what they were earning as a resident or fellow. It is natural for your standard of living to increase in the months after graduation. We support this and certainly do not expect you to spend like a resident forever. The key is to make sure your fixed expenses do not rise to an amount that would prohibit you from achieving your financial goals.

Let's pause for a moment. An observation we have made is that the first twelve months of your post-training position is one of the most crucial periods for developing your financial habits. Common mistakes include rushing into too large of a house, immediately purchasing an expensive car, and splurging on lavish trips. The typical consequence is that savings goals are severely neglected or outright ignored. As soon as you cross the threshold of expanding your lifestyle to the point of not being able to save adequately toward long-term goals, you will have a difficult time reversing course.

One common way to work toward seeking good financial habits as a newly minted doctor is to treat your first year's salary as a practicing doctor as if you merely received a 50 percent pay raise. Circumstances can make this difficult, but most *can* make this happen. You managed to live for the past three to seven years with an income equal to two-thirds of this hypothetical 50 percent pay raise, so it should still feel like an improved lifestyle. Meanwhile, you will actually be living well below your means with a substantial amount of disposable income to address your growing list of financial goals.

You will be amazed at what you can accomplish during this experimental transition year. You will enter practice with an expansive list of competing financial goals, all of which you can likely accomplish if you live well below your means. Immediate goals might include paying off credit cards and other high-interest-rate debt, building an adequate emergency fund, saving for a home down payment, replacing your 1999 Honda Civic, taking a vacation that does not require sleeping in a tent, and paying back parents for financial support they provided during your training years. If this sounds familiar, there is good reason. These are some of the most frequently mentioned short-term financial goals we hear from graduating residents and fellows.

For doctors already in practice, working through a monthly spending analysis may be a sobering experience as to how much money you truly have to plan with. Hopefully you have a large positive number for disposable monthly income that can be applied to retirement savings and other goals. If your disposable income is lower than desired, you may need to consider making changes to your spending. Larger expenses are typically more difficult to reduce than small ones. We suggest beginning by listing all expenses that occur in a typical month. Next, add categories of savings goals (retirement, college for children, etc.) before prioritizing each item. You can then decide which expenses are first to be reduced or eliminated, such as those that serve little to no purpose toward your livelihood or happiness.

## Maintaining a Proper Emergency Reserve Account

Many people are familiar with the concept of having money set aside in a rainy-day fund for unexpected costs that come up from time to time. We call this an emergency reserve account, and it allows you to pay for unforeseen expenses with cash on hand rather than accruing a balance on a credit card that may not be paid off for months. Two questions on this topic are:

1.  How much money should I have set aside for emergencies?
2.  Where should I keep this money?

A good rule of thumb for the size of your emergency fund is three to six months of fixed expenses. In Adrienne's case, she would aim to maintain an emergency reserve of $8,250 to $16,500 based on her monthly fixed expenses of $2,750. Where you fall within this range depends on your personal comfort level and backup sources of income and assets. For example, if you have a spouse who works, other cash on hand (such as savings for a home purchase), or a decent balance in a non-retirement account, then it may make sense to be closer to the three-month level of fixed expenses. It may make sense to be closer to the six-month end of this range if you are the sole income earner or do not have access to readily available backups.

Some sources of personal finance literature claim you should hold a full year's worth of fixed expenses for your emergency reserve. While this does not harm your financial plan, it may be unnecessary. The excess cash held in your bank account may earn an interest rate less than the rate of inflation, which means the purchasing power of this balance is being eroded over time due to the rising cost of living. Your emergency reserve is simply an amount of cash set aside, earning a minimal amount of interest until it is needed, to avoid creating a balance on your credit card from an unexpected cost. In the meantime, you can apply the extra cash to other areas of your plan that may be more productive, such as paying down your debts faster. We will cover this concept of opportunity cost in more detail in the Debt Management chapter. We have three criteria your emergency reserve fund should satisfy: it should be safe, liquid, and free.

"Safe" in this context means that your funds should not have any risk of losing value. For example, we would not recommend having the cash earmarked for your emergency reserve invested in the stock market, due to the unpredictable short-term fluctuations the market can experience. You may need to access this at any time, so it would be inconvenient to find you have less than needed because your investment decreased in value. We would instead suggest holding your emergency reserves in an interest-bearing, FDIC-insured bank savings account.[1] This ensures your rainy-day fund will be available in its entirety.

"Liquid" as it relates to emergency reserves means this money is easily accessible as cash or a cash equivalent. You may need several thousand dollars within a few days depending on the nature of the unexpected cost, which rules out the use of certificates of deposit. CDs are banking products that provide an interest rate slightly higher than a regular savings account. These are offered in certain dollar increments and mature in a few months to a few years from the date they are established. In the meantime, you generally cannot access the money in your CD without forfeiting the interest earned and possibly paying fees. This lack of accessibility is why CDs may not be the most appropriate choice for your rainy-day fund. Instead, we recommend holding your emergency reserve fund in a savings account that is linked to your checking account or has similar bill-paying capabilities.

"Free" for emergency reserves means exactly how it sounds. Your emergency fund should not cost you a penny. No monthly maintenance

---

[1] FDIC insured means the account is protected against loss by the Federal Deposit Insurance Corporation up to $250,000 per person per bank.

fees, minimum balance penalty fees, or any other ancillary fee to access your money.

Checking and savings accounts at traditional banks usually satisfy all three of these criteria. The downside of these accounts is the interest rates they offer are quite low. While this money should be easily accessible, it does not need to be held in a bank within walking distance. Online high-interest savings accounts are a common alternative, as these accounts tend to offer interest rates 0.5% to 1.0% higher than a traditional bank's savings account. As you will hopefully not be accessing this account frequently, it will be nice to earn a higher rate of interest on this balance in the meantime. Bankrate.com is a good resource to search for online high-interest savings accounts with banks across the country.

## Responsible Use of Credit Cards

Credit is an essential part of our economy. To put this into perspective, there is about $3 trillion of cash in the US economy, and the total amount of credit is estimated at $50 trillion. If the use of credit were to cease, our economy would revert to a cash-only system, and large purchases, such as a home, would be out of reach for most people. Credit cards allow the convenient purchase of goods and services now, with the ability to pay later when you settle your credit card balance. They are also required to rent a car and reserve a hotel room. In addition, they help build your credit score, which lenders use to assess your creditworthiness for new loans. This is important for other parts of your financial plan, such as qualifying for a mortgage. However, credit cards can severely damage your financial plan if they are not used responsibly.

Appropriate use of credit cards includes making monthly purchases and on-time payments. It is generally beneficial to have two or three cards, assuming you are disciplined with paying your balances in full each month and have no problem limiting credit card use to within your means. Your credit score is partially based on the number of lines of credit you have, so having two or three cards will help your credit score more than a single card. This does not need to be complicated. For example, you may have one card you use only for gas and groceries and another card you use for all other credit purchases. It can be also helpful to call your credit card company (or bank if you go through them for your credit card) to increase your credit limit on each card once a year. If you are looking to open a new card, then the website Cardratings.com can be a good resource to review your options and screen for certain benefits, such as cash back or travel rewards.

For every positive reason to use a credit card, there are negatives that are akin to many aspects of life where moderation is key. Detrimental credit card use includes missing payments, frequent opening and closing of cards, having large outstanding balances that are accruing interest, and multiple balance transfers between cards. As missed payments will lower your credit score, it can be helpful to set up your bank account to automatically pay the minimum due on each credit card every month so your credit score is not hurt if you forget to pay the balance in full. Your credit score will also be temporarily lowered each time you open or close a card. This is why we recommend sticking with two or three cards and not changing these unless needed. If you will be applying for a new loan or to refinance an existing loan soon, you will want to treat your credit score with care and not open or close any cards in the months leading up to your application.

Some readers may have heard that it is beneficial to carry an outstanding balance on your credit cards, which is actually not true and is harmful for a couple of reasons. First, interest will accrue on the unpaid balance, so it will cost more in the long term when you get around to paying this down. Your score will also be lowered if you are using a large percent of your available credit, known as your credit utilization, when your score is checked. For the best chance of a favorable credit score, you will generally want to keep the total balance on your credit cards below 30 percent of your total available credit limit. For example, if the total amount you could charge to all of your credit cards is $10,000, then you will want to avoid having a balance of more than $3,000 among all of your cards at a time. This is one reason why it can make sense to increase the limits on your cards annually—to allow a greater amount to be held on your cards before lowering your score.

At this point in our conversation, Adrienne looked away and wore a guilty expression.

"I'm afraid I have not been the best with my credit cards. I have quite a few cards with standing balances. A lot of this is from medical school that I haven't been able to pay off since then. I'm not sure of my exact payment history, but I probably miss a payment a couple of times a year. My credit is a mess."

We agree with Adrienne that there is room for improvement. The good news is that there are a couple of strategies we can use to clean up her credit situation. The first and simplest way to pay off your credit cards is to set up each one with automatic payments from your bank account to cover the minimum payment, and then allocate any extra money toward the one with the highest interest rate. Once the highest interest rate card is fully paid off, then allocate those payments to the next highest card and so on.

If you would like to minimize the interest you pay in the meantime, then another option is to consolidate your outstanding balances to fewer cards through balance transfers. This is exactly as it sounds; you are transferring the balance of one or more cards to a new or existing card. The receiving card may offer a starting teaser rate, often 0 percent, for twelve to eighteen months. After that time, it is common to see the rate adjust to 15 percent, 20 percent, or higher. Keep in mind if you open a new card to transfer your balance to, this will temporarily lower your credit score, so it is not wise to rely on frequent balance transfers as a long-term solution. If you do consolidate, then it can be helpful to shred and throw away the cards you have transferred the balance away from so they do not begin to accrue new balances, but also be careful about closing cards. This will usually result in reducing the average length of credit history on your active cards, resulting in a temporary reduction in your credit score. The benefits of this process include simplifying your situation and providing breathing room to pay off your balance aggressively while the interest is put on hold.

"That sounds like a good strategy. It also sounds complicated and, to be honest, I would never get around to doing this. Is there an easier way?" Adrianne replied.

Another option to remedy the credit situation for someone like Adrienne is to follow these steps:

1. Set up automatic payments from your checking or savings account to each credit card to cover the minimum due every month. This will help avoid missing future payments.
2. Pick two or three cards to keep in your wallet. Place all other cards in a drawer to be cut and discarded.
3. Each month, pick the card that is charging the highest rate of interest and pay as much as you can.
4. Keep paying the balance of the first card until it is paid off. Then move on to the card with the next highest interest rate. Repeat until all balances are paid in full.

You may have noticed that we did not add a row for credit card payments in Adrienne's spending analysis. This is because we do not want to accept this as a part of her usual spending. It generally makes sense to pay a credit card balance off as soon as possible with your disposable income. If you are worried your regular spending will consume all of your income before extra credit card payments, then we suggest increasing your payment from your bank account to the card you are currently targeting to automate this as much as possible. Another strategy is to take any lump sums of cash you are expecting, such as a tax refund or signing bonus, and apply this directly to your credit cards. A good resource to monitor your credit and learn to improve your credit score is CreditKarma.com. Their mobile app is user friendly and full of advice on improving your credit score.

**Chapter Summary**

Your financial plan begins with an honest assessment of your income, expenses, assets, and liabilities. These are captured in your net worth statement and monthly spending analysis. Maintaining an emergency reserve fund for unexpected costs and responsibly using your credit cards contribute to setting the foundation for a successful plan. You may have heard the expression about "needing to learn how to walk before you can run." This chapter has outlined four of the key "walking" steps to be learned before mastering the intermediate steps in the following sections.

### Key Takeaways

Your *net worth statement* provides a snapshot of your current financial situation by listing your assets and liabilities. The difference is your net worth. Periodically updating this document is one way to track your financial progress over time.

Your monthly cash flow is broken down into specific line items in your *spending analysis*, which can highlight areas where you may be able to reduce your expenses.

Due to the unpredictability of life, it is advisable to have an *emergency reserve fund* of three to six months of fixed costs saved in an account that is safe, liquid, and free, to act as a buffer against incurring a balance on your credit cards.

Responsibly using two or three *credit cards* will improve your credit score, which is a key component lenders use when assessing your creditworthiness for taking out a loan. Using these cards regularly and paying them off in full each month will contribute to an excellent credit score.

# CHAPTER 2

# TAX BASICS

HAVING TAKEN A few tax courses in college, the authors should know better than to include "Tax" and "Basics" in the same line. The Internal Revenue Code is a four-million-word beast that is constantly evolving, as seen with the recent adoption of the Tax Cuts and Jobs Act passed by Congress in December 2017.[1] Nevertheless, we will do what we can to make the focus of this chapter—income and capital gain taxes—as digestible as possible. Apart from filing your tax return in April, taxes are rarely a stand-alone topic. Instead, they are usually a side effect resulting from actions taken in other areas of planning, ranging from the sale of your home to retirement account distributions to estate planning. The next few pages will cover how income and capital gain taxes function. We will then apply these rules through the remainder of the book.

Please keep in mind the authors are not tax professionals and recommend consulting with one for specific tax advice.[2] Many of

---

[1] To give this some context, the Internal Revenue Code is about four times the number of words in all seven Harry Potter books combined, and nowhere near as enjoyable.

[2] Any accounting, business, or tax advice contained in this book is not intended as a thorough, in-depth analysis of specific issues, nor a substitute for a formal opinion, nor is it sufficient to avoid tax-related penalties.

the numbers that follow, such as tax rates and contribution limits to retirement plans, relate to the 2018 tax year, and we expect these to change over time.

## Income Taxes

April 15 is known as Tax Day. The weeks leading up to this are characterized by repetitive commercials for tax preparation software and finding mild-mannered accountants stressed about the looming deadline. We begin our peek into income taxes with the main parts of a tax return before seeing how our income tax system is both progressive and marginal in nature.

### Filing Status

The first step in filing your income tax return, Form 1040, is determining which of the four filing statuses you will use:

1. *Single.* You will likely file as single if you were not married on the last day of the year (December 31).
2. *Married Filing Jointly.* It is almost always beneficial for married couples to file their taxes jointly; however, in some very limited cases, it can make sense to file separately (to have lower student loan payments under certain income-driven repayment methods, for example).
3. *Married Filing Separately.* Spouses who wish to keep their finances apart may choose to file their taxes separately. Filing separately can result in lower student loan payments if you are on income-based repayment or pay-as-you-earn, though it may increase the amount of taxes you owe compared to filing jointly.
4. *Head of Household.* This status may be used for unmarried individuals who provide qualifying support for another person.

*Gross Income (Total Income)*

Once you have determined a filing status, the next step is to report your income. The IRS has a broad definition of gross income, including but not limited to:

- wages or salaries
- taxable interest
- dividends[1]
- capital gains
- IRA distributions
- business income
- income from rental real estate, royalties, partnerships, S Corporations, or trusts

Collectively, these categories are referred to as "ordinary income," apart from long-term capital gains, which we will get to shortly. If you have economically benefitted from work, investments, or another income source, you can bet the Internal Revenue Service will most likely tax you on it. Just in case they missed anything, the IRS states that "generally, you must report all income except income that is exempt from tax by law." Salaried employees will receive Form W-2 from their employer to report their salary for the year. Investment documents will generally be mailed by the administrating firm to the account owner in January or February to provide details on any taxable events throughout the year.

*Adjustments (Above-the-Line Deductions)*

After compiling all income items, the IRS allows for adjustments to be made for items, such as pretax retirement plan contributions. If your employer offers a retirement plan like a 401(k) or 403(b), then you can defer up to $18,500 of your salary into this account on a pretax basis and deduct this from your gross income. Contributions to traditional IRAs are also tax deductible if your income is below certain

---

[1] Qualified dividends are tax at long-term capital gains tax rates.

thresholds or if you do not have access to an employer retirement plan. Contributions to health savings accounts and flexible spending accounts also qualify for a tax deduction, which will be covered in more detail in the Health Insurance, HSAs, and FSAs chapter. Self-employed taxpayers have greater flexibility here, as they can deduct their health insurance premiums and half of what they pay in self-employment tax. They also have additional retirement account options, such as a solo 401(k), and can deduct up to $55,000 into these accounts—$18,500 made as the employee and $36,500 made as the employer. The much-appreciated student loan interest deduction is also subtracted from gross income. However, there is a good chance your post-training income will be too high to take this $2,500 deduction. There are additional adjustments, though these are less common, so we will skip them.

### Adjusted Gross Income (AGI)

Collectively, these adjustments are known as above-the-line deductions and subtracting them from your gross income results in adjusted gross income, also known as "The Line" in tax lingo. Your AGI is an important number because it determines your eligibility for other tax deductions, such as how much of a deduction you can take for charitable contributions. It is also the income number used to calculate your monthly student loan payments under income-driven repayment methods, which include income-based repayment, pay-as-you-earn, revised pay-as-you-earn, and income-contingent repayment. The lower your AGI, the lower your student loan payments will be.

A related number is your modified adjusted gross income, or MAGI. Your AGI is increased to arrive at MAGI by adding tax-exempt interest received through the year, as well as amounts initially excluded from gross income, like foreign-earned income. AGI and MAGI will be the same for many people. Like your AGI, your MAGI determines eligibility for other items, such as whether you can take the student loan interest tax deduction or make contributions to a Roth IRA.[1]

*Standard Deduction versus Itemized Deductions (Below-the-Line Deductions)*

We now have a choice to make with your below-the-line deductions: should you take the standard deduction or itemize your deductions? Most taxpayers automatically qualify for a standard deduction of $12,000 for single filers or $24,000 if you are married and file jointly. You will compare this to your itemized deductions, and if they are larger, then you will elect to itemize your deductions in lieu of taking the standard deduction, as this will lower your tax bill. If you itemize, then your deductions will be listed on Schedule A and include but not be limited to:

- qualified mortgage interest (You can deduct the amount of interest paid on up to $750,000 of loans used to acquire your primary residence and one other home. Interest paid on a refinanced mortgage qualifies as well.)
- property taxes
- either state and local income taxes or sales tax (up to $10,000 total when combined with property taxes)
- charitable contributions (to the extent allowed by the type of contribution and your AGI)
- medical expenses above certain thresholds (7.5 percent of AGI in 2018, 10 percent of AGI afterward)

If your itemized deductions exceed your standard deduction, then your tax liability will be lower by itemizing your deductions. If not, then it will be beneficial to take the standard deduction.

You may be familiar with personal exemptions and miscellaneous

---

[1] Taxable conversions from pretax retirement accounts to Roth (post-tax) accounts are included in your adjusted gross income and taxable income but not your modified adjusted gross income. As a result, a taxable conversion will not affect your ability to contribute to a Roth IRA.

itemized deductions, which further lower your income before you arrive at taxable income. The 2017 Tax Cuts and Jobs Act repealed personal exemptions and miscellaneous itemized deductions through 2025.

### Taxable Income and Tax Liability

After that, we input your taxable income into the tax brackets to determine your tax liability. The 2018 federal income tax brackets for each income level are listed as follows.

**2018 Federal Income Tax Brackets**

| Tax Rate | Married Filing Joint | | | Single | | |
|----------|------|------|------|------|------|------|
| 10% | $0 | to | $19,050 | $0 | to | $9,525 |
| 12% | $19,050 | to | $77,400 | $9,525 | to | $38,700 |
| 22% | $77,400 | to | $165,000 | $38,700 | to | $82,500 |
| 24% | $165,000 | to | $315,000 | $82,500 | to | $157,500 |
| 32% | $315,000 | to | $400,000 | $157,500 | to | $200,000 |
| 35% | $400,000 | to | $600,000 | $200,000 | to | $500,000 |
| 37% | $600,000 | to | No Limit | $500,000 | to | No Limit |

We notice a couple of things here. First, our federal income tax rates are progressive in the sense that the rates increase as your income does. This places a larger tax burden on higher income earners. Second, our tax system is marginal in nature, meaning only the incremental income above the lower tax bracket is taxed at the new higher rate, not all prior income. This is seen in the staircase-like graph illustrating how much income falls into each tax bracket for a couple filing their taxes jointly with $700,000 of taxable income.

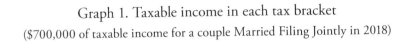

Graph 1. Taxable income in each tax bracket
($700,000 of taxable income for a couple Married Filing Jointly in 2018)

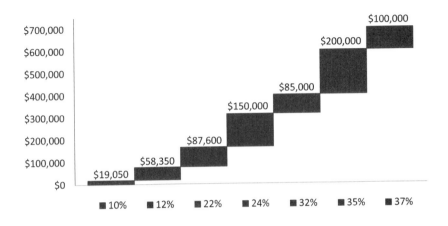

Even though this couple is in the 37 percent tax bracket, only a small portion of their income is actually taxed at their highest marginal rate. The first $19,050 is taxed at 10 percent, the next $58,350 taxed at 12 percent, and so on. Your marginal income tax rate indicates the tax effect of additional income earned or deducted. If this couple in the 37 percent tax bracket earned another $100, then they can expect to pay $37 more in taxes. The same logic applies to tax deductions. If this couple deducted another $100 from their income, it would save them $37 in taxes.

We then multiply the amount of taxable income in each bracket by its tax rate and add the results to arrive at your federal income tax.[1] This couple would have approximately $198,379 in taxes to be paid before adding other taxes and subtracting tax credits. Self-employed taxpayers would add self-employment taxes. This is also where you would pay

---

[1] The Qualified Dividends and Capital Gain Tax Worksheet in the Form 1040 Instructions shows the calculation of removing qualified dividends and long-term capital gains from taxable income. This ensures your remaining taxable income is taxed at ordinary income rates, while dividends and capital gains are taxed at their lower rates (more on this in the next section). The result is listed on Line 44 on Form 1040. Tax preparation software should do this for you.

household employment tax if you hired a nanny or other domestic employee and paid them over $2,000 during the year.[1]

## Tax Credits

Unlike deductions, which lower your taxable income, tax credits are direct dollar-for-dollar reductions in taxes owed and are therefore more beneficial than a tax deduction of the equivalent amount. These include credits for education and dependent care expenses, as well as the child tax credit of $2,000 per child. Although personal exemptions are no longer available, the December 2017 tax bill increased the child tax credit and expanded eligibility for high-income earners to claim this credit. Residential energy credits are also becoming more common as homeowners install solar panels and other energy-efficient upgrades, though there are limits to these items. Many tax credits are subject to income phaseouts, so individuals and families with high incomes may not be able to claim the full amount, or potentially any, of certain credits.

## Tax Owed or Refunded

We now arrive at your total tax—the total amount of tax owed. Your employer should be withholding estimated taxes throughout the year, which will be indicated on your Form W-2. If you earn income as a 1099 worker (self-employed or independent contractor) instead of as a W-2 employee, then you are responsible for making quarterly estimated tax payments, as you do not have an employer to withhold taxes for you. Either way, the amount already paid is hopefully close to your actual tax liability, so reconciling the difference does not result in a large tax bill or refund. That's it, another tax season behind you!

Your tax return will generally be due on April 15, unless the fifteenth falls on a weekend or holiday. If so, then Tax Day will be pushed into the following business day. If you need additional time to complete your return, you can file an extension to be granted six more months to file

---

[1] There is also a quarterly threshold amount to this number, which is lower than the annual amount.

your return. However, this extension does not delay the date when your tax payment is due.

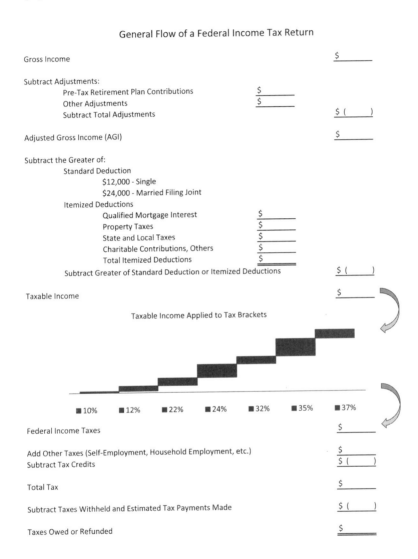

General Flow of a Federal Income Tax Return

Gross Income                                                     $ _____

Subtract Adjustments:
    Pre-Tax Retirement Plan Contributions        $ _____
    Other Adjustments                            $ _____
    Subtract Total Adjustments                                   $ ( _____ )

Adjusted Gross Income (AGI)                                     $ _____

Subtract the Greater of:
    Standard Deduction
        $12,000 - Single
        $24,000 - Married Filing Joint
    Itemized Deductions
        Qualified Mortgage Interest        $ _____
        Property Taxes                     $ _____
        State and Local Taxes              $ _____
        Charitable Contributions, Others   $ _____
        Total Itemized Deductions          $ _____
    Subtract Greater of Standard Deduction or Itemized Deductions   $ ( _____ )

Taxable Income                                                  $ _____

Taxable Income Applied to Tax Brackets

■10%    ■12%    ■22%    ■24%    ■32%    ■35%    ■37%

Federal Income Taxes                                           $ _____

Add Other Taxes (Self-Employment, Household Employment, etc.)   $ _____
Subtract Tax Credits                                           $ ( _____ )

Total Tax                                                      $ _____

Subtract Taxes Withheld and Estimated Tax Payments Made         $ ( _____ )

Taxes Owed or Refunded                                         $ _____

## Alternative Minimum Tax

In addition to the regular income tax formula, there is an alternative system that ensures high earners with a large amount of deductions pay at least a minimum amount of tax, sensibly called the alternative minimum tax, or AMT. However, do not mistake "alternative" to mean you have a choice. If your income and deductions result in you paying a higher amount of tax with the AMT calculation, then you must use the alternative minimum tax. Further details on the AMT are beyond the scope of this book, but be aware that you may be subject to it. Your tax preparation software or accountant should alert you if the alternative minimum tax applies to your tax return.

### State and Local Taxes

So far, we have ignored state income taxes apart from using them as an itemized deduction. Most states have a state income tax, and while a few have a flat tax rate system, the majority of these have a marginal tax bracket system similar to the federal income tax calculation. Florida is a commonly referenced state without an income tax, and for good reason. Its many retirees are drawn not only to its warm weather but also to the lack of state income tax benefitting their retirement distributions that would be taxed in other states. The Tax Cuts and Jobs Act limited the amount of state and local taxes that taxpayers can deduct from their federal income. Taxpayers can now only deduct up to $10,000 of state and local taxes when combined with property taxes. If your state does not have a state income tax, then the $10,000 cap applies to property taxes combined with the actual amount of sales tax paid.

### If Tax Rates Seem High Now ...

We previously mentioned the tax code is constantly evolving, though this may not be apparent from year to year. If we look back to 1913 when the federal income tax was created, we see that today's highest income tax rate of 37 percent is historically low compared to what it has been for much of the past eighty years.

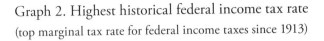

Graph 2. Highest historical federal income tax rate
(top marginal tax rate for federal income taxes since 1913)

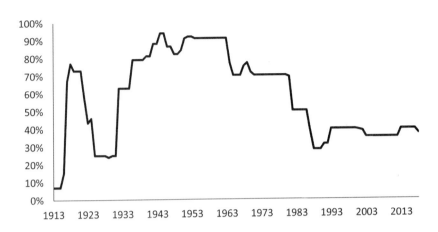

Keep in mind this graph shows only the highest marginal rate and not the rates of lower tax brackets, nor the dollar amounts needed to reach each bracket. Because of this, a quick glance may be misleading. We need a different metric to measure how much tax we are paying now compared to past years. Instead of focusing on the highest marginal rate, we turn our attention to effective tax rates. You can think of your effective tax rate as your average tax rate weighted by the dollar amount in each tax bracket. Put another way, it is your total income tax divided by your gross income. Our couple in the previous example had taxable income of $700,000 after their deductions and exemptions. Let's say their gross income before these subtractions was $750,000. If they did not have any credits or other taxes, then their total income tax of $198,379 divided by their $750,000 of gross income leads to an effective tax rate of 26.5 percent, far lower than their highest marginal rate of 37 percent, due to much of their income being taxed at lower rates.

How do effective tax rates today compare to those in the past?

Favorably for most Americans. Effective tax rates for the lowest 80 percent of income earners are about 3 percent lower than their trailing thirty-five-year average according to a Congressional Budget

Office report. However, most doctors are in the top 5 percent to 10 percent of earners, if not the top 1 percent. The CBO report paints a different picture for households in the top quintile. Those in the 81 to 99 percentile of income earners saw an effective tax rate of 23.2 percent in 2013, only slightly lower than the 23.8 percent average over the past thirty-five years. Households in the top 1 percent were the only demographic with 2013 effective tax rates above their thirty-five-year average. Their effective tax rate of 34 percent was 3.4 percent higher than their average rate over the past three and half decades. While this is helpful to see where rates have been, it does not give us much indication where effective tax rates may be going over the next thirty-five years. We will have to wait to see how economic, political, and social pressures influence new tax legislation.

## Capital Gain Taxes

With income taxes in our rearview mirror, we turn our attention to capital gains tax, which are levied on the gain on the sale of a capital asset. What qualifies as a capital asset? Assets held for investment are a common example, such as shares of stock or mutual funds.[1] Partnership interests and properties are also capital assets. The first step in calculating a capital gain is to determine the asset's *basis*, roughly defined as how much you paid to acquire it. The asset's basis may be adjusted up or down from certain items, such as depreciation claimed on a property or a step up in basis due to death of the property owner. We also expect the asset's value to change over time, hopefully in a positive direction, though you do not owe taxes on the gain until you dispose of the asset. Let's walk through an example to see this in action.

You recently purchased two shares of stock (units of ownership) in a large, publicly traded coffee company for sixty dollars apiece. Over the next eleven months, the company's sales exceed expectations, and

---

[1] A mutual fund is a collection of individual securities pooled together and managed as a portfolio by the portfolio manager and his or her team of analysts and traders.

its stock price increases to eighty dollars. You now have a twenty-dollar gain on each of your shares, though this is an *unrealized* gain because you have not yet sold your shares. They have simply appreciated in price, but there has not yet been a taxable event to trigger payment of tax. Pleased with this performance, you sell one of your shares and continue holding the other. This action realizes the twenty-dollar gain in the share sold and creates a taxable event, resulting in capital gain taxes being owed. How much? This depends on your holding period. Your eleven-month holding period causes this gain to be treated as a *short-term* capital gain, which is taxed at your highest marginal income tax rate. This can be as high as 37 percent, resulting in $7.40 of capital gain tax to be paid. Another month goes by, and the price of your remaining share appreciates to ninety dollars before you sell it a few days after your holding period passes twelve months, realizing a thirty-dollar *long-term* capital gain. Long-term capital gains are currently taxed at the following rates, depending on your income tax bracket:

- 0 percent for taxpayers in the 10 percent and 12 percent tax brackets
- 15 percent for taxpayers in the 22 percent, 24 percent, 32 percent, and 35 percent tax brackets
- 20 percent when taxable income reaches $425,801 (single taxpayers) or $479,001 (married filing joint)[1]

Long-term capital gain tax rates have also varied over time, though not quite as much as income tax rates.

---

[1] These dollar amounts are adjusted annually for inflation after 2018.

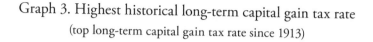

Graph 3. Highest historical long-term capital gain tax rate
(top long-term capital gain tax rate since 1913)

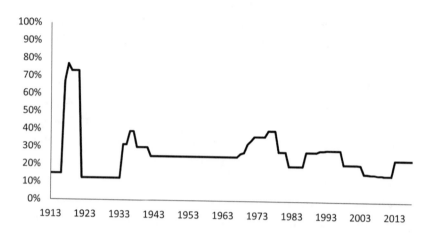

Single taxpayers with income over $200,000 and married taxpayers filing jointly above $250,000 will pay an additional 3.8 percent tax on their net investment income above these thresholds, which includes realized capital gains (with income defined as the taxpayer's MAGI). Your thirty-dollar long-term capital gain could therefore result in as little as zero dollars in taxes but will more likely be taxed at 15 percent, 18.8 percent, or 23.8 percent, resulting in $4.50, $5.64, or $7.14 in taxes. It is generally beneficial to avoid creating short-term capital gains and instead delay realizing the capital gain until it is long-term for the lower tax rates.

In addition to the normal function of capital gain taxes, there are a few rules that can help you avoid paying capital gain taxes entirely.

*Exemption on the Sale of Your Home*

Your home is a capital asset, so appreciation of its value and subsequent sale could cause you to realize a capital gain, potentially a large one. Section 121 of the Internal Revenue Code provides an exclusion for the gain realized on the sale of your primary residence. If you have lived in your home as your primary residence for two out of the last five years, then you can exclude $250,000 of gain from the sale. Married taxpayers can each claim the exclusion, avoiding taxes on up to $500,000 of gain. Keeping your previous home as a rental property is one example of where this can be applicable. Once you have been a landlord for over three years, then you will have no longer lived in the property as your primary residence for at least two out of the past five years and will not be able to claim the exclusion when you sell.

*Step up in Basis upon Death*

If a relative or friend were to pass away and leave a capital asset to you, then its basis will be adjusted to fair market value at the date of death.[1] This will usually result in the inherited asset's basis being "stepped up," eliminating any unrealized gain that accrued before death. For example, if your uncle had a non-retirement investment account with holdings valued at $30,000 and basis of $10,000 when he passed away, the basis would be stepped up to $30,000. You could then sell all investments in the account for $30,000 and not pay any capital gain taxes.[2]

*Capital Losses*

While capital assets often appreciate, they can also decrease in value resulting in a capital loss if you sell for less than its basis. This is certainly not the goal with investing, but is sometimes unavoidable. The silver lining is that you can use realized capital losses to offset capital gains to reduce your tax bill. If your capital losses exceed your capital gains for the year, then you can use $3,000 of excess capital loss to lower your taxable income and pay less in ordinary income tax. Any additional capital loss is carried forward to offset future capital gains and ordinary income until it is fully exhausted. One caveat is that capital losses from personal assets, such as the sale of your primary residence or car, cannot be used to offset capital gains or income.

---

[1] Or six months later if the alternative estate valuation date is elected.

[2] Different rules apply if the asset is jointly owned, the deceased lived in a community property state, or if the asset counts as income in respect to a decedent, such as an annuity.

## Chapter Summary

The Internal Revenue Code is, for better or worse, much more complicated than our cursory overview. For now, an understanding of the ordinary income and capital gain tax basics outlined in this chapter will suffice. We will revisit these concepts and build upon them in the upcoming sections. We must also remember that the tax code is a living document, continually being molded by new legislation offered by Congress and influenced by the prevailing political parties. This was demonstrated with the 2017 Tax Cuts and Jobs Act, called the largest tax overhaul in thirty years. To complicate matters, some of these updates are permanent changes, while others expire after 2025. Rules that seem commonplace today have by no means been around forever. Roth IRAs—a staple in retirement planning—only came into existence in 1997. It is unrealistic to think today's tax rules will remain the same throughout your career and into retirement. Though we do not know what new laws will arise, we can at least anticipate a changing tax landscape in the decades to come.

### Key Takeaways

Calculating your ordinary income tax begins by defining your filing status, then reducing your gross income by deductions and exemptions to arrive at your taxable income. Your taxable income is run through the tax brackets and their respective rates to determine your federal income tax owed. Our income tax system is *marginal in nature*, meaning only the incremental amount of income that exceeds the lower tax bracket's upper limit is taxed at the new higher rate, not all previous income.

The *alternative minimum tax* is a separate income tax formula designed to prevent taxpayers with a large amount of deductions from having a low effective tax rate.

Compared to tax rates in the past, our highest marginal rate today is relatively low. Your *effective tax rate* is the average rate at which you pay taxes at, weighted by how much income is taxed in each bracket. Current effective tax rates are slightly below their thirty-five-year average for households earning in the top 20 percent of Americans, though are above average for the top 1 percent.

*Capital gain taxes* are assessed on realized capital gains. Long-term capital gain rates have historically been lower than ordinary income tax rates.

*You are allowed to exclude $250,000 of capital gain from the sale of your home* if you have lived in it as your primary residence for at least two out of the last five years. If you are married, then your spouse is allowed to exclude an additional $250,000 of gain.

Most inherited capital assets qualify to receive a *step up in basis* to their fair market value, eliminating any capital gain if they are sold immediately afterward.

After being netted against capital gains, remaining *capital losses* then reduce ordinary income by $3,000 each year. They are carried forward indefinitely and used to offset future capital gains and ordinary income until the entire capital loss has been exhausted.

The Internal Revenue Code has changed significantly since the federal income tax originated in 1913. We expect it to continue to evolve in the years ahead.

# CHAPTER 3

# DEBT MANAGEMENT

BECOMING A DOCTOR often results in a significant amount of debt taken on, usually in the form of student loans and credit card balances. Auto loans and home mortgages are other common debts to acquire in training or soon afterward. These liabilities come with different balances, interest rates, and repayment terms, making it difficult to prioritize which debts should be paid off first and how this fits within your overall financial plan. This chapter will cover a few rules of thumb with regard to efficiently managing debts. We will then expand on these concepts in the following sections that focus on student loans and home buying.

To start, let's establish a uniform understanding of the term *debt*. Although *Merriam-Webster* defines debt as an amount of money you owe to a person, bank, company, or other entity, we can also express the meaning of debt as: borrowing an amount of money from your future self to access money now, knowing you will have to pay back a sum greater than the amount borrowed.

If we use the latter meaning of debt, we can view taking on debt as a method of accelerating your spending beyond a level your current income and assets allow. Lenders stand ready to provide this capital, though not without a cost.

## The Role of Interest

Interest is a fundamental part of our economy, and most people are familiar with it in one form or another. It may be the interest you pay on your student loans or mortgage, or the interest received on the balance in your savings account. What is it and how does it work? The idea behind interest is that it is more desirable to have money you can use now than money you cannot use until a future point in time. After all, you can use the ten-dollar bill in your pocket to buy a sandwich right now, but the deli will likely not accept your promise to pay ten dollars next year as payment. Our economy is full of people and businesses that have capital but do not need to use it at the moment, and other people and businesses that need capital and are willing to pay a price to have it now instead of later. This price is expressed as interest. When you take out a mortgage to buy your home, your payments back to the bank are part repayments of the principal loan balance and part interest that the bank charges you for using their capital. The same idea applies to the interest you earn on your savings account. You are not currently spending this balance, so you allow the bank to use it in their lending operations, and in return, they pay you interest on the balance deposited. Apart from a few rare debts that carry a 0 percent interest rate, all other debts will charge you interest for the use of this balance.

## Opportunity Cost

Opportunity cost is a term used in economics to mean tradeoffs with limited resources, such as time or money. Formally, opportunity cost is the cost of the most beneficial alternative that was not chosen because a different option is pursued. When you choose to use your resources to do option A, you are giving up the opportunity to pursue option B and the economic benefit that comes with it. For example, going to medical school for four years meant that you gave up the opportunity to join the labor force and earn an income during that period. As it relates to debt repayment, the concept of opportunity cost quantifies how much each debt costs to hold on to. For example, a credit card balance of

$1,000 with an annual interest rate of 20 percent will result in $200 of interest that will accrue after a year (ignoring the compounding effects of interest charged monthly in this example). An auto loan of $1,000 with a 4 percent interest rate will generate only $40 in interest over a year. One way to think of these debts is that the credit card balance is a more expensive debt to have than the auto loan. Interest is accruing faster on the credit card than auto loan, so it is a more efficient use of your money to aggressively pay off the 20 percent credit card than the 4 percent auto loan.

From an interest-minimization standpoint, the most efficient way to pay down multiple debts is to rank them by their after-tax interest rates and pay the minimum due on all of them, except one—the debt with the highest rate—and pay extra on this one to accelerate its repayment.[1] Once this debt is paid off, then apply the amount you were paying on the original highest-rate debt toward the balance with the next highest rate, and so forth. Mathematically, this will minimize the total amount of interest paid over the life of all your debts. This strategy has us considering the opportunity cost of each debt.

**What about the Balance?**

Some sources of personal finance literature claim the best way to pay off multiple debts is by ranking them by balance and paying extra toward the debt with the smallest balance first, then the next smallest balance, and so forth. While it is natural to have some emotional satisfaction when a debt is completely paid off, this method is less efficient than paying debts in order of interest rate and will result in paying more interest over the life of all loans. Let's use a simple example to see this in action:

---

[1] The after-tax interest rate for debts with tax-deductible interest is the stated interest rate multiplied by (1 − highest marginal income tax rate). For example, if the stated interest rate on a home mortgage is 4 percent and the borrower's highest marginal income tax rate is 24 percent, then the after-tax interest rate is 4% x (1 − 24%) = 3.04%. For debts whose interest is not tax deductible, such as credit cards, the after-tax interest rate is simply the stated interest rate.

- Credit card balance of $10,000 with a 20 percent interest rate and minimum monthly payment of $300.
- Auto loan balance of $6,000 with a 4 percent interest rate and minimum monthly payment of $300.
- In addition to the two minimum monthly payments of $300, you are also paying $400 extra each month toward one of these debts

First, let's see in the following table how much interest you would pay if we prioritized your debts by balance and applied the extra $400 payment toward the 4 percent auto loan first. The following table shows the payment schedule with this strategy, which includes interest being accrued as each debt is paid off.

Table 1: Extra payments applied toward auto loan

| Month | Auto Loan (4%) | Credit Card (20%) |
|---|---|---|
| 1 – 8 | $700 | $300 |
| 9 | $498 | $502 |
| 10 – 18 | $0 | $1,000 |
| 19 | $0 | $261 |

The first eight months have you applying the extra $400 toward the auto loan. By the ninth month, the auto loan is fully paid off, and you begin paying the full $1,000 toward your credit card balance from months ten through eighteen. Both debts are paid off after nineteen months with $2,260.67 in total interest paid in this example. Now let's see how much interest you would pay if we prioritized your debts by interest rate and applied the extra $400 payment toward the 20 percent credit card first.

Table 2: Extra payments applied toward credit card

| Month | Credit Card (20%) | Auto Loan (4%) |
|-------|-------------------|----------------|
| 1 – 16 | $700 | $300 |
| 17 | $318 | $682 |
| 18 | $0 | $731 |

The second scenario has you applying the extra $400 each month toward the credit card balance through sixteen months until it is paid off at the start of the seventeenth month. It then only takes you another month to pay off the rest of the auto loan. The total interest paid in this example is $1,730.96 over eighteen months. You would save $529.71 by paying off these debts in order of interest rate rather than by balance because you are giving less time for the credit card to accrue interest at 20 percent.

**The 7 Percent Rule**

In addition to paying off their debt balances, another goal many doctors have early in their careers is to increase contributions to their long-term savings plan. Retirement planning is often put on hold while in training, so there is some catch-up to do. This book devotes several chapters on retirement and investment planning, but we want to revisit the concept of opportunity cost as we coordinate this with your debt management plan. The question to ask is, What "cost" am I incurring by paying down my debts aggressively and forgoing the opportunity to invest for retirement?

We know to quantify the cost of debts by their interest rates, but how do we quantify investing for retirement? This is trickier because we do not know what return you will earn on your investments. Though a simplistic way of thinking, one way to estimate the potential benefit of investing is to look at what you could have earned historically based on returns in the past. The eighty-year period from 1937 through 2017 saw the US stock market, measured by the S&P 500 Index, have an average annual return of 11.9 percent per year.[1] Keep in mind that past performance does not indicate future returns, and 11.9 percent is an average, with returns being much higher and lower in some years. This at least gives us a basic idea of the returns you may be giving up by not investing in the stock market and instead allocating your resources elsewhere.

We prefer to be conservative in our assumptions and future projections, which leads us to a concept we call the 7 percent rule, given that annual stock market returns have averaged 7 percent to 9 percent over certain time periods. This rule helps differentiate between "good debts" below 7 percent and "bad debts" above 7 percent. Good debts commonly include mortgages and student loans, both of which are appropriate uses of borrowing. Bad debts include consumer debts, such as credit card balances. The 7 percent rule advises we aggressively pay off debts with an interest rate above 7 percent before investing in the stock market, while debts below 7 percent should be balanced among other priorities in your financial plan, such as saving for retirement and building an emergency reserve account.

If your debt with the highest interest rate is at 4 percent and if you expect the return on an investment in the stock market will average greater than 7 percent per year, then the opportunity cost of aggressively paying down your debt at the expense of not investing in the market would be the difference of 3 percent. In this example, it would be beneficial to pay the minimum on your debt and instead use your cash to invest in the stock market, potentially earning significantly more over the long term. On the other hand, it would be advantageous to aggressively pay down the balance of your credit card with a 20 percent interest rate in lieu of investing in the stock market because we would not expect the stock market to provide a return consistently greater than 20 percent.

---

[1] Standard & Poor's 500 Index is an index of about five hundred large US company stocks and is a commonly used benchmark for the US stock market. Indices mentioned are unmanaged and cannot be invested into directly.

One area of managing debts we have not yet discussed is the emotional side. We understand some people may be more comfortable with having debt than others. If you happen to be the type who cannot stomach the thought of owing money to anyone, regardless of the cost of borrowing, then you can consider ignoring the opportunity cost and should work toward paying off debts below 7 percent quicker than their minimum payments. This is okay as long as you understand the consequence of this may be delaying your retirement date or needing to save a higher percent of your income toward retirement.

**Chapter Summary**

Debt will be a significant part of most doctors' financial plans, particularly early in their careers, so it is important to use efficient repayment strategies. The concepts of opportunity cost and the 7 percent rule help organize which debts should be paid off aggressively and which should be balanced with other areas of your plan. The following debt-related chapters will turn the focus to student loans and home buying.

---

**Key Takeaways**

The *cost of borrowing* is expressed as interest. Lenders charge you interest on the amount of the principal balance borrowed for you to accelerate your spending and pay for items your income and assets cannot currently afford (paying for medical school or a home with your cash on hand as examples).

As we turn to paying off your debts, we consider the *opportunity cost* of doing so: what alternatives (and their financial benefits) are you giving up by applying your limited resources to paying down one of your debts instead?

---

We define efficient debt management as the strategy that minimizes the total amount of interest paid among all debts. This is done by *focusing on the interest rate*, rather than the balance, of each debt and prioritizing repayment in order from highest interest rate debt to lowest.

As we look outside of debts and into other areas of your financial plan, we use the *7 percent rule* to separate higher interest rate debts that should be aggressively repaid from lower interest rate debts that we want to balance with saving for retirement and other goals.

# CHAPTER 4

# STUDENT LOANS

MICHAEL HAD RECENTLY started his internal medicine residency, and student loans were his top concern. He wanted to know which repayment method to select when the grace period for his medical school loans was over.

"Some of my colleagues suggested one of the options with payments based on my income to allow my loans to be forgiven, but I'm not sure if my career path will qualify me for this program. I plan to do a fellowship, but after that, I'm not sure how I would like to practice," Michael explained.

Student loans can be one of the more difficult pieces of your financial plan, not because they are very complicated but because how to best repay them depends on several factors that may not be clear today or even for a few years. One of these factors is your post-training employer, as Michael mentioned. In addition, student loan repayment methods are subject to future legislative proposals. As of 2018, there is serious debate in Congress about changing the income-driven repayment methods and the public service loan forgiveness program. We suggest visiting StudentLoans.gov for current information.

"I have $180,000 in student loans at 6.80 percent. I have also received flyers from private lenders offering to refinance my loans to a lower interest rate. I'm not sure which repayment method is the best fit for me now and will also keep my options open in the future. All of this is causing me a fair amount of stress …"

We understand where Michael is coming from. Many doctors have expressed similar feelings, especially those recently out of school. His loan balance is the size of a small mortgage, and it will be around for several years. With that said, let us consider a few things:

- First, the average student loan balance of a doctor recently graduated from medical school is around $190,000. While Michael's balance seems like a large number, and it is, he is right where many of his peers are.
- Second, whenever you are feeling stressed about your loans, we would encourage you to remember *why* you took these out. Your student loans paid for your medical education so you could become a doctor and do what you love. Working in a white coat would likely have been impossible without them.
- As a young, poor medical student, you made a promise with your future, not-so-poor attending self to pay for your education. Your attending self agreed to give $180,000 of income, plus interest, to your student self so you could practice medicine and have a comfortable lifestyle. In return, your student self agreed to work hard through medical school and residency to earn your attending position. Your student self is halfway through your end of the deal. Once you finish training, it will be time for your attending self to pay off your student loans.
- While you do not know exactly where your career path will lead or what future repayment options may develop, we do know your current options with their benefits and drawbacks.

The path to becoming a doctor is not an easy one. This coveted title is earned after undergraduate college, medical school, residency, and possibly fellowship—the first eight of these years often financed by student loans. They can have a positive impact by allowing you to pursue a career in medicine and earn a high income. In this regard, student loans can be one of the best investments you will ever make. However, they can also burden your financial plan more than necessary if not properly handled. This chapter will begin by providing an overview of student loans and the types of loans available. We will then compare repayment methods and their pros and cons before concluding with common questions and how loans affect your overall financial plan.

## Student Loan Overview

Across America, there are over $1.5 trillion of student loans outstanding, making student loans the second largest type of personal debt owed only behind mortgages. Student loans commonly rank near the top when young doctors list their main financial goals and concerns. Approximately 75 percent of doctors who graduated medical school in 2017 owed student loans, and of those who did, 83 percent of graduates had balances over $100,000. As mentioned previously, the median student loan balance for a graduating medical student is around $190,000. If you have more than this, you are in good company; half of your peers do too. According to the College Board, the average tuition for a year of undergraduate education at different college types for the 2016–2017 school year was:

- $9,650 at public universities for in-state students
- $24,930 at public universities for out-of-state students
- $33,480 at private universities

Average tuition for a year of medical education was:

- $31,202 at public medical schools for in-state students
- $55,040 at public medical schools for out-of-state students
- $52,558 at private medical schools

If we multiply these numbers by four to obtain the cost of each degree, we see how the cost of education quickly rises.

### Table 1. Average cost of undergraduate,
### medical, and combined degrees (2017)
(four years of each undergraduate and medical school education)

| Public, In State | Public, Out of State | Private |
|---|---|---|
| Cost of Undergraduate Degree | | |
| $38,600 | $99,720 | $133,920 |
| Cost of Medical Degree | | |
| $124,808 | $220,160 | $210,232 |
| Cost of Combined Degrees | | |
| $163,408 | $319,880 | $344,152 |

In today's world, the cost of becoming a doctor can be estimated between $160,000 and $350,000 in tuition alone. Room and board costs are estimated at another $10,000 to $15,000 per year. Your student loan balance may be lower than this range if you received family support, scholarships, or worked through college. However, if we add general living expenses, interview expenses, and, for some, the cost of providing for a family in training, we can see how many doctors have student loan balances in excess of this. If you are on the higher end of this range, do not feel alone; many of your peers owe similar amounts.

It is important to acknowledge this as an intentional decision to allow you to pursue a career in medicine. Do you remember how hard you worked to get here? Remember those hours in organic chemistry and studying for the MCAT, medical school applications and interviews? There were countless times when you could have given up, and many of your undergraduate peers did, but you did not. You persevered. You survived the cut! We encourage you to view your student loans like a badge of honor.

With that said, we imagine they are a badge you would prefer to not wear forever, so let's talk about getting rid of them.

## Types of Student Loans

Before we analyze loan repayment methods, we must first understand the various types of student loans, as this determines which repayment options they qualify for. The two broad categories student loans fall into are federal and private. In general, federal loans offer the most flexibility among repayment choices. Private loans are a whole different animal. Keep in mind the student loan landscape is always evolving, and the specific details of each loan type, such as the interest rate, may have changed since publication.

### *Federal Loans*

Federal loans are usually the majority of a doctor's balance, unless they have been refinanced with a private lender (more on this later). The three main types of federal student loans are Perkins, Stafford, and PLUS loans. The two most notable differences between these are the interest rate and repayment options available.

As of 2017, newly issued Perkins loans carry an interest rate of 5.00 percent, and interest does not accrue until you begin repayment. You must demonstrate financial need to receive a Perkins loan. One caveat with Perkins loans is that you may need to consolidate them with another loan to allow them to be eligible for certain repayment methods.

Stafford loans are the most common type of federal loan we come across. Borrowers who took Stafford loans between 2006 and 2013 carry balances at 6.80 percent, though Stafford loans issued in recent years offer slightly lower interest rates for new borrowers. Borrowers may receive a 0.25 percent reduction in their interest rate if they make automatic monthly payments. Stafford loans differ by how interest accrues or does not accrue while in school and training. If a loan is *subsidized*, then no interest is charged before a loan is in repayment (technically the government pays the interest charge while in training, but it has the effect of interest not accruing). If a loan is *unsubsidized*, then interest will accrue immediately, and capitalize annually, adding to the original loan balance.

PLUS (Parent Loan for Undergraduate Students) loans carry the highest interest rate at 6.84 percent for new borrowers, though we often see rates between 7.5 percent and 8.5 percent for balances originated in the recent past. Interest continues to accrue on PLUS loans while in school or training. One word of caution regarding PLUS loans is the difference between PLUS loans for graduate students and PLUS loans for parents. Graduate PLUS loans are eligible for income-based repayment and public service loan forgiveness, while parent PLUS loans are not. If parent PLUS loans are consolidated with other loans, then the entire new loan balance will be ineligible for public service loan forgiveness (more on this in the next few pages). It is generally not advisable to consolidate parent PLUS loans with other loan balances because of this.

Primary care loans (PCLs) are a fourth, less common type of federal loan. If you are practicing or intend to practice in primary care and can demonstrate financial need, then you may have taken out primary care loans. PCLs currently carry an interest rate of 5.00 percent, and the interest does not accrue while in training, similar to Perkins loans. However, unlike Perkins loans, PCLs cannot be consolidated and are not eligible for income-based repayment or public service loan forgiveness. More information can be found online at the Health Resources and Services Administration (HRSA) website by searching for primary care loans.

*Private Loans*

We categorize any nonfederal loans as private loans for simplicity, though we would like to point out that these loans are diverse, and some share characteristics closer to federal loans than other private loans. The main types of nonfederal student loans are those issued by private lenders (such as banks) and those directly provided by teaching institutions, both undergraduate and graduate. Loans taken out from universities may allow for full or partial forgiveness if the borrower provides their services in the state for a period of time, commonly in states with rural or underserved populations.

In general, two of the main factors to consider with private loans are the interest rate and the level of required payments, as both will affect your cash flow and ability to pay off other debts. While federal loans have fixed interest rates, private loans often have interest rates that are variable. These rates are commonly tied to an interest rate benchmark, such as the bank's prime rate, plus one or two percentage points, and will fluctuate with the current interest rate environment. Payment requirements can also vary among private loans. They may require no payments in training, monthly payments, or a different frequency, such as one payment per quarter.

## Student Loan Repayment Methods

"Finally, the part I've been waiting for. Which repayment method should I choose?" asked Michael.

Before doctors commit to a plan, you first need to understand your available options. There are two general ways you will become free of your student loans—repayment and forgiveness.

- Repayment is similar to paying off other debts, such as a mortgage. There is an original loan balance, or principal, that is charging you interest. You determine the term length over how long you wish to pay off your balance, and the lender inputs the term, current loan balance, including any interest that has been capitalized (added to loan balance), and interest rate into an amortization table. This produces a schedule for how much you will pay each month to completely pay off the current loan balance and all interest charged over the life of the loan.

- Forgiveness is preferable to repaying them; however, not all doctors or all loans are eligible for loan forgiveness. There are several programs that may fully or partially forgive your loan balance that have become popular in recent years. According to the Association of American Medical Colleges, nearly half (46 percent) of recent medical school graduates were planning to enroll in one of the loan forgiveness programs.

One of the key factors in determining which repayment option is most appropriate is how you choose to practice and your employer's classification.

### Deferment

Deferment means you are deferring, or delaying, payments on your student loans until a later date because of additional training. No payments are due and no interest accrues on subsidized loans; however, interest continues to accrue on unsubsidized loans. Deferment as a longer-term option throughout training is now rarely offered with federal Stafford loans, which has largely been changed to forbearance for borrowers who do not make payments in training.

Michael's monthly payment under deferment would be zero dollars.

### Forbearance

Borrowers who elect to go on forbearance for their student loans also do not make payments while in training, but interest continues to accrue on all loan balances (subsidized and unsubsidized). Forbearance is allowed for a financial hardship, and most physicians in training easily qualify for this. If you had to begin normal monthly payments on your large loan balance while earning a typical resident salary, you would likely have a difficult time paying general living expenses. It can make sense to go on forbearance if you have other debts that take priority, such as a credit card balance with a higher interest rate, or are unable to make payments on one of the other options. Borrowers can deduct up to $2,500 of student loan interest paid; however, this would not be available under forbearance as the borrower avoids making any payments. Once your forbearance or deferment period is over, then you must select one of the following repayment methods.

Michael's monthly payment under forbearance would be zero dollars.

## Standard Ten-Year

You can think of the standard ten-year repayment term as being similar to a fifteen-year fixed mortgage. These level payments are a function of the loan balance, interest rate, and repayment term. Your lender will use these factors as inputs to create an amortization table of 120 equal payments, with each payment being part interest and part principal. The majority of the early payments are used to pay interest, with a small portion being applied to reduce the loan balance. Over time, the principal is decreased and generates less interest, resulting in a larger portion of each payment applying toward the principal.

With a balance of $180,000 at 6.80 percent, Michael's estimated monthly payment under the standard ten-year repayment option would be about $2,071.

## Extended Twenty-Five-Year

If the standard ten-year option is similar to a fifteen-year mortgage, then the extended twenty-five-year repayment plan is similar to a thirty-year fixed mortgage. The concept is the same as the standard ten-year option—loan balance, interest rate, term, and fixed payments—but each payment is lower because the repayment term is stretched over a longer period. The extended twenty-five-year option will result in more interest being paid over the life of the loan, but you can make additional payments above the minimum without penalty.

Michael's estimated monthly payment under the extended twenty-five-year repayment option is about $1,249.

## Graduated

With graduated repayment, payments begin low and gradually increase over a ten- to twenty-five-year period. While the initial low payments can be appealing, borrowers should be aware of the higher payments in later years, which may conflict with other goals within your financial plan.

Michael's estimated monthly payment under the ten-year graduated repayment option would begin at around $1,195 and eventually increase to around $3,585.

*Refinance with a Private Lender*

If you do not plan to have your loans forgiven through the public service loan forgiveness program (covered in the following section) or another loan forgiveness plan, then your goal should be to pay the least amount of interest possible on your student loans while balancing this with other priorities. One option that has become popular is refinancing your federal loans to a lower interest rate with a private lender. For example, Michael's $180,000 balance at 6.80 percent paid over ten years results in payments around $2,071 a month and total interest of about $68,573. If he were to refinance to a fixed rate of 4.50 percent over ten years, then his monthly payments would fall to $1,865 with total interest paid being $43,859, saving $24,714 in interest over the life of his loan.

Refinancing to a lower rate can be beneficial, but there are a few catches when changing federal loans to private loans. First, private loans are not eligible for public service loan forgiveness, so you would be giving up the opportunity to take advantage of this program. The government is generally more flexible with going onto forbearance if you experience a financial hardship, whereas a private lender could send you to collections if you are unable to make the monthly payment. Most private lenders also require you to start paying your loan immediately, which may not be realistic for a physician in training. If you find yourself in this situation, you might consider limiting the private lenders you are considering to the ones that allow minimal payments during residency and fellowship.

It is important to carefully weigh the pros and cons of refinancing your federal loans before moving forward with this irrevocable decision. If there is even a small chance you may benefit from public service loan forgiveness, then it may be beneficial to keep your options open by not refinancing until your career plans are more established.

The methods we have covered so far relate to the first way of eliminating your student loan balance—repayment. The payment options that follow list the ways your loan balance may be forgiven.

## Public Service Loan Forgiveness (PSLF)

Public service loan forgiveness (PSLF) is not a repayment method itself but a result of several of the following repayment options that are dependent on your income, known as income-driven repayment (IDR) options, or the standard ten-year repayment. Under PSLF, your eligible loans are forgiven after 120 qualifying monthly payments while working in qualifying employment.

### Eligible Loans

Only federal Direct Loans are eligible for PSLF (Direct Stafford, Direct Grad PLUS, or consolidated Direct Loans). Private, state, parent PLUS, Perkins, and Federal Family Education Loans (FFEL) are not eligible to be forgiven under this program. FFEL and Perkins loans may be consolidated into a Direct Loan to become eligible for PSLF. If you need to consolidate your Perkins and FFEL loans into a Direct Loan, you can do this at www.studentloans.gov. However, one stipulation to be aware of is that any qualifying PSLF payments already made on Direct Loans will not count toward loan forgiveness for the new Direct Consolidation Loan. For this reason, consolidating existing Direct Loans with non-Direct Loans may not be beneficial, as you would have to restart your PSLF payments on this new balance. Parent PLUS loans would not be eligible even if they were to be consolidated with Direct Loans, as the resulting loan would be entirely ineligible. You are also unable to consolidate a private loan into a federal loan. A good resource to see how your federal student loans are classified is the National Student Loan Data System (NSLDS) at www.nslds.ed.gov.

### Qualifying Payments

Your 120 qualifying monthly payments do not need to be consecutive but do need to be made under a qualifying repayment plan after October 1, 2007. They must be made in full and on time; otherwise they will not count toward the 120 needed for forgiveness.

Qualifying repayment plans include:[1]

- Income-Contingent Repayment (ICR)
- Income-Based Repayment (IBR)
- Pay As You Earn (PAYE)
- Revised Pay As You Earn (REPAYE)
- standard ten-year

Repayment plans that do not qualify for PSLF include:

- extended twenty-five-year
- graduated repayment (unless monthly payments under a graduated method are at least equal to the standard ten-year payment amount)

*Qualifying Employment*

Your employment is another factor in determining eligibility for PSLF. The government-provided Public Service Loan Forgiveness Employment Certification Form defines an eligible employer as:

> A qualifying organization is a Federal, State, or local government agency, entity, or organization or a tax-exempt organization under Section 501(c)(3) of the Internal Revenue Code (IRC). Service in an AmeriCorps or Peace Corps position is also qualifying employment.
>
> A private not-for-profit organization that is not a tax-exempt organization under Section 501(c)(3) of the IRC may be a qualifying organization if it provides certain specified public services.

---

[1] Payments under another repayment plan may also qualify for the public service loan forgiveness program as long as your monthly payment is at least the amount of the standard ten-year payment.

Public health services are one of the "certain specified public services" listed. Most teaching hospitals qualify as PSLF eligible employers from their 501(c)(3) tax-exempt status. Your eligibility after training will depend on whether you stay with a qualified employer. If you work for a qualified employer and plan to take advantage of PSLF, we would encourage you to clarify how your employment is actually defined. Some hospitals consist of both a nonprofit 501(c)(3) entity and a for-profit entity. If this is the case, then you will want to check which organization pays your salary. If you are paid fully or partially from the for-profit entity, then your employment may not qualify for PSLF. Qualifying employment includes working full-time, defined as an average of at least thirty hours per week.

"That must be the forgiveness program my colleagues were talking about. They also mentioned that this program may be eliminated in the future. Is that true?" Michael asked.

There are rumors that some congressional budgets have proposed reducing or eliminating public service loan forgiveness. However, as of the date of this book being published, nothing has been decided yet. For doctors who plan to take advantage of PSLF but suspect the government may cap or cut the program, one alternative is to continue making the minimum payments to qualify for PSLF and also make additional contributions to a savings or investment account. If PSLF is not available at the end of the 120th payment, then they can use the funds saved in the meantime to make a lump sum contribution toward their loan balance.

"Ten years is a long time to know how I may be practicing medicine. Can you tell me more about the repayment methods that would allow my payments to qualify for PSLF?"

Qualifying repayment plans fall into two types—the standard ten-year we talked about earlier and the income-driven repayment options. To take full advantage of PSLF, you will want to pay as little as possible through your 120 payments to leave the largest balance left to be forgiven. As the standard ten-year repayment will result in the loan balance being fully repaid by the 120th payment, the income-driven repayment options are the best choice when planning on PSLF. The similarities of these options include …

*Similarities among Income-Driven Repayment (IDR) Options*

There are several similarities among the four forms of IDR, including:

- *Payments based on discretionary income.* For all forms of income-driven repayment, discretionary income is defined as your adjusted gross income (AGI) minus 150 percent of the poverty level for your family size. You must recertify your repayment method each year by documenting your income, marriage and tax filing status, and family size. The recertification process will recalculate your monthly payment for the following year.
- *Spouse's income considered.* Your spouse's income is also included in the payment calculation if you are married and file your taxes jointly. However, your spouse's income will not be considered if you file your taxes separately (for all IDR plans other than REPAYE). This can be more complicated in community property states.
- *Forgiveness after twenty or twenty-five years.* In addition to qualifying for PSLF, all forms of income-driven repayment result in any remaining balance being forgiven after twenty or twenty-five years of payments (depending on the repayment plan) if you do not work for a PSLF-qualifying employer. This amount forgiven at the end of the twenty- or twenty-five-year period will be taxable as income, whereas the balance discharged under PSLF will not be taxed.

In addition to our summary of the four IDR plans, a good resource for information on these is the list of frequently asked questions provided by Federal Student Aid (part of the US Department of Education) at StudentAid.gov.

## Income-Contingent Repayment (ICR)

Income-contingent repayment is the oldest form of income-driven repayment. ICR payments are calculated as 20 percent of your discretionary income. ICR is generally not selected anymore, as other IDR options allow for lower payments based on lower percentages of discretionary income. There is also no cap on what ICR payments may rise to when your income adjusts after training, whereas other forms of IDR limit your payments to what they would be under the standard ten-year repayment term based on when you enrolled in IBR or PAYE.

| | |
|---|---|
| Payments calculated as: | 20 percent of your discretionary income |
| Treatment of spouse's income: | Included in calculation if file taxes jointly<br>Not included if file taxes separately |
| Cap on monthly payment: | None |
| Balance forgiven (if not PSLF): | After twenty-five years |

Assuming Michael is single and did not work during his last year of medical school, his initial monthly payment under ICR would be zero dollars if he filed for ICR at the start of his intern year. His payments under ICR will increase over the years as Michael recertifies at higher income levels.

## Income-Based Repayment (IBR)

The first upgrade to income-contingent repayment came as income-based repayment. One improvement to IBR included decreasing payments to 15 percent of discretionary income. Unlike ICR, IBR requires an initial eligibility requirement to enroll, which is simply having your calculated IBR payment be less than what payments would be under the standard ten-year repayment method. Most doctors in training satisfy this. Once you are in IBR, then your income no longer matters in determining your eligibility when you recertify; it only serves to determine your payment amount, but you cannot become ineligible for IBR due to your income increasing. If your income is high enough, IBR will cap payments at the standard ten-year repayment level calculated when the borrower enrolled in IBR. This limit has the effect of accruing a balance to be forgiven for PSLF, with the accrued balance being the difference between the standard ten-year repayment level and the amount paid below the standard ten-year amount (often far below this while in training).

| | |
|---|---|
| Payments calculated as: | 15 percent of discretionary income (if not a new borrower) 10 percent of discretionary income for new borrowers (new borrowers did not have an outstanding student loan balance when they took out a Direct Loan on or after July 1, 2014) |
| Treatment of spouse's income: | Included in calculation if file taxes jointly Not included if file taxes separately |
| Cap on monthly payment: | Capped at the payment amount under the standard ten-year plan, based on loan balance and interest rates when enrolled in IBR |
| Balance forgiven (if not PSLF): | Twenty-five years (not new borrowers) Twenty years (new borrowers) |

For example, let's say Michael enrolled in IBR when he started residency and his monthly payments were based on his income during his last year of medical school, which was zero dollars. His monthly IBR payments will be zero dollars for his intern year. We previously calculated his monthly payment under the standard ten-year repayment level to be $2,071. Each month that Michael "pays" zero dollars that

counts as a qualified payment for PSLF, another $2,071 is accrued that
will not have to be repaid if Michael realizes loan forgiveness after 120
months due to the cap on what payments could rise to. Once IBR has
adjusted to his income of $55,000 for a full year as a resident, then his
estimated monthly IBR payment would be about $460, still far below
the standard ten-year rate.

Let's fast-forward to when Michael is in practice and his income is
high enough so his IBR payment hits the monthly cap at the standard
ten-year level. Michael has been making his lower IBR payments through
residency and his three-year fellowship, so he only has four additional
years of IBR payments before the balance is forgiven by PSLF. At the
beginning of the seventh year, his payments will be capped at the amount
he would pay under the standard ten-year method, based on the amount
owed when he entered IBR ($2,071 a month). If the balance will be
forgiven in four years, then the amount forgiven is the remaining balance
and interest that will accrue minus the next forty-eight payments at
$2,071 a month. Said another way, Michael will pay approximately
$99,429 over the next four years, and his loan balance at the end of that
period will be forgiven.

If you are going to take advantage of PSLF, then the goal is to pay
as little as possible leading up to your 120th qualifying payment. It is
therefore advantageous to begin IBR (or one of the other IDR plans)
as early in training as possible. If Michael had entered IBR a year after
he started his residency, then he may still benefit from having his loans
forgiven, but he would have paid a higher total amount over ten years
and have had less forgiven at the end. This is because he will have to pay
an additional twelve payments of $2,071 a month based on his attending
income rather than his initial twelve payments of zero dollars as an
intern. *If you are recently out of medical school or early in your training
and are considering taking advantage of public service loan forgiveness, then
it is generally in your best interest to enroll in an income-driven repayment
option as soon as possible to start your 120 payments at a low income level.*

"I also heard something about a new version of IBR. Can you tell
me more about this?"

There are two forms of income-based repayment, depending on when you took out your loans. The new type of IBR, called "IBR for new borrowers," is available to borrowers who did not have any outstanding Direct or FFEL loans when they took out a new Direct Loan on or after July 1, 2014. One update for new borrowers is a lower monthly payment at 10 percent of discretionary income, rather than 15 percent if you are not a new borrower. If you stay on IBR but do not qualify for PSLF (this rarely makes sense for doctors), then new borrowers see their balance forgiven after twenty years, compared to twenty-five years for the earlier version of IBR.

Michael's estimated payment under IBR for new borrowers would be about $308 a month once he has recertified based on his resident income of $55,000.

*Pay As You Earn (PAYE)*

Pay As You Earn is similar to IBR for new borrowers but with a different eligibility requirement. To enroll in PAYE, you must not have had an outstanding Direct or FFEL loan balance as of October 1, 2007, and also must have taken out a Direct Loan on or after October 1, 2011. Only Direct Loans are eligible to be on PAYE. Like IBR for new borrowers, PAYE payments are based on 10 percent of your discretionary income and are capped at the amount you would have paid on the standard ten-year, calculated when you entered PAYE. Loan balances are forgiven after twenty years under PAYE, if they are not forgiven earlier from PSLF.

| | |
|---|---|
| Payments calculated as: | 10 percent of discretionary income |
| Treatment of spouse's income: | Included in calculation if file taxes jointly<br>Not included if file taxes separately |

| Cap on monthly payment: | Capped at the payment amount under the standard ten-year plan, based on loan balance and interest rates when enrolled in PAYE |
|---|---|
| Balance forgiven (if not PSLF): | Twenty years |

Michael's estimated monthly payment under PAYE would be zero dollars for his first year. The same example we covered with Michael going through IBR for PSLF would apply if he were to use PAYE to qualify for PSLF.

One item to note is that the cap on monthly payments under IBR and PAYE is calculated when you enter into one of these repayment plans. Because of this, switching from IBR paying at the 15 percent discretionary income level to PAYE at the 10 percent discretionary income level may not be beneficial, due to the monthly payment cap being recalculated to a higher limit based on interest that has accrued while on IBR. The extra amount you may pay after training due to the higher cap may outweigh the small savings on your payments while in training.

## Revised Pay As You Earn (REPAYE)

In case student loan repayment options were not confusing enough, the government rolled out a fourth IDR option called Revised Pay As You Earn, or REPAYE. Revised Pay As You Earn is similar to PAYE. Both are only available to Direct Loans, payments are generally 10 percent of discretionary income, and it is a qualified repayment plan for PSLF. Two notable differences include how spousal income affects payment amounts and the payment limit. With PAYE, spousal income is not considered in calculating monthly payments if you file your taxes separately rather than jointly. With REPAYE, monthly payments are based on the combined incomes of both spouses, regardless of tax filing status. This means REPAYE payments may be much higher than PAYE payments if your spouse earns a substantial income. Whereas PAYE caps payments at the standard ten-year level, REPAYE does not have a limit and payments may be above the standard ten-year amount if your income is high enough.

| | |
|---|---|
| Payments calculated as: | 10 percent of discretionary income |
| Treatment of spouse's income: | Included in calculation regardless of tax filing status |
| Cap on monthly payment: | None |
| Balance forgiven (if not PSLF): | Twenty years for undergraduate loans Twenty-five years for graduate school loans |

Michael's estimated monthly payment under REPAYE would be zero dollars for his first year. After that, payments would depend on his income and family size.

**Loan Forgiveness Other Than PSLF**

In addition to loan forgiveness through PSLF, there are other programs that may forgive or repay your student loans.

*National Institutes of Health Loan Repayment Program (NIH LRP)*

The National Institutes of Health Loan Repayment Program (NIH LRP) can be a good option if you are engaged in certain areas of research. If you commit to at least two years of conducting qualified research funded by a domestic nonprofit organization or US federal, state, or local government entity, then the NIH may repay up to $35,000 of your qualified student loan debt each year. Qualified loans including those taken out to pay for undergraduate, graduate, and medical school education. There are intramural loan repayment programs if you are an NIH employee, but most doctors conduct research at universities or other nonprofit organizations and would therefore be considered for the extramural loan repayment program. Areas of qualified research for the extramural LRP include:

- clinical research
- pediatric research
- health disparities research
- contraception and infertility research
- clinical research for individuals from disadvantaged backgrounds

The NIH LRP is a competitive program and requires an application. You can visit the NIH's website at www.lrp.nih.gov for more information on this, including eligibility requirements and tips for writing a strong application.

## Underserved Areas

Certain locations of the country offer assistance in loan repayment, commonly in areas with populations with limited access to health care. For example, the Montana Rural Physician Incentive Program provides a financial incentive to physicians to practice in underserved areas of the state by repaying up to $100,000 of student loans over five years as a nontaxable benefit. Other loan repayment programs can be found at the Association of American Medical Colleges (AAMC) website for loan repayment, forgiveness, and scholarship programs. Over sixty programs offer various ways of student loan repayment or forgiveness by providing services to their populations, often in locations designated as health professional shortage areas (HPSAs) or medically underserved areas (MUAs), which may be rural or urban. If practicing in an underserved area appeals to you, then this can be a great opportunity to work in a setting you enjoy and accelerate your loan repayment.

## Military Service

Joining our nation's armed forces is an admirable decision and offers many benefits, including the ability to have your loans forgiven by serving. More so than the other loan forgiveness and repayment programs, military service is a lifestyle choice and a major commitment. Repayment terms vary by military branch and program, but doctors who choose this route generally must serve at least three to five years in a location not of your choosing, which may include areas of conflict and time apart from your family. Incentive packages may include annual bonuses and substantial loan repayment each year. However, military positions pay significantly less than civilian positions, so you will want to consider the lost earnings over this time if you are thinking about joining the armed forces.

## Common Questions

There are many options for how to become free of student loans, though there is no one-size-fits-all recommendation for each doctor every time. Here are a few of the more common questions on student loans.

### Should I consolidate my federal loans?

It usually does not make sense to consolidate your loans simply for the sake of consolidating. When you consolidate, the interest rate on the new loan is the weighted average of the interest rates on the loans being consolidated, rounded up to the nearest eighth of a percent. This prohibits you from applying extra payments toward balances at higher interest rates because your entire balance is at one rate. The most common exception is when Direct Loan consolidation is required to allow loans to qualify for PSLF.

### To refinance or not to refinance?

Refinancing your federal loans to a lower interest rate with a private lender can significantly reduce your total payments. The most apparent drawback to refinancing is losing the option to take advantage of federal loan forgiveness through public service loan forgiveness. As the status of your future employer will determine your eligibility for loan forgiveness, the first step is to ask yourself, "Do I intend to work for an employer that will allow me to qualify for public service loan forgiveness?"

If your answer is yes—you intend to work for a nonprofit, tax-exempt 501(c)(3) organization (such as most teaching hospitals), government entity, or another qualifying employer—then taking advantage of public service loan forgiveness can be beneficial. The decision will then depend on how far along you are in training, your anticipated post-training income, spouse's income, and loan balance, all of which determine how much loan balance you may have forgiven. If the estimated amount of loan forgiveness is large, then refinancing may not be in your best interest, and you may be better served by continuing toward the 120th payment under PSLF. If the estimated amount of loan forgiveness is small, then it may make sense to refinance to a lower rate if this would lower the total amount you would pay over the life of your loans.

If your answer is no—you do not intend to work for a PSLF-qualified employer—then it may make sense to refinance your student loans with a private lender. About a dozen banks and other lenders are currently offering to refinance student loans at interest rates that are usually much lower than the interest rates on Stafford (6.80 percent) or Grad PLUS (7.90 percent) loans for graduates of the past several years. For example, competitive fixed interest rates for a ten-year repayment term are around 4.50 percent to 5.50 percent as of 2018. Once your loans are refinanced, your payments will be based on the current balance, interest rate, and term length, rather than your income. A few lenders provide the option to make minimal payments while in training.

One word of caution before you refinance your loans is that it is an irrevocable decision. Your federal Direct Loans will no longer qualify for PSLF after they are refinanced with a private lender. For this reason, we encourage you to think carefully before refinancing your loans. If there is a small chance you may work for a PSLF-qualifying employer, then you may want to keep this option available and leave your federal loans in a qualified IDR plan until you are certain of your post-training plans.

In Michael's case, refinancing with a private lender will likely not be his best option, at least not yet. He is early in his training (and therefore has several years of low payments under an IDR option), he has a fairly large loan balance, and he is considering working for a PSLF-qualified employer. It is generally advisable for someone like Michael to revisit his post-training plans periodically to see if refinancing later is appropriate.

*How should I file my taxes based on my repayment method?*

If you are married and repaying your loans under an income-driven repayment option, then your spouse's income adds another layer of complexity by increasing your household adjusted gross income, and therefore your discretionary income, which determines your IDR payments. One option to counter this with IDR methods other than REPAYE is to file your taxes separately, which results in only your income being considered. The downside is that the tax brackets for Married Filing Separate are more compressed than Married Filing Jointly, meaning filing separately could result in a higher tax bill. Filing separately also results in a much lower income phase-out range for making direct contributions to Roth IRAs, and the tax deduction for student loan interest payments is prohibited. This is further complicated if you live in a community property state, as your combined income may be deemed to be earned equally by both you and your spouse.[1] While you may have a larger balance forgiven by filing separately, this may be overshadowed by the additional taxes you and your spouse pay along the way. You will therefore need to weigh the benefit of lower payments against the cost of higher taxes. If it is time to recertify for your IDR payments and you are not sure how best to file your taxes, then consulting with a CPA or other tax professional for a tax projection under each filing status can help with this decision.

*How do my student loans affect my overall financial plan?*

Student loans affect your financial plan in two main ways—cash flow and creditworthiness. The most noticeable aspect of your student loans is their monthly cash outflow, which directly decreases your ability to fund other areas of planning. For example, Michael's $180,000 loan balance at 6.80 percent paid over ten years results in monthly payments of $2,071.

---

[1] Community property states include Arizona, California, Idaho, Louisiana, Nevada, New Mexico, Texas, Washington, and Wisconsin. Community property tax laws differ by state.

This equates to the principal and interest payments on a $420,000 mortgage at 4.25 percent over thirty years. Paying both of these debts would cost approximately $4,137 a month. If Michael wanted to keep his total monthly debt payments at $4,137 but had another $70,000 of loans at 6.80 percent (adding $806 to his monthly student loan payments), then he would only be able to afford a $256,000 mortgage.

Your loan balance and payments also affect your ability to qualify for other loans, such as a mortgage. One metric lenders use to assess your creditworthiness is your debt-to-income ratio, which is your total monthly payments of your debts divided by your gross monthly income. Even if you are not yet paying on your student loans or are paying on an IDR plan, lenders may consider your entire student loan balance and what your payments may increase to when considering your eligibility for a new loan.

**Chapter Summary**

We covered a lot of material in this chapter, and for good reason. For doctors, student loans tend to stay as one of the top financial concerns for many years. We began this chapter with an overview of student loans and how prevalent they are; three out of four doctors graduate medical school with student loans, and four out of five borrowers have balances over $100,000. We then reviewed the types of student loans and available repayment plans before concluding with several common questions.

Before we move on from student loans, we would like to leave you with one last takeaway:

*If you are not sure which repayment plan to choose, get help now. The longer you wait, the more it could cost you over the life of your loans.*

From here, we will cover home buying as it fits into a doctor's financial plan. This must be balanced with student loans, as many doctors have a goal of becoming homeowners within their first few years of entering practice.

## Key Takeaways

The median student loan balance for a graduating medical student is $190,000, so half of your peers owe more than this.

Doctors generally become free of their student loans in one of two ways—by repaying them or through a loan forgiveness plan. Public Service Loan Forgiveness (PSLF) discharges eligible student loans after 120 qualifying payments.

To benefit the most from PSLF, doctors will commonly enroll in one of the income-driven repayment (IDR) methods. These include Income-Contingent Repayment (ICR), Income-Based Repayment (IBR), Pay As You Earn (PAYE), and Revised Pay As You Earn (REPAYE).

If you will not be benefitting from PSLF, then *refinancing your student loans to a lower interest rate with a private lender* can reduce the amount of interest you will pay over the life of your loans. However, this is an irrevocable decision, so you will want to carefully consider this before refinancing and forever giving up PSLF.

In addition to PSLF, there are *alternative loan forgiveness programs* for doctors who work with underserved populations, conduct qualifying research, or join the armed forces.

Student loans affect other areas of your financial plan, so it is important to develop a strategy with them, even if this means making payments of zero dollars under an income-driven repayment plan early in residency.

Laws change, and it is possible that PSLF, as we know it today, will not be the same program in the future. New legislation may reduce or eliminate the amount of loans forgiven, hopefully grandfathering existing borrowers into the favorable program we have come to be familiar with.

# CHAPTER 5

# HOME BUYING

SARAH RECENTLY COMPLETED her orthopedic surgery residency and was eager to purchase her first home. Her contract with a private practice group included a base salary, along with production-based compensation, though she acknowledged it may be a while before this amounted to a significant source of her income. One of her main concerns was fitting a mortgage payment into her monthly budget with existing payments toward student loans and other expenses.

"My current lease ends in six months, so I would like to own a home by then to avoid having to renew my lease or find another temporary residence," explained Sarah. "I have an idea of the area I would like to live in, but other than that, I am not sure where to begin."

Many new doctors share Sarah's feelings about home buying— optimistic but also cautious of adding another component to an already complicated financial plan. This chapter will provide an overview of the home-buying process, specifically for early-career doctors. We will begin by reviewing the professionals you will be working with in this process. We will then define some of the common terms you will come across when buying a home and the types of mortgages available. After that, we will walk through each step in a home purchase before concluding with the pros and cons of refinancing your mortgage if you are already a homeowner.

## The Players

As you work through the home buying process, it will be helpful to know the key players who will help you through this and the roles they perform.

*Real estate agent.* A real estate agent represents you in the transaction. The seller will have their own agent, known as the listing agent. Common tasks for real estate agents include finding and showing homes, as well as negotiating the terms of the purchase. You can think of your real estate agent as your "muscle" in the home-buying process. A good agent will also be able to refer you to a loan officer or broker, appraiser, and inspector. Your Realtor's fee is paid by the seller, so it is free to you to work with a real estate agent as the buyer.

*Loan officer.* An employee of a bank or other lending institution that assists you in securing a loan. The loan officer's role is to take your information and explain it to the loan underwriter to get you approved for a mortgage.

*Loan underwriter.* An employee of a bank or other lending institution who assesses your creditworthiness and approves your loan.

*Mortgage broker.* An independent broker who has access to many lenders and can help you shop the loan market to obtain financing. Using a mortgage broker is an alternative to going directly through a lender and working with a loan officer.

*Inspector.* An inspector will perform a thorough evaluation of the property and will provide an assessment of the home's general condition. They note anything that could affect the property's value, such as water damage, but do not give an estimate of the property's value. The inspection is usually performed after your offer on a home has been accepted and before closing.

*Appraiser.* An independent appraiser will provide an assessment of the property's value. During your home purchase, your home will be appraised after your offer has been accepted and the home has been inspected but before final closing. The appraised value is also important if you are planning to refinance your mortgage or want to have private mortgage insurance taken off your current loan.

*Financial advisor.* A financial advisor's role in the home-buying process is to make sure you are aware of how your new home and mortgage fit within your overall financial plan. Their job is to educate you on the various financing options, as well as help you decide which type of loan and how much is appropriate for your situation.

## Types of Mortgages

Mortgages will have a combination of the following features, such as an adjustable-rate conventional mortgage or a fixed jumbo mortgage.

*Interest Rate*

*Adjustable-rate mortgage (ARM).* The interest rate is fixed for an initial time period and then adjusts, usually annually, based on a measure that tracks interest rates. They generally have a thirty-year repayment period and begin with an interest rate lower than a fixed mortgage, but the interest rate then adjusts up or down based on the current interest rate environment. Common term lengths for ARMs are three-, five-, seven-, and ten-year fixed-rate periods. For example, a 7-1 ARM will carry a fixed rate for the first seven years and will then adjust annually based on interest rates at the time of adjustment.

*Fixed mortgage.* The interest rate is fixed for the entire loan. Fifteen- and thirty-year fixed mortgages are the most common term lengths.

*Loan Size*

*Conventional.* Loans under $453,100 (in most regions) that conform to established guidelines. Conventional loans do not require as extensive underwriting as jumbo loans.

*Jumbo.* Loans above $453,100 (in most regions). Jumbo mortgages are perceived as higher-risk loans than conventional loans and therefore usually have an interest rate that is slightly higher, as well as require more documentation before being approved.

*Other Loans*

*FHA Loan.* Mortgages that are insured by the Federal Housing Administration (FHA). These loans are only issued by certain lenders and are designed for low-income to middle-income borrowers, though there are no income limits on who can apply for an FHA Loan. They require a small down payment, currently 3.5 percent of the home's value. They also come with a fairly sizeable private mortgage insurance payment and therefore tend to be more expensive than other types of mortgages over the life of the loan.

*Physician loan.* Special mortgages structured for doctors that require less than a 20 percent down payment and do not have private mortgage insurance.

*VA loan.* Special mortgages available to those who have served in the military. They provide financing for the full amount of the home value with no money down.

## Common Terms

You will encounter several terms through the home-buying process that you may not be familiar with. These are some of the more common terms you may hear.

*Debt-to-income (DTI).* The ratio of monthly debt payments over monthly gross income, including your future mortgage payments. Lenders generally like to see a DTI under 43 percent to qualify for the best mortgage rates available.

*Earnest money.* A deposit of money made by the buyer into an escrow account. Earnest money shows the seller that you are serious about buying a home. Your earnest money will not be refundable after a certain point in the purchase.

*Escrow.* Escrow may refer to the neutral third party who holds the buyer's down payment and other settlement costs before releasing these to the seller. The term escrow may also refer to the account used to hold this money, known as an escrow account.

*FICO score.* A commonly used measure to assess a borrower's creditworthiness. When people mention their credit score, they are usually referring to their FICO score, which has a range of 300 (poor credit) to 850 (best credit).

*Full credit and income approval.* A mortgage underwriter's approval of your creditworthiness after thorough review of all financial documents, including income statements, credit history, and current debts. The mortgage underwriter will perform this after you have had your offer accepted. The lender will require the mortgage underwriter's formal authorization with a full credit and income approval before they release the funds to purchase your home. You may also request to have an underwriter review all of your documents and provide a full credit and income approval before submitting an offer, but they will review everything again prior to closing.

*Good faith estimate (GFE).* A legal disclosure lenders must provide you that lists a potential loan amount, interest rate, and all fees involved with the mortgage.

*Loan-to-value (LTV).* The ratio of a home's mortgage balance (and any home equity debt) divided by the home's value. For example, purchasing a home with a 20 percent down payment will result in a loan-to-value ratio of 80 percent as the buyer has paid 20 percent of the home's value upfront and has taken a mortgage for the remaining 80 percent.

*Points (discount points).* One point is 1 percent of the mortgage balance. Discount points refer to paying an additional amount upfront to lower the interest rate of the loan. The decision whether to pay for points should be made on a case-by-case basis and in consideration with other factors, such as how long you plan to own the home before selling and the interest rates on your other debts.

*Preapproval.* The process of getting preapproved for a mortgage, in which your credit report is formally checked and financial documents are reviewed. Once you have been preapproved, the bank will state how much they will lend to you and their proposed interest rate. You will work with either a loan officer or mortgage broker to get preapproved with a lender.

*Prequalification.* An informal process done with a lender to receive an estimate of the mortgage you may be able to qualify for (amount and interest rate). Prequalification does not run your credit report and does not guarantee you will be approved for a loan with the characteristics in the estimate. This is an optional step that can help you understand what loan terms you may be looking at, but other than that, it does not provide any value in the home buying process.

*Principal, interest, taxes, and insurance (PITI).* The components of a total monthly mortgage payment.

- principal—the loan balance
- interest—the cost for borrowing money

- taxes—property taxes
- insurance—homeowners insurance and potentially private mortgage insurance

*Private mortgage insurance (PMI).* A form of insurance that reimburses the lender in the event the borrower defaults on their loan. It protects the lender if you are unable to make your mortgage payment, so the borrower does not benefit from PMI. Mortgage insurance is usually paid by the borrower and often required when making a down payment of less than 20 percent of the home's value.

## Let's Buy a Home!

Now that we have a basic understanding of the key terms and players in the home-buying process, let's buy a home from start to finish. The first order of business is to determine whether buying a home is appropriate at this time or whether renting would be more favorable. Once you have decided that you want to purchase a home in the coming months, you will then need to get financing squared away. You can then go home shopping with your agent, make an offer, and close on your home.

### Is buying a home appropriate at this time?

We often hear doctors in training mention buying a home as a priority. Owning a home can be a valuable part of your financial plan, and we support becoming a homeowner when it also makes sense financially. Renting can feel like a waste of money, whereas buying a home can be viewed as a good investment. With that said, purchasing a home and taking on a mortgage is a large commitment and is not always appropriate. There are numerous costs, fees, and taxes in buying, owning, and selling a home.

In general, it is difficult to come out ahead financially if you buy and sell a home in a short period of time, such as over the course of your training. First, there are costs related to buying your home, such as fees related to originating your mortgage and the appraisal. Once in a home, the costs of maintenance and taxes are usually much higher than renting. In addition, the majority of your payments during the first few years of your mortgage will go to paying interest, and very little will be applied to pay down the principal balance. Another item to consider is the value of your home. Home prices have historically risen over long periods of time. However, they can decrease significantly in the short term, as we saw in the housing and financial crisis of 2007 through 2009. There is also the cost of selling a home (usually 5 percent or 6 percent of the home's value as Realtor fees), as well as taxes on the gain realized from the sale if you have not owned and used the home as your primary residence in two out of the last five years. For these reasons, doctors should move slowly with home buying after weighing the pros and cons, especially while in training. As you transition into practice, it can make sense to rent for at least three to twelve months to make sure you like your new employer, your colleagues, and the area before buying.

With that said, we can sympathize with not wanting to move multiple times and understand some people may want to buy a home around their start date after training. If you are one of these people, then we encourage you to consider the consequences of having to move within a short amount of time if your new position does not work out. By renting initially, you can get a feel for your position to have a better idea whether it will be a good long-term fit.

*Prefinancing: Items to Consider*

Once you have determined you would like to buy a home in the coming months, there are several items to consider before you begin talking with a lender and real estate agent.

One of the most important assets you have when buying a home is your credit score. Lenders will use this to determine how risky of a borrower you are, so you will want to treat your credit with care in the months leading up to your purchase. This includes paying off any balances on your credit cards, not signing up for any new credit cards or closing existing ones, and minimizing the number of hard inquiries that could decrease your credit score (such as taking out an auto loan). One resource that can provide periodic estimates of your credit score is Credit Karma, which has an app and can also be accessed through their website at CreditKarma.com. Mint.com also provides credit score updates for its users. Keep in mind that Credit Karma and Mint may not give you the exact FICO score that mortgage lenders use in determining your credit. These two websites are starting points to give you a sense of where your credit rating stands.

The next item to consider is your cash flow. Before you fall in love with your dream home, you will want to know how much house you can afford. To answer this, you need to work through a detailed spending analysis and include *all* changes to your income and expenses that affect your ability to make your mortgage payments. Common changes for new doctors who have recently finished training include the following:

*Student loan payments.* In training, your student loan payments will likely be either zero if on forbearance or a few hundred dollars a month if your repayment method is dependent on your income. Your student loan payments will adjust soon after graduation and will depend on your repayment method, loan balance, interest rate, and income. You will want to factor your higher student loan payments into your budget before adding estimated mortgage payments, as your student loan payments can increase to a few thousand dollars a month. If you are considering refinancing your student loans to a lower interest rate with a private lender, you will want to consider how a home purchase and mortgage may affect your ability to refinance your student loans. Banks will usually require your debt-to-income ratio to be below a certain number. If your mortgage payments are too large compared to your income, they may prohibit you from refinancing your student loans. Firms that refinance student loans have their own debt-to-income requirements, so you will want to consider how taking on a mortgage will affect your ability to refinance your loans.

*Saving for retirement.* Doctors typically begin saving for retirement later in their lives due to their extensive training, so you have some catch-up to do. You will want to include your target retirement savings goal in your spending analysis *before* adding a mortgage payment. You have already been putting off seriously saving for several years, so you will not want a large mortgage payment to inhibit your ability to fully save for retirement.

*Higher taxes.* In training, your modest income will result in a fairly small amount owed in taxes. The amount you pay in taxes will be much larger once you have a full year of practicing income. Your income taxes may also be higher if you move to a new state with higher state income taxes than the one you moved from.

*Childcare costs.* You will want to include costs of childcare if you have a young family or will be starting a family. These include daycare and potentially private school tuition. If providing for your child's higher education is a priority, then you will also want to factor in monthly contributions to a college savings account.

*Decrease or loss of spouse's income.* If your spouse plans to decrease or stop working in the future, then you will want to plan around your ability to pay the mortgage with this in mind.

*Other discretionary spending.* You learned to live frugally through your years of training. When your income adjusts after graduation, your standard of living and discretionary spending naturally rise with it. You may want to buy a new car or take your family on vacations. If you would like to afford them with your new home, then you will want to factor these costs into your budget before taking on your mortgage.

*Future income increases.* Conversely, if you expect your income or your spouse's income to increase significantly in the near future (when you leave training or if you become a partner in your practice, for example), then you can factor this into your cash flow. However, if you purchase a home now with your future income in mind, then you may feel "house poor" until your income adjusts. Future income is not always guaranteed, so we suggest proceeding cautiously when factoring this in.

The key point with these items is to come up with an accurate idea of what your desired lifestyle will look like from an income, tax, spending, and saving point of view immediately prior to taking on a mortgage. This will help you determine how much you can spend each month on your home while allowing you to have the lifestyle you want. It is important to consider all of these factors to avoid becoming house poor, which is when a mortgage payment consumes such a large amount of your income that you have difficulty meeting your other financial obligations. Your home will likely be your largest monthly bill for decades, so it is critical you do not overextend yourself. You can then use your desired monthly payment to solve for an estimated home value to aid in narrowing your search.

You will also want to make sure the money you have earmarked for your down payment is in good order. This means having your down payment in your savings account for potentially ninety days before closing. The length of time may vary by lender, but most banks require at least two months of statements in your savings account that do not show the money as a deposit. If you will be using your signing bonus or if a relative will gift you the money for your down payment, then you will likely need to have this money settled in your bank account at least two to three months before applying for a loan. The lender may disallow your down payment funds if the paper trail on your bank statements does not show a clear record of this.

*Home Financing: Deciding on a Lender*

Now that we have an idea of how much house you can afford to buy, let's look into how to finance your home. The two main professionals who will help you obtain financing are a mortgage broker and loan officer. A mortgage broker is an independent broker who has access to many lenders and will help you shop the loan market. They can be a good fit if you have poor credit, as they will know which lenders are more favorable for your situation. However, financing may take longer with a mortgage broker because they do not work for a lender and must relay information between you and the lender. A loan officer is employed by a lender, and their job is to help borrowers secure a mortgage through the lender, usually a bank or credit union. They will have direct access to their lender's mortgage terms and loan underwriters, so turnaround time can be shorter than with a mortgage broker. We will assume you decide to work with a loan officer for the rest of this chapter, so how do you find the best lender?

If you walk into a bank and ask them what rate they will offer you on a mortgage, they will likely want to run your credit. Each time they do this, your credit score will drop slightly if multiple checks are done outside of a thirty-day period, as it tells other lenders that you are planning to take on additional debt and are therefore a riskier person to lend to. Your credit score will recover in a few months, but this could pose a problem if you want to close on your home soon. Remember, your credit score is one of your most valuable assets in this process, so you will want to treat it with care. If your credit drops below the lender's minimum score at any point during the loan origination, underwriting, or closing, then the lender can retract their offer, and the whole deal could be off.

If you would like to get into a home before you are able to save a 20 percent down payment, then narrowing your search to lenders who have physician loan programs or a VA loan can help. Physician loans are often a good option for new doctors, as they allow you to get into a home with a down payment far less than 20 percent and do not require mortgage insurance. Five percent to 10 percent down payments are common, though there are a few 0 percent down loans available. By requiring less than a 20 percent down payment, physician loans allow you to avoid prepaying on a low-interest debt and instead apply thousands of dollars to other priorities, such as debts that carry a higher interest rate.[1] There are about two dozen lenders across the country with physician loan programs, though most are regional and only a few are national. You can compare their features with an informal estimate or a formal preapproval

---

[1] In certain regions, most notably the Bay Area of California, physician loans are not as effective due to the competitive real estate market requiring at least a 20 percent down payment for your offer to be considered.

to select your top choice, considering factors such as the interest rate, fees, amount of down payment required, total amount of cash due at closing, and monthly payment.

If you apply to get preapproved with multiple lenders, then you will want to do so within a short time period, as your credit score will not drop for having your credit run multiple times for the same reason within thirty days. The preapproval process will require a few signed forms (which can usually be completed electronically), income documentation, and bank statements to show your assets and where your down payment will come from. The bank will also run your credit report (which will show all your debt, all lines of credit, and your payment history). The lender will then issue a one-page letter that states the mortgage balance you are preapproved for and the interest rate, which are both subject to change until you lock the interest rate. Once you lock the interest rate, you then have period of usually thirty to sixty days in which the interest rate on your preapproved loan will not change. Your preapproval letter is your ticket to go house shopping with your Realtor.

## Home Buying: Shopping, Making an Offer, Closing

This is the fun part we have been waiting for. With your preapproval letter in hand, it is time to find a Realtor, go house shopping, make an offer, and close. Your mortgage lender can likely refer you to a real estate agent they work well with. Finding a good team is an undervalued component of this process. A real estate agent and lender that are familiar with each other can make this a smoother purchase and ensure the necessary steps are completed in a timely manner. If there is poor chemistry between the two, it can cause headaches and sometimes result in a sale falling through.

Alternatively, real estate agents can be found online or in the real estate section of the local newspaper. You will want an agent who is familiar with the local market, has purchased several houses in the area you are considering, and ideally has experience working with doctors. Do not worry about paying for their services; real estate agents are paid by the seller. When you begin working with your Realtor, you will first give them your criteria of where you want to live and how much house you can afford. Try to paint the picture for your agent with as many details as possible. If good public schools are a priority, be sure to mention this. Real estate agents are helpful, but they will commonly show you homes that are at the high end or slightly over the price range you quote them. Because of this, you may want to quote them the lower end of your price range so that even homes they show above this are still affordable.

Your agent will generally facilitate the actual house shopping in one of two ways. They may send you listed properties via email so you have a pool to pick from. You can then select which ones you are interested in and schedule a time to visit them with your Realtor. The other method is scheduling a day or two in which your Realtor will take you on a tour of several properties. Either way, you will have the option to write an offer during an onsite visit when you are touring homes with your agent. Once you decide to make an offer, your agent will write the offer letter and submit this to the seller and their listing agent.

Your Realtor will know to write a few key clauses into your offer. The first one is an inspection contingency, which gives you the option to cancel or renegotiate your offer if the inspection reveals water, termite, or other significant damage. The last thing you want is to find out your new home needs expensive structural repairs before you move in. An escalation clause is another component of your offer that can make a difference in a competitive housing market. This clause allows you to submit an initial offering price that may increase up to a limit based on competing offers. For example, if your offer on a property is $450,000, but you would be willing to pay up to $475,000, then your agent will write in an escalation clause up to $475,000. This will automatically increase your bid to beat any offers above $450,000, up to $475,000. If a competing bid came in at $460,000, then your escalation clause would be triggered and your offer would be increased to the next increment above $460,000 (usually in $1,000 to $5,000 raises).

The seller will then either accept your offer or counter with a higher offer. Once you have agreed on terms, you have the property under contract and usually then have thirty to forty-five days to close. Your Realtor will outline the remaining steps from the date your offer is accepted until the day you move in. One of the first items after your offer is accepted is to send a copy of the agreement to your lender. You and your Realtor should be communicating regularly with your loan officer to make sure your financing is in good order. Your loan officer will be in contact with the loan underwriter, who will perform a final review of all financial documents, including income statements, credit history, and current debts before formally authorizing your mortgage and releasing the lender's funds.

This is also when you will finalize how your loan will be structured. A fixed-rate loan can be an appropriate option if you plan to own the property for a long time and want to lock in an interest rate for the entire loan term. This is a good strategy if interest rates are low, like they were in 2008 and the following years. An adjustable-rate mortgage (ARM) can be appropriate if you expect to own the home for a short period of time, such as five to ten years. An ARM can also make sense if interest rates are high, like they were in the 1980s, and are expected to be lower once the fixed term of the ARM expires. However, there is always the risk that rates could increase even higher, which would raise your mortgage payments after the initial fixed-rate period. You will also decide how much of a down payment to make and whether you wish to pay for points to buy down the interest rate. These decisions will depend on how long you expect to own the home and your other debts.

Your Realtor will concurrently order the inspection for an assessment of the home's general condition, noting anything that could affect the property's value, as well as getting a formal appraisal of the home's value. In the meantime, your Realtor will work with you to make sure your earnest money is in the escrow account in time. From here, it is up to your Realtor and loan officer to finalize the rest of your purchase and take you through closing. You will want to check in with them one to two times a week to make sure everything is on track. Once the boxes are unpacked, be sure to relax and enjoy your home; you've earned it!

## Refinancing an Existing Mortgage

In general, it can be beneficial to refinance your mortgage in a couple of situations. The first is if you have an adjustable-rate mortgage and wish to lock in a fixed interest rate for the remainder of the loan term. Let's say you took out a 5-1 ARM when interest rates were fairly high, with the expectation that after five years rates will be lower and your interest rate will adjust downward. It is now past five years since you took out your loan, and rates are indeed lower, so your interest rate has decreased. If you suspect interest rates may increase in the future, then refinancing to a fixed mortgage to secure a low rate for the remainder of your mortgage can make sense. The second case is if you have a fixed loan and current market interest rates are now lower than the interest rate on your loan. You could potentially refinance to lower the amount of interest you are paying. For each of these, you will want to consider how many additional years you plan to own your home before refinancing to ensure you break even on the costs to refinance.

## Chapter Summary

Owning a home can be rewarding, both emotionally and financially. Buying a home, however, can be stressful and can create a financial burden for decades if not done carefully. You will want to work with a loan officer who is familiar with different types of loans and is able to write physician loans if a low down payment is desirable. Ongoing and clear communication among your home buying team will help avoid last-minute surprises that could derail your careful planning. As a doctor navigating the home-buying waters, you must be aware of the pitfalls in this process and how your home fits within your overall financial plan.

## Key Takeaways

Two of the key players in your home purchase will be your *real estate agent* and *loan officer* (or mortgage broker).

Thirty-year fixed mortgages are the most common loan structure, though alternatives include adjustable-rate mortgages and fifteen-year fixed loans.

*Physician loans* are mortgages structured for doctors that require less than a 20 percent down payment and do not have private mortgage insurance.

As you begin the home buying process, *be aware of how your mortgage payments fit within your overall financial plan.* The lender will likely approve you for a larger mortgage than you should responsibly take on, and your real estate agent may show you houses at the higher end of your price range. It is important to consider your mortgage payment as it relates to your cash flow, as you do not want this to handicap your ability to save for retirement or achieve other goals.

Existing homeowners can *refinance their mortgage to a lower interest rate.* There is a cost to do this, so calculating the breakeven time between refinancing costs and amount saved each month can aid in making this decision.

# CHAPTER 6

# RISK MANAGEMENT

ALONG WITH MAINTAINING a balanced budget, having the proper level of emergency reserves, and responsibly handling your debts, managing various risks rounds out the foundation for a successful financial plan. This is one of the most important areas of planning because the consequences of failing to mitigate risks can be disastrous. The term "risk" has different meanings depending on the context in which it is used. For example, one way to view risk is the loss of capital due to market fluctuations with regard to investments. In this section, we will think of a financial risk as an event that directly results in a loss of property, a loss of income, or expenses owed. We will consider two key characteristics of each risk: the *probability* of the risk occurring and, if it does, the *severity* of it. With these in mind, we look at four ways to manage risks—by avoiding, reducing, retaining, or transferring them.

*Avoid.* You can *avoid* a risk by not putting yourself in a position to be exposed to it. For example, you can avoid the risk of getting a speeding ticket by driving under the speed limit. This is a good choice when both the probability and severity of a risk are high. However, certain risks are unavoidable, such as the risk of a malpractice claim if you practice medicine. The chance of a professional liability claim is always present no matter how careful you may be.

*Reduce.* If you cannot avoid the risk, you can aim to *reduce* the risk. An example of this would be brushing your teeth daily and going to your dentist on a regular basis to reduce the chance of tooth decay.

*Retain.* Risk *retention* means accepting to pay the consequences of the risk yourself. This is a good option when the severity of the risk is low. For example, by not purchasing the warranties on electronics, you accept the cost of replacing these items if they break. This is an acceptable risk to retain because the replacement cost is low.

*Transfer. Transferring* risk is often done in the form of insurance. This is appropriate with low-probability, high-severity risks that could be financially devastating if they occur. You purchase an insurance policy and transfer the financial risk from yourself to the insurance company. The insurance carrier receives small premium payments from many policyholders so it can make large claim payments to the unlucky few who experience this risk. When you buy insurance, you accept an affordable, known cost in the form of premium payments to shift the burden of a potentially large, unknown cost to the insurance company. Purchasing flood insurance to protect your home is one example. You may be willing to buy flood insurance for the peace of mind that you will be reimbursed for this loss if you live in an area that is prone to flooding. A major flood may not happen very often, but if it does, it could be difficult to replace your home if you do not have insurance.

We will focus on transferring risk in the form of insurance for the remainder of this section and following chapters that cover various types of insurance.

In today's world, we have found it is easy to become overinsured by purchasing coverage for many risks that you do not actually need to protect. Fortunately, we feel deciding whether to buy insurance for a certain risk is fairly simple by asking yourself the following question: if this risk happens, could it ruin me or my family financially?

If your answer is no—this risk would not ruin you—then it can make sense to not buy insurance and instead self-insure against this risk with the money set aside in your emergency reserves. Warranties on electronics are a good example. Think of your friend who jumped in the pool with his phone in his pocket. Three summers in a row. He is likely not too pleased with himself each time, but he is also probably not financially ruined because of it either. If the result of a risk is limited to hundreds or even a few thousand dollars, you may be better off retaining this risk by directing the cost of what you would have paid on the warranty to your emergency reserve account.

If your answer is yes—this risk could ruin you—then it makes sense to consider buying insurance to protect against this risk. Four risks we will cover over the next several chapters include:

*Medical expenses.* If you break a bone, find a tumor, or have another condition requiring health care services and do not have medical insurance, this would be scary both medically and financially. Doctors know as well as anyone how quickly medical bills add up, so it is important to have health insurance to pay for these costs.

*Lawsuits.* Many doctors enter medicine to follow their passion of helping and healing people, with the ability to earn a nice income as an afterthought. However, the public's perception of doctors is that you are wealthy, and because of this, doctors generally have a higher probability of being sued for personal and professional liability claims than other occupations. Malpractice, tail, and personal liability insurance can protect your assets and income if you are the subject of a lawsuit.[1]

*Disability.* You have invested heavily in yourself with the time, energy, and resources to become a doctor and have a lot of income to earn, particularly if you are in the early stages of your career. If a long-term disability were to put you out of work for an extended period of

---

[1] Tail insurance is also known as extended reporting coverage and extends the period over which you are covered for professional liability claims if your malpractice insurance is claims-made. It is explained in more depth in the Professional Liability Insurance chapter.

time, it could be difficult to maintain the standard of living you were accustomed to while practicing. Properly structured disability insurance replaces income lost from the inability to work in your own occupation as a doctor in your specialty.

*Death.* If you have anyone who is financially dependent on you, especially if you are the primary or sole income earner for your household, then guarding against an unexpected passing with life insurance will be an important part of your planning.

The common theme among these risks is their level of severity. If any of them were to occur, then we are not talking about hundreds or thousands of dollars; we are talking about *hundreds of thousands or millions of dollars* of expenses or lost income. Most people do not have this much in their emergency reserve, so using insurance is the preferred method to manage large risks that cannot be avoided. The following chapters will expand on these risks and the lines of insurance that protect against them.

---

### Key Takeaways

Four ways to deal with financial risks include *avoiding, reducing, retaining,* or *transferring* them.

Risks that cannot be avoided and could be financially devastating if they occur are candidates to transfer to an insurance company by purchasing insurance. These are difficult to self-insure against because of their severity.

---

CHAPTER 7

# HEALTH INSURANCE, HSAs, AND FSAs

WHILE HEALTH INSURANCE is an essential part of a financial plan, health savings accounts (HSAs) and flexible spending accounts (FSAs) can be beneficial but are not vital for your plan to be successful.

### Health Insurance

Most doctors have a thorough understanding of how health insurance works, so we will only cover a few basics before moving on. Health insurance is generally provided by your employer at no cost or a subsidized cost to you. From the standpoint of properly managing health care-related risks, we do not have a preference on the type of health insurance to select as long as the cost of expensive procedures or treatments would be covered at limited cost to you. One suggestion is to make sure you have enough in your emergency reserve account to cover the full out-of-pocket maximum for your health plan. Once you have reached this amount, the insurer pays for the remainder of covered benefits. The specific health plan selection (HMO versus PPO, deductibles and copayments, providers you can see within your network, etc.) is up to your preference on how you would like your health care to be provided and paid for.

If you will be taking time off between the completion of your training and start of your next position, you may need a short-term health insurance policy for you and any dependents to bridge the gap in coverage. The default choice for this is to sign up for COBRA to continue your previous employer's health insurance, which can be a retroactive election after a qualifying event; however, this can be an expensive option. An alternative is to secure short-term health insurance through your state's exchange or an independent health insurance broker.

On the other side of medical insurance, with you being the provider of health care services, the largest development in recent years has been the introduction of the Affordable Care Act in 2010. Since then, there have been efforts to repeal it or certain aspects of the ACA, such as the mandate that people must have health insurance. Like taxes, health care legislation is a highly politicized topic. Future developments could include further dismantling of the Affordable Care Act or a swing to the other side of the spectrum with universal health care gaining momentum, depending on which party holds power in Congress and the White House.

## Health Savings Accounts (HSAs)

A health savings account is an account used to save for future health care costs. It is designed to help pay for expenses that are not covered by a high-deductible health plan (HDHP) and therefore requires you have an HDHP to be eligible to contribute to an HSA. The tax advantages of HSAs include:

*Pretax contributions.* You can deduct your HSA contributions from your income when filing taxes, resulting in a lower amount of taxes owed. HSA contributions must be made by the due date of your tax return, which is usually April 15 of the following year. The 2018 contribution limits are $3,450 for an individual and $6,900 for a family. An individual over age fifty-five can make an additional $1,000 contribution, and a married couple with both spouses over fifty-five can make an additional $2,000 contribution.

*Tax-deferred growth.* Your HSA contributions can be invested and grow without being taxed.

*Tax-free distributions.* HSA distributions used for qualified unreimbursed medical expenses are not taxed. Nonqualified distributions (those not used for qualified health care expenses) are taxed as ordinary income and subject to a 20 percent penalty if you are under age sixty-five. Once sixty-five or older, there is no penalty for nonqualified distributions, but the amount withdrawn is taxed as income.

Employers may also contribute to their employees' HSAs as part of their benefits package. If you are comfortable having a high-deductible health plan and your employer offers an HSA, then making contributions to this account can be a tax-advantaged way to save for future medical expenses.

## Flexible Spending Accounts (FSAs)

Flexible spending accounts are similar to health savings accounts with pretax contributions and distributions for qualifying expenses not being taxed as income. However, there are a couple of major differences, the first being contributions to FSAs that have not been used by the end of the calendar year are forfeited. This "use it or lose it" feature of FSAs makes these accounts unattractive unless you are certain you will use the full amount contributed by the end of the year.[1] In 2018, individuals could contribute up to $2,650 to their FSA. Due to the limited time to use the funds in an FSA, contributions cannot be invested like in an HSA.

Your employer may also offer a dependent-care FSA, which allows pretax contributions to pay for dependent care expenses so you can work. Daycare for your child is one example of an eligible expense. Annual contributions are limited to $5,000, and unused amounts are forfeited at the end of the year. If you know you will have at least a certain amount of

---

[1] Employers may allow employees the option to carryover up to $500 of unused funds to the next year.

qualifying expenses, then using a dependent-care FSAs can be a favorable way to pay for them.

## Chapter Summary

Doctors have a front-row seat to view the sometimes-staggering cost of health care for a single patient. Fortunately, health insurance will likely be provided by your employer, and you will need only to select which plan best suits your needs. Your employee benefits summary will also list whether an HSA or FSA is provided, and if so, you can reduce your tax bill by making contributions into these.

---

### Key Takeaways

The high cost of health care makes medical insurance a necessity, though it should be provided by your employer at a subsidized cost to you.

*Health savings accounts (HSAs)* and *flexible spending accounts (FSAs)* are accounts that offer tax-advantaged ways to pay for current and future health care expenses.

---

CHAPTER 8

# PROFESSIONAL LIABILITY INSURANCE

MEDICAL MALPRACTICE CLAIM. The very phrase can be enough to create a knot in any doctor's stomach. Being the subject of a professional liability claim is not only time intensive and stressful, but it may also be difficult to recover from financially if you are not properly insured. This section will focus on the two most common lines of insurance that protect your assets and income in the event of a professional liability claim—malpractice and tail insurance.

Let's first take a look at some of the numbers regarding medical malpractice claims. A *New England Journal of Medicine* article found the following insights after analyzing a study conducted from 1991 through 2005 covering over 40,000 doctors.

- Each year during the study period, 7.4 percent of doctors had a malpractice claim brought against them.
- Each year during the study period, 1.6 percent of doctors made an indemnity payment due to a malpractice claim.
- Across all specialties considered, the median indemnity payment made was $111,749, while the mean was $274,887 due to a small number of significantly higher payments (in 2008 dollars).

Roughly one out of fourteen doctors faced a malpractice claim each year, and about one out of sixty-two made a payment. When they did, however, the amount owed was generally above $100,000. This low-probability, high-severity profile is what we look for when deciding to transfer a financial risk to an insurance carrier by purchasing insurance. To put it another way, ask yourself this question: if my employer did not provide malpractice insurance for me, would I get it on my own?

Many doctors would. Why? Not because you are a careless practitioner and think there is a high chance you will get sued, but because even if you are very careful, there is a small chance you could face a claim with a large financial consequence.

Fortunately, malpractice insurance is often provided by your employer at no cost to you as part of your benefits package. It pays the fees for your attorneys to represent you and the amount owed to the patient or their family in the event of an adverse decision in a professional liability claim. Each malpractice insurance policy has two coverage limits. The per-occurrence limit is the maximum amount the insurer will pay on a single claim. The aggregate limit is how much an insurer will pay in total in a single year. Common limits are $1 million per occurrence and $3 million aggregate or $2 million / $6 million, though they can be higher. If your employer does not provide malpractice insurance, then it is advisable to purchase an individual policy. This is often the case if you are a solo practitioner or moonlight outside of your regular employer.

In addition to the amount covered, we also need to understand *when* your malpractice insurance will protect against a claim. The two types of malpractice insurance are "occurrence" and "claims-made." Occurrence malpractice insurance covers claims that occur when the malpractice policy is in force, regardless of when the claim is filed. For example, let's say a surgeon was allegedly negligent when performing an operation in 2016. The patient appeared to be fine following the procedure, but she then fell ill and died two years later in 2018 because of complications. Her family filed a malpractice claim against the surgeon shortly after. The surgeon would be covered for this claim with occurrence malpractice insurance if his policy was in force in 2016 when the operation occurred, even though the claim was filed two years later and even if the surgeon had insurance through a different malpractice carrier in 2018.

Claims-made coverage protects you from a malpractice claim only if you are continuously covered by the same company when both the act happened and the claim is filed. In the previous example, the surgeon would have needed a claims-made policy to be continuously in force from 2016 through 2018 to protect against the claim. The original claims-made policy that was in force in 2016 would not have been activated in 2018 if the surgeon had switched malpractice insurance companies between the act and claim, which can be the case with employment changes. If this were the case, then the surgeon would have needed to purchase extended reporting coverage, also known as tail insurance, to extend the period over which the original claims-made policy would be in effect because the next malpractice insurance policy would not cover prior acts.

Initial contracts with a new employer often require doctors to be covered for potential liability claims arising from past employment. Tail insurance is the most common way to fulfill this if your past employer's coverage was claims-made. The cost of tail insurance can be significant, depending on your specialty, and is either paid by your old employer, you, or both parties. If you are responsible for acquiring tail coverage and fail to do so, your past employer can purchase it for you and send you an invoice for reimbursement.

What does this mean for doctors? One way to view tail insurance is as the cost to leave an employer if you are responsible for obtaining it following termination of employment. Teaching hospitals provide tail insurance for their graduating residents and fellows or have occurrence malpractice insurance. However, once you are evaluating post-training positions, you will want to be aware of which employers require you to purchase tail coverage. These offers may not be the best fit if you are considering another employment change in the near future, such as going back to training for a fellowship.

## Business Liability Insurance

In addition to malpractice and tail insurance, business liability insurance should be considered if you have your own practice. This type of liability insurance protects against claims that are not due to professional negligence but rather those resulting from an event on your business premises that causes bodily injury or property damage. For example, business liability insurance would cover attorney fees and possible settlement costs if a patient fell and injured themselves in your waiting room. This is clearly not due to practicing medicine carelessly, so your malpractice insurance would not be triggered, but the patient could still sue for reimbursement, and you may need insurance to cover litigation costs.

## Chapter Summary

Dealing with a professional liability claim is never an enjoyable process and can be financially difficult to recover from without the necessary insurance. Residents and fellows can depend on their teaching hospital to provide malpractice insurance and, if needed, tail coverage upon graduation. These are two benefits we would encourage you to keep in mind when deciding on future positions after training. The added responsibility of owning your practice means considering business liability insurance in case of a liability claim at your clinical location arising from events other than professional negligence.

**Key Takeaways**

*Malpractice insurance* protects against professional liability claims and is either occurrence or claims-made. *Occurrence* malpractice insurance covers claims that occur when the malpractice policy is in force, regardless of when the claim is filed. In contrast, *claims-made* coverage protects against a malpractice claim only if you are continuously covered by the same company when both the act happened and the claim is filed.

If you were previously covered by a claims-made malpractice policy and change employers, securing *tail insurance* may be needed to cover you for the period that your prior malpractice policy does not.

Practice owners need to consider *business liability insurance*, which protects against claims from events on your business premises rather than those due to professional negligence.

## CHAPTER 9

# AUTO, HOMEOWNERS, AND UMBRELLA LIABILITY INSURANCE

IN ADDITION TO professional liability claims, you also want to be adequately protected in the event of a large personal liability claim. These arise outside of the workplace but can still result in a significant financial burden. This chapter will focus on the four main lines of property and casualty insurance—auto, homeowners, renters, and umbrella liability—which provide basic protection for your assets and income if you are sued for an event on your property or while driving.

**Auto Insurance**

Most people have auto insurance if they own a car or drive one regularly, as it is required by law. Some insurers emphasize their cost competitiveness, while others promote their claims coverage and service. If you are unhappy with how much you are paying or the level of service you are receiving, you may want to switch to another company. Independent of your carrier, there are two types of coverage that apply if you are deemed to be at fault in an accident. The first type reimburses the other party for damage you cause and includes three liability limits:

*Bodily injury per person.* The maximum amount your auto insurance policy will reimburse to each person injured or killed.

*Bodily injury in aggregate.* The total amount your auto insurance policy will pay to all people injured or killed.

*Personal property.* The maximum your insurer will reimburse for damaged or destroyed personal property, such as the cost to fix or replace the other vehicle(s).

For example, a policy with limits of $100,000 / $300,000 / $50,000 would pay a maximum of $100,000 to any one injured person, $300,000 among all injured people, and $50,000 for personal property damaged. The maximum liability limits are often required before an insurer will allow you to purchase umbrella liability insurance.

The second half of an auto insurance policy relates to covering your vehicle, including comprehensive and collision, as well as your deductible. Like with health insurance, the deductible is how much you pay out of pocket before the insurer begins covering your claim. If your deductible is $250 or $500, then you can lower your cost of insurance by increasing your deductible to the maximum, usually $1,000 to $1,500. While paying $1,500 would not be ideal, this amount is low enough to reasonably self-insure with your emergency reserve. Collision insurance reimburses for damage to your vehicle if it collides with an object, like a tree or another vehicle. Comprehensive insurance, also called other than collision, reimburses for damage that happens to your vehicle, such as a tree falling on your car, hail, or if your car is stolen. These are commonly bundled together in an auto insurance policy, but they are not required. If you drive an older vehicle that is not worth much, you may want to discontinue paying to protect your car and instead apply the savings to your reserve account or the cost of your next vehicle.

## Homeowners Insurance

Your home will likely be your largest physical asset and would be difficult to replace if it were heavily damaged or destroyed. Homeowners insurance reimburses you for damage to your home, unless the loss is due to an excluded risk, such as an earthquake or flood. If you live in an area that is susceptible to an excluded risk, then an endorsement (specialized add-on) or separate specialized policy is advisable to fill the gap in coverage. Homeowners insurance also has a limit on the maximum it will pay in the event of a large liability claim.

## Renters Insurance

You can purchase renters insurance if you are a tenant living in someone else's house or apartment. It will reimburse you for the loss of property, such as a stolen bicycle; however, the limit is fairly low on certain items. You may want to add an endorsement to reimburse more than the initial limit covered if you have high-value personal property, like jewelry. Renters insurance also protects against liability claims that occur on your premises or for which you are deemed to be negligent (leaving the stove on resulting in a fire, for example).

## Umbrella Liability Insurance

Auto, homeowners, and renters insurance have limits on how much they will pay out, often between $100,000 and $500,000. While these numbers seem large, they can easily be exceeded. For example, let's say one of your colleagues is driving home one evening when he is hit and killed by a driver who was texting at the wheel. The negligent driver's auto insurance would pay a grand total of $100,000 if this were the bodily injury limit per person. Your colleague's spouse will not be satisfied with only receiving $100,000 because your colleague was on track to make millions of dollars over the course of his career. His spouse has every right to sue for additional payment and will likely do so. Court proceedings will generally determine how much the spouse is entitled to receive based on the present value of your colleague's future earnings, human life value, or another calculation.

How would this play out if you were the driver being sued for a large amount, such as $3 million?

Your auto insurer would pay up to the per person bodily injury limit specified on your policy. If this were only $100,000, then where does the other $2.9 million of the settlement come from? Your creditors would begin by seizing your unprotected assets, such as cash in bank accounts and investments that are not in protected accounts. In some states, they can even force you to sell your home to repay the debt if you have a certain amount of equity. Your creditors would then look to your income by garnishing a portion of your take-home pay until the claim is fulfilled.

This would be a nightmare scenario. As most people do not have a spare $2.9 million in their checking account, it is reasonable to consider insurance to protect against such a risk. Umbrella liability insurance is designed precisely for this. It pays the remainder of a claim, up to the umbrella's limit, once the claim has exceeded the limits of the underlying auto or homeowners insurance policy. If you had an umbrella liability insurance policy in the previous example, then this would be activated after your auto insurance paid $100,000. The rest of the settlement would have been fulfilled by the umbrella policy if you had at least $3 million of coverage, therefore protecting your assets and income from creditors.

Like a professional liability claim, the probability of having a personal liability claim may be small, but its impact can be severe. Fortunately, umbrella liability insurance is inexpensive and usually costs ten to twenty-five dollars a month per million of coverage. Some insurers provide a discount for having multiple lines of insurance with them, making the net cost even less. Another item to keep in mind is that your carrier will likely require you to increase the liability limits of your underlying auto, home, or renters insurance to their maximum before allowing you to purchase an umbrella policy.

When should you get umbrella liability insurance? It is never too soon to secure an umbrella policy. A claim could arise tomorrow, and it would be unfortunate if you became responsible for a large payout without it. Umbrella policies come in blocks of $1 million, though a minimum of $2 million or $3 million is generally advisable, especially as your income increases and assets grow.

## Chapter Summary

This chapter provides a basic understanding of the main types of property and casualty insurance. In addition to adequate auto, homeowners, and renters insurance, we also want to protect your assets from a personal liability claim. Remember, doctors are generally more likely to be sued than other occupations because the public's perception is that you have deep pockets and can afford to pay a large claim. Umbrella insurance is an often-overlooked form of insurance and a valuable asset protection tool to guard against lawsuits that occur from events outside of work.

### Key Takeaways

*Auto insurance* pays claims resulting from a car accident on a per-person, people-in-aggregate, and property-damage basis.

*Homeowners and renters insurance* cover claims that arise on your property, as well as the loss of personal property. Floods, earthquakes, and certain other risks are excluded from basic homeowners and renters insurance and can be covered by adding endorsements for these specific events or by purchasing a separate policy designed to cover these events.

*Umbrella liability insurance* is activated when the liability limits on your underlying auto, homeowners, and renters insurance are exceeded. Umbrella policies are issued in increments of $1 million and protect against large personal liability claims.

# CHAPTER 10

# DISABILITY INSURANCE

WE FIRST MET with Ben near the end of his anesthesiology residency. He had not yet secured disability insurance, but this was one of his top priorities after a family member had recently been injured.

"My sister broke her leg skiing last weekend," Ben explained. "And this got me thinking about my own health. I was on the slopes with her, and it could easily have been me who hit the icy patch that caused her injury. A broken leg is painful and inconvenient, but fortunately, she will make a full recovery. I don't know what I would do if something happened to me and I couldn't go back to work."

We share Ben's concern. There are many important parts that go into building your financial plan but not many as vital as making sure you can still get by if you cannot work. Disability insurance is designed to do just this—provide a benefit to replace your income if you are unable to practice in your area of medicine.

"I heard my colleagues talk about disability insurance and think I have this through my teaching hospital. Is that enough? And if not, what do I look for if I need to get disability insurance on my own?"

You invest a significant amount of time, energy, and money to be able to practice in your specialty and earn millions of dollars throughout your career. Think back to the last chapter that covered home, auto, and umbrella liability insurance. Your creditors look at your future earnings as an unprotected asset and can garnish a portion of your wages if you do not have enough personal liability insurance to fully cover a large claim. If your creditors in a lawsuit view your unearned income as an asset, then so should you. Properly protecting your income in the event of a long-term disability is one of the most important planning steps you can take, particularly if you are early in your career with the majority of your lifetime income still to be earned.

## Protecting Your Most Valuable Asset

What do we mean when we say "protecting your most valuable asset"? Well, if we continue to think of your unearned income as an asset, we see that the future income for a young doctor will be much larger than any physical assets they will buy. Incomes vary depending on your specialty and how you decide to practice, so we will use Ben as an example. Let's say that Ben expects to earn $300,000 his first year out of training. If he plans to work for thirty years, then he is already on track to earn $9 million over his career, not including production bonuses, cost of living raises, or promotions increasing his base salary.

Your home will likely be your largest physical asset purchase in your lifetime, but even a very nice house may only cost one or two million dollars. If your million-dollar house were destroyed and you did not have homeowners insurance (hopefully never the case!), it would be unfortunate. However, if you could still earn a high income, you could get by and eventually rebuild your home or buy another. If you experienced a long-term disability that erased millions of dollars of future income, you may not be able to recover.

## Types of Disability Insurance

Disability insurance is classified in several ways: short-term versus long-term; government social security disability insurance versus employer-provided group versus individual; and how disabled you have to be to receive a benefit, known as the definition of disability. With the multitude of options available, it can be difficult to know how each one may affect you.

Short-term disability insurance policies have short waiting and benefit periods. They often begin paying a benefit immediately or after one to two weeks, but the benefit may only last a few months. Females expecting to have children tend to be interested in short-term disability insurance more than other demographic groups, given the possibility of pregnancy complications. Insurance companies are aware of this adverse selection (tendency of people of who have a higher chance of experiencing a risk to be more interested in buying insurance to protect against it), and short-term disability insurance is therefore offered only in group plans through an employer. In addition, short-term disabilities fail our "Does this risk ruin me?" screening question. You will hopefully have an emergency reserve account to self-insure against a disability lasting three to six months. If your reserve is not fully funded, you may experience a minor hardship if you are unable to work for a few months but can likely make a full financial recovery afterward. In contrast, long-term disabilities affecting your ability to work for years could result in permanent impairment of your finances.

Long-term disability insurance may be provided through several sources, though these offer different levels of protection. Social security disability insurance contains the most restrictive contract language and requires your disability be so severe that it renders you unable to engage in any substantial gainful activity and is expected to last at least twelve months or result in death. We would not recommend doctors rely on this language. Because of this, doctors will commonly use individual disability insurance or a combination of individual and employer-provided disability insurance to protect their incomes against a long-term disability.

### Employer-Provided Group Disability Insurance

Most medium and large employers provide group disability insurance as part of their benefits package. Smaller employers, such as private practices with only a few partners, may or may not have a group disability insurance plan. If group insurance is provided, it is often free and does not require any health screening to qualify. With these positives aside, there are several limitations worth mentioning. The first is that group insurance only replaces a portion of your income, commonly 50 percent or 60 percent, and the benefit has a dollar limit, usually $10,000 to $15,000 per month. In addition, any benefit paid out to you will be taxable at ordinary income rates when employers pay the premium for the group plan (and include this cost as a business expense to lower their tax burden). This combination of a partial and taxable benefit results in a sizable gap between your pre-disability after-tax (net) income you were taking home while working and the net benefit received after paying taxes on the group disability insurance proceeds.

The following graph provides a visual illustration of this.

*Gross income.* This is your total pretax income while working.

*Net income.* This is your after-tax, or take-home, income you receive in your bank account when working. If we assume roughly a third of your income goes to taxes, then your net income would be 67 percent of your gross income.

*Group disability insurance benefit.* This is your pretax benefit amount received from your group disability insurance plan. Sixty percent is a common income replacement ratio. This amount is limited to the lesser of the income replacement ratio or the monthly dollar cap, which may result in a true income replacement ratio of less than 60 percent for high-income earners.

*Net group disability insurance benefit.* This is your after-tax group disability insurance benefit, as taxes are owed on the gross amount of group disability insurance benefit received. If we again assume a third of income going to taxes, this decreases your net group disability insurance benefit from 60 percent to 40 percent of your gross income. This would leave a gap of about 27 percent of gross income between what you were taking home before and after a disability.

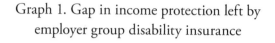

## Graph 1. Gap in income protection left by employer group disability insurance

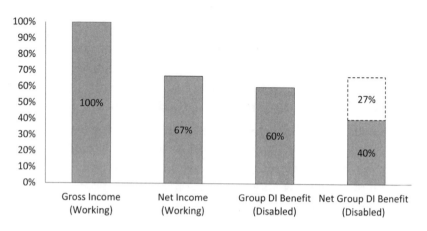

Most doctors, and Americans in general, base their lifestyle on an amount close to their full take-home income, which covers normal expenditures, student loan payments, and retirement savings. Decreasing this amount by over a third (from 67 percent down to 40 percent of gross income) would require a corresponding decrease in standard of living, such as relocating to a less desirable neighborhood to accommodate a lower mortgage payment. Also keep in mind that regular disability insurance only replaces income and does not reimburse other benefits lost, such as 401(k) or 403(b) employer-matching contributions or years of service accrual if your employer offers a pension. Last, most disability insurance benefits end at age sixty-five or sixty-seven, so it will be necessary to have extra funds saved on the side to provide for your later years after benefits cease.

Another limitation inherent in group disability insurance is just that: it is a group plan. This means it is one master contract between your employer and the insurance carrier, and you are simply a participant in the plan. Either of these two parties can modify the policy provisions or cancel the contract without your permission. As an employee, you hold a certificate of insurance, but your name is not on the actual plan contract. Most group plans are not portable either, meaning you are not able to take your coverage with you if you leave your current employer.

The last prominent downside of group disability insurance is the most important. This is referred to as the definition of disability and is the contract language within the policy that must be satisfied for you to qualify as being disabled. The ideal definition of disability is known as "own occupation," which means you are considered disabled if you are unable to perform the material and substantial duties of your own occupation. A strong definition of disability will then define your occupation in easy-to-understand language, with the insurance carrier often using your current procedural terminology (CPT) codes to define your occupational duties. In simple terms, if you can no longer perform the duties you were previously doing for wage or profit, then you are disabled and will receive a benefit from your disability insurance. If you are able to work in another occupation and choose to do so, you can earn any amount of income in your new position, and the full benefit will continue to be paid as long as you still cannot work in your original occupation that was deemed to be your occupation before the disability.

Group disability insurance will normally begin with some variation of own-occupation language but will then usually revert to less favorable wording, known as an "any occupation" definition of disability, after two years or so. This impacts how disabled you need to be to continue collecting your benefits. If you are now deemed to be able to perform any gainful occupation you may reasonably be suited to do based on your education, training, or experience, then you will no longer be considered disabled and will cease to continue receiving a benefit. We do not recommend doctors rely on this wording to protect millions of dollars of future income.

*Individual Disability Insurance*

"Okay, so what I understood from the last part is that my employer's disability insurance is a nice free benefit but should not be the only source to protect my income. What are the pros and cons of individual disability insurance?" Ben asked.

Whereas group disability insurance is an automatic benefit if offered, an individual policy requires health screening to qualify, and the cost is then paid by the policyowner. Once these are satisfied, the strengths of an individual policy mirror the limitations of group coverage.

*Full income protection.* Individual disability insurance allows you to protect almost all of your net income.

*Tax-free benefit.* The monthly benefit dollar amount you purchase with an individual policy will be received tax-free because you are paying the insurance premiums with money that has already been taxed.

*Your policy.* Individual policies are customized to your requested specifications and are your property. The insurance carrier cannot cancel or modify your policy features. You are also able to take your policy with you when you change employers or move to a different state.

*Own occupation definition of disability.* The definition of disability remains the stronger own occupation language through the full benefit period with individual disability insurance.

In addition, most individual disability insurance policies will include other features, or riders, that are not always found on group plans. These can include the following:

*Residual disability.* If you are partially disabled and have a loss of income, then a partial benefit will pay, often as a percentage of income lost. This can extend to when you have recovered from your disability and are back to work full-time, but your earnings have not yet reached your pre-disability income level (such as lower productivity due to a decreased patient load).

*Future increase option.* An additional benefit amount you can purchase to add to your base monthly benefit without having to repeat health screening. This allows you to increase your benefit periodically as your income rises over your career, even if you have had an adverse change in health.

*Inflation protection (cost of living adjustment).* Every year on disability claim, the benefit amount will increase by inflation over the prior year up to the cap (often 3 percent or 6 percent). This helps your monthly benefit keep pace with the rising cost of living if you are disabled over several years.

*Catastrophic benefit.* An extra benefit is paid each month if you are severely disabled. The catastrophic benefit helps pay for additional health care costs if you have difficulty performing the normal activities of daily living.

**Common Questions**

"That all sounds good and has reminded me of several questions I had been meaning to ask," mentioned Ben.

*What happens to my student loans if I am disabled and cannot make the payments?*

Depending on your situation, you may be able to delay payments on your federal student loans by claiming deferment or forbearance for a limited period of time. Federal loans will only be forgiven if your disability is deemed to be "total and permanent." Furthermore, if you were previously planning to have your loans forgiven through public service loan forgiveness, then you will stop accruing payments to count toward the required 120 needed for loan forgiveness until you are back to work at a qualifying employer at least thirty hours per week and resume making payments under a qualified repayment method. Private student loans may or may not be forgiven, depending on the terms set by the lender.

*What do I look for when considering individual disability insurance?*

Begin by limiting your search to the handful of insurance carriers that provide an own occupation definition of disability. As each of these companies rate risk differently depending on the applicant's health, activities, gender, and medical specialty, the company that may be a good fit for your colleague may not be the best fit for you. An independent financial advisor or disability insurance agent who has access to all of the own occupation carriers can help facilitate the screening process. This can be useful when the carrier that was initially thought to be the best fit provides a restricted offer due to a preexisting condition that another carrier may be more lenient on. Using an independent advisor for disability insurance also reduces conflicts of interest with insurance products by allowing the advisor to go through a variety of companies to better suit your needs (as opposed to a captive advisor who is affiliated with a specific insurer or otherwise biased to recommend one company over another).[1]

*I'm earning $50,000 as a resident now, but my income will increase three to ten times when I finish training. How do I ensure my income continues to be protected?*

Doctors go through an exciting transition when their income increases by many times overnight. Residents and fellows commonly obtain a small policy to protect their modest income in training, which includes a rider generally referred to as the future increase option. This provides the option to increase your benefit in the future based purely on financial underwriting, without having to repeat the medical underwriting required to initially secure coverage. If the cost of your primary residence, student loan payments, and overall living expenses have risen since graduation, it may be difficult to meet your higher obligations if your disability insurance benefit has not been adjusted to your new cash flow needs.

For example, in training, you may only need to replace $4,000 of monthly, take-home income, so you purchase a disability insurance policy with a $4,000 base monthly benefit to fit within your resident

---

[1] You can check whether a financial advisor is affiliated with or employed by an insurance company at FINRA's Broker Check website at brokercheck.finra.org.

budget. This policy includes the future increase option rider allowing you to purchase another $11,000 of benefit for a total of $15,000. After training, your income and expenses show you now need to protect $9,000 of income each month. You could submit income documentation to the insurance carrier to prove your higher earnings to qualify for the $9,000 benefit amount. You would then increase your $4,000 base policy by using $5,000 from the future increase option pool for a new monthly benefit of $9,000. The remaining $6,000 of future increase option benefit could then be accessed for later increases as needed.

*When should I get individual disability insurance?*

We would answer this question with one of our own: do you rely on your income today? The answer to this question is a clear yes for most doctors early in their careers. You may receive assistance from a group plan for a period of time, but your student loan payments and general living expenses would remain, if not increase due to additional health care and rehabilitation costs. Depending on the severity and duration of the disability, a long-term disability could certainly result in an affirmative answer to our "Does this ruin me?" question when deciding whether to insure against a risk. Apart from the current protection need, one of the most pressing reasons to secure an individual policy is the health screening involved to qualify. Disability insurance requires an applicant to go through medical underwriting to prove they are fairly healthy. A change in health, sometimes even a minor one, can result in a limited offer that may exclude the preexisting condition or result in the inability to qualify at all.

Now, we know some readers may not be the biggest fans of insurance. We understand where you are coming from. Insurance planning is the opposite of exciting for most people. If this includes you, then you can take comfort in knowing we do not view disability insurance as a forever product. In fact, once you secure it, we like to start counting down the days until you can reduce your coverage or cancel it altogether. What does this day look like? We simply ask another version of our original question: if your income went to zero for the rest of your life, how would you feel? If you would be terrified at the prospect of paying your student loans, paying your mortgage, putting children through college, saving for retirement, and covering general living expenses without income, then this is an indicator you are still reliant on your income to maintain your lifestyle. Keeping your disability insurance is therefore advisable. If the aforementioned priorities have been completed and you could comfortably live on your investment earnings or other sources of passive income for the rest of your life, congratulations! You are now financially independent from your income and should feel as if you are *choosing* to go to work each day as opposed to *needing* to work.

**Business Forms of Disability Insurance**

Business equity is often one of largest assets for owners, who may be relying on the business income stream or sale proceeds to fund their retirement. Insurance planning in this area is similar to insuring other significant assets, such as your home. While individual disability insurance should cover your personal finances, your practice may be left exposed if proper planning has not been done. Doctors who own their practice or are partners in one should consider additional forms of disability insurance to ensure the continuity or smooth succession of their business in the event of a disability. These include policies designed for business overhead expense (BOE) replacement, covering the disability of a key person, and funding buy-sell agreements.

The goal for business overhead expense, or BOE, disability insurance is to pay for operating expenses if the owner or another significant employee is unable to support the business due to a disability. Expenses needed to be covered include office rent, support staff payroll, supplies, other insurance, taxes, and utilities. Key person disability insurance is meant to replace the income lost from a disability of a key employee. This may be an owner, another doctor who generates considerable revenue, or an employee who performs a significant role for the business. The insurance proceeds are paid to the business and often used to hire a temporary or permanent replacement for the disabled worker. In simple terms, buy-sell agreements are contracts between owners of a business that outline how a business will be operated and owned by the remaining parties in the event of a disability, death, retirement, or other change in circumstance of one of the owners. For example, a buy-sell agreement may state that if an owner becomes disabled, the remaining owners will buy out the disabled owner's share of the partnership. A disability insurance policy structured to fund this buy-sell agreement would pay a benefit to the business entity or other partners to then purchase the disabled owner's share of the practice.

## Chapter Summary

This chapter has covered the various types, features, and applications of disability insurance. Let's put that aside for now and take a moment to reflect on your path to becoming a doctor.

For many of you, this began in high school, taking advanced classes to gain acceptance to a good university. Then came the long nights and missed parties, the lab groups and organic chemistry exams. The premed track for undergraduates is not known for being a breeze. It may seem long ago, but you were likely somewhat stressed leading up to the MCAT and medical school interviews. Then relief, excitement, and a little fear of what lay ahead when your acceptance letters arrived. Life accelerated through medical school. Two years of learning the human body inside and out, diseases, and treatments culminated in the Step 1 Exam. Then rounds, match day, a longer white coat, a move, your new colleagues … and now today. The path to becoming a doctor is not an easy one.

Now take a moment to think about how you picture life in the years ahead.

Some of the images that come to mind may include owning a home, having children, going on vacations, putting kids through college— maybe even seeing them go to medical school themselves—and having a comfortable retirement. The responsibilities of being a doctor will remain, but life outside of work can be quite good for doctors and their families.

Upon first glance, this chapter may appear to focus on a financial product, but that would be missing the larger meaning, failing to see the forest for the trees, as the saying goes. This chapter is really about respecting the enormous investment in time, energy, and resources to get to where you are today. It is about providing for you and your loved ones in the event of an unfortunate "what if?" What if I cannot work tomorrow? This chapter is about holding on to as much of the good life you pictured if an injury or illness renders you unable to practice medicine.

---

### Key Takeaways

The future income of an early-career doctor dwarfs any tangible asset you will buy throughout your lifetime. For this reason, paired with the idea that a long-term disability at this stage of your career could cause a significant hardship, *insuring your income with an own occupation disability insurance policy is one of the most important planning steps you can take.*

You may have group disability insurance provided by your employer, though *doctors should not rely on these group plans for their only income protection, due to their limitations.* These include partial income protection and a taxable benefit, as well as less specific contract language for the definition of disability than we like to see (often reverting to an "any occupation" definition after a short period of being on claim).

*Own occupation disability insurance* protects your ability to work as a doctor in your medical specialty by paying you a benefit if you cannot perform the material and substantial duties of your own occupation, even if you are able to work in another occupation outside of your area of medicine.

Residents and fellows will often secure a small individual disability insurance policy that has the *future increase option (FIO) rider*, *which allows you to increase the benefit amount after training without having to go through health screening again.*

In addition to protecting their personal financial plan, business owners should consider forms of disability insurance that ensure the value of their practice is not eroded if they, another owner, or a key employee becomes disabled. These include disability insurance policies to cover *business overhead expenses (BOE)*, replace income lost from a *key person*, and fund *buy-sell agreements*.

# CHAPTER 11

# LIFE INSURANCE

ERIN AND MARK were expecting their first child later in the year when we began meeting. While they were excited about becoming parents, they were also nervous about their upcoming changes and whether they were adequately prepared. Erin had recently completed her otolaryngology residency and was the newest of four surgeons at an ear, nose, and throat clinic. Mark was a high school teacher and was considering taking time off to care for their child. They had not made any adjustments to their financial plan to accommodate their growing family, and chief among their concerns was the topic of life insurance.

"We rely mostly on my income to support us, so I want to make sure Mark and our kid will be okay if I am not there for them," Erin explained. "We just bought a home in a good neighborhood, and we wouldn't be able to pay the mortgage on Mark's income alone."

"And if I take a year or two away from teaching, then we will be solely reliant on Erin to cover our expenses," Mark added. "We're young and healthy, so we didn't think we needed life insurance in the past. Now, with our new home and baby coming, we feel the need for life insurance has become more real."

Our thinking is right in line with Erin and Mark's. The responsibilities of being parents extend not only to the physical and emotional care of their child but also the financial side. It is not fun to think about, but a key topic for young families is to proactively plan for an unexpected passing.

"I've heard of several types of life insurance, so we would like to learn more about the differences and what may be appropriate for us. We are also not sure how much life insurance we need," Erin continued. "Overall, we would like a few pointers on life insurance and what young families, like us, should know."

This dialogue with Erin and Mark exemplifies the mindset of many new or soon-to-be parents. This chapter will focus on life insurance, which pays a death benefit to a beneficiary or beneficiaries if the insured passes away. Life insurance can be used for a variety of purposes within a financial plan, the most common of which is as protection for dependents. Other areas where life insurance can be applicable include estate planning or as an accumulation vehicle to complement investment accounts in a long-term savings plan. In the business setting, life insurance may be needed to take out a commercial loan, lessen the financial hardship from the loss of a key employee, or facilitate business succession planning. We will expand on each of these reasons throughout this chapter, as well as give an overview of the different types of life insurance.

## For Protection Needs

An early passing of a loved one can be one of the most heartbreaking experiences to go through. We imagine long and healthy lives for us and our family, rarely anticipating a premature death. Unfortunately, these tragedies occur from time to time, whether from an auto accident or losing the battle against an illness. Dealing with this can be emotionally draining, and family members of the deceased are financially affected as well. A life insurance benefit can help alleviate financial concerns as a family prepares to face a different future than the one planned on.

In the most basic sense, life insurance protects against the risk of living too short. It provides a benefit to the surviving spouse, children, or other beneficiaries if the insured (the person whose life was insured by the policy) passes away. An unexpected death, especially of the primary income earner, could be catastrophic for dependents who relied on the insured's financial support. Life insurance proceeds can allow the surviving spouse to take time off work and then go back part-time, or potentially not at all. They are also used to provide additional funding for retirement or to pay off a mortgage, allowing the family to remain in their home. Parents may also like the idea of using life insurance to pay for their children's education if they are not there to see them through college.

The answer to how much life insurance is appropriate depends on your current situation and future plans. There is no standard approximation for exactly how much you may need to be adequately insured. One rule of thumb you may have heard is to have ten times your annual income in life insurance death benefit. For example, if you earn $200,000, then this rule would suggest you be insured for $2 million. We would caution anyone relying on this as an accurate estimate of your life insurance need. This would be similar to saying each person needs to consume 2,000 calories a day. This is clearly not true, as some people need less than this and some need significantly more, depending on their body and physical activity, among other factors. Elements that affect your need for life insurance include but are not limited to the following:

- current assets and debts
- current and future living expenses for dependents
- number of children
- how much you would like to provide toward the cost of your children's education
- the surviving spouse's income potential
- the surviving spouse's life expectancy
- estimated inflation
- estimated rate of return on investments

If your spouse has a high income, you have a small family, your children are already independent or will be soon (or you do not plan to have children), and you have a small mortgage, your need may be less than ten times your income to be adequately insured. Conversely, your need may be more than ten times if your spouse makes little or no income, you have young children who will be dependent for many years, or you have a large mortgage. The online calculator at LifeHappens.org provides an estimate of how much life insurance may be needed when considering several of these factors.[1]

How would your family use a life insurance benefit? A portion of the benefit would be applied toward present costs, such as final medical bills, funeral costs, or to pay off a mortgage. The rest would then be invested to generate an income stream to fund living expenses for dependents. The life insurance company will provide alternate options for receiving the death benefit, but the lump sum option is generally the preferred choice. Life insurance benefits are passed through the insurance contract and avoid probate because of this.[2] They are also received free of income tax, though are included in the taxable estate of the insured unless specifically removed, such as through the use of a trust.

An often-overlooked need for life insurance is protection for a nonworking spouse or a spouse who is not the primary income earner. While the amount of life insurance needed will be less than that of the primary income earner, receiving a benefit can help the family avoid a strain on their lifestyle. Doctors regularly work over forty hours a week, and a non-doctor spouse may provide the majority of childcare or other duties to support the household. Even if they are not earning an income, a spouse is certainly providing an economic benefit. For example, if Mark were to take time away from work to care for their baby and subsequently passes away, Erin may decrease her workload to spend time raising their child, pay for a full-time childcare professional, or both. The burden of these would be reduced by Mark having life insurance.

---

[1] LifeHappens.org is a nonprofit organization dedicated to raising awareness on various risks and insurance topics.

[2] Probate is the process of distributing assets included in the deceased's probate estate through court proceedings. We expand on the topics of probate, trusts, and how assets pass to heirs at death in the Estate Planning chapter. Mention of estate planning in this book is for educational purposes only. We are not attorneys, and formal estate planning advice should be received from an estate planning attorney.

## For Estate Planning

"That makes sense on the protection side and has brought up a question about my uncle," mentioned Erin, looking a little embarrassed. "He is quite wealthy, and because he does not have a spouse or any children, he may be leaving the majority of his money to my parents, my sister, and me. This is hopefully not for many years, but we may be inheriting several million dollars at some point. How would this change our situation?"

This would change Erin and Mark's financial plan significantly, particularly around the use of life insurance. Inheriting millions of dollars would reduce or potentially eliminate their protection needs altogether. Instead, it may create an estate planning need for life insurance to pay estate taxes owed upon death.

Estate taxes are part of the unified transfer tax system, which taxes assets gifted while alive and those transferred upon death. Transfer taxes are complicated, and working with an estate planning attorney is advisable if they may apply to you. This may be the case if the combined value of your lifetime taxable gifts and your taxable estate is above the federal estate tax lifetime exemption amount, which was approximately $11.2 million in 2018.[1] The top estate tax rate is 40 percent on assets above the exemption, so the estate may owe a large amount in taxes if it is valued over $11.2 million.[2] Estate taxes are due within nine months from the date of death, which can be problematic if a significant portion of the estate is in illiquid assets, such as real estate. Having life insurance proceeds provide an infusion of cash to cover estate taxes can be beneficial to avoid having to sell estate assets in a short period of time.

---

[1] The 2017 Tax Cuts and Jobs Act temporarily increased the lifetime exemption to $10 million, an amount that is adjusted based on inflation that occurs after 2011. This indexing caused the lifetime exemption amount to be approximately $11.2 million in 2018. This temporary increase expires after 2025, when it is scheduled to revert back to a base of $5 million, also set in 2011 and indexed for inflation.

[2] This ignores the portability of the unused exemption amount from a spouse or the use of credit shelter trusts. Going into sufficient detail on these topics is beyond the scope of this book. An estate planning attorney will be able to explain whether using one or both of these strategies is advisable.

## As an Accumulation Vehicle

"I heard one of my partners talking about using life insurance as part of his retirement savings plan. Is this similar to using life insurance for estate planning?" asked Erin.

These two uses are related, however quite different in how they would be implemented. Before we go into detail on this, we need to understand the two main versions of life insurance, term and permanent. We will then build on this to explain how life insurance may be used in a savings plan.

## Term Life Insurance

Term life insurance is temporary coverage that provides protection for a certain period of time, after which the policy expires if the insured is still alive. If the insured dies during the term period, the death benefit is paid to the beneficiaries. Common term periods are ten, twenty, or thirty years but can be longer. The vast majority of term life insurance policies expire without paying a claim, which is why term coverage is the least expensive form of life insurance per dollar of benefit. This type of life insurance is often the most appropriate when there is a protection need, but the budget is fairly tight, such as having a young family while in training.

At the end of the term period, the policyowner has a few options with their policy. First, they may let their coverage expire. This can be appropriate if they no longer have a need for life insurance. Alternatively, most companies allow you to extend the term length for additional one-year periods at a time. This option is known as "annual renewable term" and is not very popular because the cost greatly increases after the fixed-cost term period. Last, some companies allow you to convert all or a portion of your term life insurance benefit to a permanent life insurance policy without having to repeat the health screening. This can be useful if you still have a need for life insurance after the term policy will expire (such as a mortgage to cover or dependent children), but you have experienced a change in health for the worse since you initially secured the term policy. Without the conversion option, you may not be able to qualify for a new term policy, or, even if you can, the new policy may be at a more expensive health rate.

## Permanent Life Insurance

In contrast to term insurance, permanent life insurance is designed to last for one's entire life and pay a death benefit when the insured passes away. The cost of insurance is higher because the probability of a claim being paid is greater than with term insurance. In addition to being used for protection needs, it can also be implemented for accumulation purposes. The objective for why you may choose to use this in your plan will determine which version of permanent life insurance may be suitable and how it should be structured.

Before we go into more detail on this topic, we need to acknowledge the divided reputation this product has earned. There are not many areas of financial planning in which public opinion is more polarized than permanent life insurance. Why is this? Permanent life insurance has favorable tax advantages and asset protection benefits, but it has been recommended when not appropriate, not structured in line with the policy's objective, or not well explained by the insurance agent or financial advisor as to how the policy may perform. As with all areas of financial planning, we encourage you to form your own opinion on this subject.

This section of the book will not make an argument for why you should avoid permanent life insurance, nor will it be a ringing endorsement. Instead, the goal is to add clarity to a complicated financial product so you can decide whether you may or may not want to consider this in your plan. We will first provide an overview of how permanent life insurance works before reviewing the common versions. This section will conclude with several points about permanent life insurance to keep in mind if you already own a policy or plan to in the future.

With all forms of permanent life insurance, policy owners typically pay a premium greater than the minimum cost of insurance required to keep the policy in force. The extra amount paid goes to a reserve account called the "cash value," hence why it is also called "cash value life insurance." The cash value can earn interest, or gain or lose value, depending on the type of policy used, and can be accessed during the insured's lifetime with certain tax advantages (more on this aspect later). If you will be using this product in your financial plan, then you first need to decide your objective for the policy. The two main goals for permanent life insurance are to either maximize the internal rate of return on the cash value accumulation or on the benefit paid upon death (otherwise known as the "death benefit"). If the policy's objective is not clearly defined or if the policy is not structured for this objective, then it may not perform as expected. This is one of the main causes of disappointment with cash value life insurance.

If the primary function of the policy is to grow the cash value component to be accessed while alive, then the most efficient way to structure the policy is to minimize the death benefit (which will minimize the cost of insurance) and *maximize premium contributions* allowed for the chosen death benefit amount. Policy owners may use permanent life insurance in this capacity as a complement to their long-term savings plan to help fund their retirement. To efficiently grow the cash value, policy owners will want to make consistent premium payments every month. Missed contributions will result in less efficient cash value growth, so a high amount of discretionary income is needed before funding a permanent life insurance policy for this objective.

If the permanent policy is to be used primarily for the death benefit, then the goal will be to pay the *lowest amount of premiums* for a given death benefit (or have the largest death benefit for a given premium amount). This will result in the highest return on premiums paid when the death proceeds are distributed to beneficiaries. Policy owners may use life insurance in this capacity for protection beyond the period of a term policy, to add liquidity to their estate, or for business planning purposes.

You have likely noticed the previous two paragraphs are conflicting with their opposite goals. It is difficult for a policy to be efficient at accumulating cash value while simultaneously maximizing the death benefit amount. The manner in which a policy is structured at the start will have an exponential effect in the long run, so it is important to have a clear objective of what this is aiming to accomplish before beginning a permanent life insurance policy.

### Types of Permanent Life Insurance

Now that we have covered the two main objectives for permanent life insurance, we can review the different types available. Four common versions of permanent life insurance are whole life, universal life, variable universal life, and indexed universal life insurance. With each of these, the cash value grows without being taxed, though the manner in which the cash value grows is one of the key differences between them. The following paragraphs list some of the defining traits of each version.

### Whole Life Insurance

Whole life insurance is characterized by a fixed death benefit amount and fixed monthly premium. The cash value grows by a combination of a low guaranteed minimum interest rate and discretionary dividends determined by the carrier. Dividends granted by the insurer each year are based on several factors, including their realized versus expected death claims and investment earnings on the reserve funds held in their general account. Insurance carriers typically invest their excess cash conservatively, primarily in fixed-income securities, such as bonds. This influences how much of a dividend the insurer may be able to provide to policyowners. As interest rates have been declining since the early 1980s and causing bond yields to fall with them, dividend rates on whole life policies have generally been decreasing over the past few decades. Policyowners should keep in mind that dividends are not guaranteed, and insurers can decrease or skip dividend payments as they see fit. Whole life dividends are not taxable until they exceed the policyowner's total premium payment, or basis, at which time they begin to be taxed as ordinary income. The primary appeal of whole life insurance stems from the guaranteed death benefit and minimum interest rate; however, potential policyowners should understand this may be at the expense of greater cash value upside provided by other versions of permanent life insurance.

## Universal Life Insurance

In contrast to the rigid structure of whole life policies, universal life insurance policies provide flexibility by allowing policyowners to change their monthly premium and death benefit. Insurers credit interest to a universal life policy's cash value based on interest rates. These policies originated in the early 1980s when interest rates were at their peak. As with whole life dividend rates, universal life interest crediting rates have decreased steadily over the past couple of decades. Interest rates are near all-time lows at the time of this book's original publication, so universal life policies are generally not an attractive choice for long-term cash value growth. The primary appeal of a universal life policy over a whole life insurance is the policyowner's flexibility to pay more or less into the contract as they choose. Universal policies may have a guaranteed minimum interest crediting rate, like whole life policies. Policyowners also have the option for an increasing death benefit, so the combination of a policy's face value (original death benefit amount) and cash value growth may exceed the policy's original death benefit amount.

## Variable Universal Life Insurance

The next development in the world of permanent life insurance came as variable universal life insurance. Like traditional universal policies, variable universal policies provide flexible death benefit and premium amounts. The difference is how the cash value earns its return. With variable policies, the cash value is invested into subaccounts, which are similar to mutual funds, a type of investment whose value depends on the performance of its underlying holdings (much more on mutual funds in the investment section). Policyowners now have the option to invest in the stock market within their life insurance. This can be attractive during rising markets, such as the bull market of the 1990s. However, subaccounts may lose value in a declining market, such as the dot-com recession of the early 2000s. This can be problematic for variable life insurance policy owners because the policy's cash value decreases as its subaccounts lose value, but the policy's cost of insurance and administrative fees remain and continue to be paid out of the policy's shrinking cash value. This can cause the policy to cannibalize its previous growth and, in a worst-case scenario, require the policyowner to pay more into the policy to keep it from lapsing.

*Indexed Universal Life Insurance*

Indexed universal life insurance policies also exhibit flexible death benefit and premium payments; however, their cash value growth is different from both traditional universal life and variable life policies. As its name indicates, cash value returns of indexed policies are tied to a market benchmark index for an investment asset class. The defining characteristics of indexed policies are their floor and ceiling on the amount of interest credited to the cash value over the interest-crediting period, commonly twelve months. The floor, or lower limit, of indexed policy returns is often 0 percent but can be slightly higher. The ceiling, or upper limit, typically ranges from around 12 percent to 16 percent. For example, the cash value's return may track the performance of the S&P 500 Index, which represents about five hundred of the largest US companies and is bound by a floor of 0 percent and a ceiling of 13 percent. In this scenario, contributions to an indexed policy's cash value would earn the following returns (ignoring policy expenses):

> From January 1 to the following January 1, the S&P 500 Index increased 8 percent. The contribution made on January 1 (along with previous January contributions and their growth) would have been credited an 8 percent return (within floor and ceiling limits).

> From February 1 to the following February 1, the S&P 500 Index increased 20 percent. The contribution made on February 1 (along with previous February contributions and their growth)

would have been credited a 13 percent return (ceiling of 13 percent applies).

From March 1 to the following March 1, the S&P 500 Index *decreased* 10 percent. The contribution made on March 1 (along with previous March contributions and their growth) would not have received an interest credit or seen its value decrease (floor of 0 percent applies).

With indexed life insurance, policyowners forego some of the upside return by accepting the ceiling's cap to receive the insurer's guarantee their cash value will not lose value during periods of negative index performance.[1] The floor is an attractive feature, particularly if there is a market downturn when the policy owner is accessing the cash value through withdrawals or a policy loan. This provides the policyowner a source of income that is unaffected by poor market performance, allowing them to avoid selling other portfolio assets for a loss (stock or bond funds that may have decreased in value in the market decline, for example). Due to the low cash value return rates of whole and universal life insurance and the downside risk of variable policies, indexed policies have become an alternative choice for policy owners looking for cash value accumulation.

*How Cash Value Is Accessed While Alive*

"You mentioned that the cash value can be accessed while we're alive. How?" asked Mark. "Is it similar to taking a withdrawal from an investment account?"

---

[1] Life insurance companies are able to do this by investing most of the premium contributions in a bond portfolio that will grow to a specified value within a year with a high degree of confidence, creating the floor. They invest the rest of the premium contribution (apart from policy expenses) in call options on the underlying index, which increase in value with an increase in the value of the index. This allows the insurer to provide returns similar to the index during periods of positive index performance.

The end result is similar, but how a policyowner receives the funds is not as straightforward as simply taking a distribution from the cash value. Policyowners are able to first withdraw the total amount of premiums they have paid tax-free from the cash value. The premiums were paid with after-tax money, so they are not taxed again upon withdrawal. After this, any growth in the cash value that is distributed is Taxable as ordinary income. To avoid this, policy owners will take a loan from the life insurance company not by taking a loan *from* your cash value but rather *against* it by pledging it as collateral for the loan.

Loans do not count as income, nor do they represent gains on capital assets, so neither income nor capital gains tax applies to the loan amount disbursed. Instead, the insurer must charge interest on the amount borrowed for this to qualify as a loan, but policyowners usually have the option for a "wash loan" in which the insurer credits back the same amount of interest being charged so the net interest rate charged is 0 percent. To be clear, policy owners generally do not plan to pay back this loan amount. The loan is simply the method used to benefit from the cash value that has grown over time.

There are a couple of aspects with policy loan provisions to keep in mind. First, the amount of loan disbursed and any accrued interest will be subtracted from the death benefit paid to beneficiaries if the insured passes away with the loan outstanding. Second, withdrawing too much or taking too large of a loan may cause the policy to lapse, which would result in adverse tax consequences (the entire amount of cash value growth would immediately be taxable as income). If you have a permanent life insurance policy and are either currently or will soon be accessing your cash value, it is advisable to work with a knowledgeable professional to avoid this pitfall.

### Considerations with Permanent Life Insurance

"Wow, you were right; this can get complicated. Do you see us using permanent life insurance?" asked Erin.

Not at the moment. Remember, Erin and Mark's primary need for life insurance today is protection against an early passing, which is satisfied by term life insurance. With that said, it can be beneficial to have the option to convert all or a portion of their term life insurance into a permanent policy in the future. Starting with fully convertible term insurance is a nice way to get adequate protection at a low cost, secure coverage at your good health rate when younger, and keep your options open in the years to come. If you do use permanent life insurance at some point, there are a few other items to consider.

*Cost and expenses.* Due to the higher probability of a death benefit being paid with permanent life insurance, the cost is higher compared to a term policy for the same death benefit amount. Term life insurance premiums are generally fixed, whereas the cost of insurance for permanent policies increases each year. Permanent life insurance policies also have surrender charges in the early years of the policy, which decreases the amount of cash value available within the first ten to fifteen years and makes them inefficient for short-term growth.

*Adequately funding cash value.* If using permanent life insurance for cash value accumulation, the most efficient way to fund the cash value is to make the maximum premium contributions allowed for a given death benefit amount. Contributing significantly less than this will result in too much of the premium going to the cost of the insurance and too little going toward the cash value. Beware of advisors or insurance agents who recommend "target funding" a universal, variable universal, or indexed universal policy if the goal is cash value accumulation, as this will underfund the policy and result in inefficient cash value growth. All versions of universal life insurance allow policy owners to skip premium payments; however, this will cause the cost of insurance to be drawn from the cash value, decreasing growth. For this reason, policyowners should have a high discretionary cash flow before starting a permanent policy so they do not have to skip payments.

*Avoid becoming a modified endowment contract (MEC).* While you do not want to underfund a permanent policy, you also do not want to overfund it by too much either. Doing so may cause the policy to become a modified endowment contract, or MEC. This will result in the policy losing its tax advantages of nontaxable premium withdrawals and policy loans.[1]

*Conservative illustrations.* If you are considering a permanent life insurance policy, the financial advisor or insurance agent you are working with is required to provide you with an illustration. This is a hypothetical projection showing how the cash value may grow over time with assumed premium contributions, cash value rates of return, and loan amounts taken. These should be shown with conservative rates of return, and the advisor should emphasize that rates of return listed are not guaranteed.

*Beneficial asset protection treatment.* In many states, the cash value is a protected asset from creditors in the event of bankruptcy or a lawsuit. This can be helpful for doctors who are at risk for higher personal or professional lawsuits than non-doctors.

As the last few pages have shown, permanent life insurance is a complicated product and should be properly understood before implemented. Benefits include a death benefit that will be in place for the policyowner's entire life, strong asset protection laws in many states, cash value that is not taxed while it grows and can be accessed while alive without being taxed, and in some versions, the cash value will not decrease even if the market does. Drawbacks include a higher cost of insurance than term coverage, potentially low cash value rates of return, and extra expenses if the cash value is accessed within the first several years. The decision whether to use permanent life insurance in your financial plan should be made on a personal basis after careful consideration of the pros and cons.

---

[1] With policies that have become a MEC, withdrawals and loans are taxed as income. If distributions are made before the policy owner is fifty-nine and a half years old, a 10 percent penalty applies on the amount withdrawn or loaned unless they are due to a disability or annuity payment.

## Business Uses of Life Insurance

"No kidding. There is definitely a lot to consider with permanent life insurance. I agree starting with term life insurance makes the most sense," acknowledged Mark.

"On another note, the lead partner in my practice mentioned wanting me to have life insurance soon. I think he meant as it relates to my role in the practice rather than for my personal planning. Is this common?" asked Erin.

Yes, it can be common for a business, especially small practices like Erin's, to own life insurance on key employees or owners. Practice owners may purchase life insurance for several reasons relating to the acquisition, growth, and eventual sale of their business. Life insurance may serve as collateral for a commercial loan needed to start your practice or buy an ownership interest. It can also be used to protect the business from a worker's unexpected passing that could result in a hardship for the practice. Due to the tax advantages of permanent life insurance, businesses may use this to create executive compensation plans to reward owners or key employees. Last, life insurance can facilitate the succession planning of a business if an owner passes away.

### Collateral for Business Loans

Erin does not yet have an ownership stake in her practice but expects this to change soon. Partnership offers are usually made after the second or third year of employment. In some cases, there may be no explicit buy-in required of the new partner. In these scenarios, the new partner will commonly earn below the market rate of compensation for their specialty before they are allowed to share in the company's profits. Other practices may have a specific acquisition cost per share of ownership, and the new partner will need to buy in, generally in one of two ways. First, the practice may defer a portion of the new partner's income toward the buy-in cost until it is repaid. Alternatively, the practice may require an upfront lump sum payment. The new partner will either need to have a substantial amount of cash available for the purchase or may need to borrow this amount. If a loan is taken out from a bank or credit union, the lender will usually require the borrower to have life insurance as collateral for a loan above $50,000. This arrangement is known as collateral assignment and designates the lender as the assignee. The borrower assigns their life insurance policy as collateral for the loan so the lender will receive a portion of the death benefit in the amount of the loan balance outstanding if the borrower passes away before the loan is fully repaid. The remainder of the life insurance death benefit then goes to the beneficiaries listed on the policy.

### Protection for Key Employees

The reason the head of Erin's practice may want her to have life insurance is likely due to protection needs for the partnership. Erin will account for a substantial portion of the practice's revenue once her patient load increases, as she is one of four providers. An unexpected passing could cause a hardship to the practice with decreased billings and the potential need to hire a temporary or permanent replacement. For this reason, small businesses will commonly secure key employee life insurance on owners or employees who contribute a significant amount of revenue or provide duties that are vital to ongoing operations. Businesses may also purchase life insurance to cover business overhead expenses (BOE), such as staff costs and office rent, if Erin's income disappears. While Erin is the insured, the business entity will be the policyowner and beneficiary to receive the policy's proceeds for both key employee and BOE life insurance.

### Executive Compensation Plans

Employer-provided retirement plans, such as 401(k) plans, generally limit total contributions to $55,000 per year.[1] While this should provide plenty

---

[1] Section 415 of the IRS tax code limits the total amount that may be contributed into a qualified defined contribution retirement plan to $55,000 for the 2018 tax year. This is split into employee salary deferrals of up to $18,500 or 100 percent of the employee's salary, whichever is lower. Employers can make up to $36,500 of matching contributions or profit-sharing contributions to reach the total of $55,000. In addition to this, workers age fifty and over can make catch-up contributions of up to $6,000 per year for a total of $61,000.

of room for most workers to accumulate retirement funds, many doctors will save more than this annually, especially since salaried employees can only contribute $18,500 from their income. Employers who wish to reward executives or key employees with a larger retirement benefit may establish an executive compensation plan that can discriminate in favor of high-income earners and does not have to be available to rank-and-file employees. These plans do not receive the beneficial IRS tax treatment that qualified retirement plans do, so employers will often choose to use permanent life insurance to fund them due to the tax advantages of cash value growth and policy loan options. These are broadly known as nonqualified deferred compensation plans, though there are different types and ways of structuring them. Erin's partnership may establish and fund one of these if they would like to have an extra benefit to recruit and reward valuable employees.

*Business Succession Planning*

As with planning for an owner's disability, businesses should also plan for an unexpected passing of an owner. Failing to do so could jeopardize the continued growth of the practice and cause discord between the remaining partners and family members of the deceased owner. Business owners often have a large amount of their personal wealth tied to their equity share of a business and likely want this value to be inherited by their family. Unfortunately, this may not happen smoothly if the necessary planning steps are not taken in advance. The instructions for a business succession plan can be found in a document called a buy-sell agreement, which is a legal contract that outlines how a business will be owned and operated by the remaining partners if one of the partners dies or is otherwise unable to continue their managerial or medical duties. Life insurance provides the funding that allows the buy-sell agreement to be implemented. Let's see how this may play out in Erin's partnership.

We have fast-forwarded a few years, and Erin is now an equal partner in her clinic along with Adam, Carolyn, and Dave, with each doctor having a 25 percent ownership share. Referrals to new patients are picking up, operating rooms are rarely vacant, and the partners are beginning to think about expansion plans. The practice is rolling! Then the unthinkable happens. One evening after work, Erin receives a call from Donna, Dave's wife, informing her that Dave died in a car accident on his commute home. Erin, Adam, Carolyn, and their staff are stunned. After she regains her composure, Erin remembers they had worked with an attorney on legal documents for the business around the time she became a partner.

The attorney explains that if a partner dies, their buy-sell agreement states the remaining partners will buy the deceased partner's ownership share. The beneficiary of the deceased partner's ownership share, Donna in this case, is obligated to sell her ownership share to Erin, Adam, and Carolyn.[1] Until then, they have the privilege of running their practice with her. Erin and the other partners are on good terms with Donna, but Donna does not have a medical background, and the partners are concerned her interests may not be aligned with theirs. Donna may want to use her share of the practice's profit to fund her two kids' college, pay off her mortgage, and maintain the lifestyle she has been accustomed to, rather than fund the practice's expansion plans. In short, this may be an inconvenient arrangement for Erin and the other partners.

Now that the buy-sell has been triggered, Erin and the other partners will be buying Donna's equity share at a predetermined sale price. The agreement should clearly outline how the business is to be valued, using either a stated formula or a method for obtaining the practice's value. If the practice were valued at $12 million between practice assets and projected revenue growth, then Erin, Adam, and Carolyn need to come up with $3 million to buy Donna's 25 percent ownership share. Each partner may not have a spare $1 million, so using life insurance to fund

---

[1] Cross-purchase and entity buy-sells are two forms of buy-sell agreements. In a cross-purchase buy-sell, each partner owns a life insurance policy on every other partner. Cross-purchase agreements tend to be more common with small firms, as the number of life insurance policies needed grows quickly with the number of owners. They are more tax efficient than entity buy-sell agreements due to the increased cost basis remaining partners receive when they buy the deceased partner's equity share. Erin's practice must have a cross-purchase agreement, as the doctors themselves will be buying the ownership shares from Donna. In an entity buy-sell, the business entity itself owns life insurance policies on each partner and purchases the equity share from the deceased partner's beneficiary.

the buy-sell agreement can be useful. In this example, Erin, Adam, and Carolyn would each own a $1 million life insurance policy on Dave's life, so when he passed they would each receive the $1 million death benefit to fund their purchase of Donna's ownership interest. If the life insurance policies on each partner were not in place, then the buy-sell would be considered unfunded. This could result in an unfavorable outcome because Donna may be allowed to sell her ownership share to an outside party if the remaining partners are not able to complete the purchase within the timeframe outlined in the agreement.

## Common Questions

"We asked to learn more about life insurance, and we certainly have," said Erin. "I know our session today is almost over, so I wanted to cover a few questions before we finish …"

*What happens to my student loans if I pass away?*

Federal student loans are discharged upon death and do not become the obligation of surviving family members or your estate. PLUS and private lender loans are treated differently. PLUS loans may be discharged at the death of either the student or the parent. If due to the student's death, parents will file Form 1099-C (Cancellation of Debt), and the amount of discharged PLUS loans will be taxable as income. This may increase the parents' tax bill substantially. Private loans may or may not be discharged, depending on the lender and whether you had a cosigner when you took out the private loan. If you did, then your cosigner may be responsible for paying back the loan balance, possibly immediately depending on the situation. Having life insurance to provide a benefit to parents or your cosigner could help them avoid a financial strain if you were to pass away with PLUS or private student loans outstanding.

*What should I look for when considering life insurance?*

When looking into term life insurance, we would suggest a carrier whose term life insurance is fully convertible to a number of permanent life insurance types at any point throughout the term to keep this option available. We would also encourage you to work with an independent financial advisor or insurance agent when considering not just life insurance but any financial product. Working with someone who is not employed by or affiliated with an insurance or investment company can reduce a conflict of interest when considering which life insurance carrier for your protection.

*When should I get life insurance?*

At the latest, we view life insurance as a necessary part of your plan if someone comes to mind as being in a difficult financial situation if you were to pass away. This is usually a family member but not always. In Erin's case, Mark and their future child are dependent on her income and would need to make significant changes to their planned lifestyle if Erin were to die unexpectedly. The health screening needed to qualify for life insurance is another factor to consider. Even if you do not have a financial dependent today, it may make sense to look into an inexpensive term life insurance policy to qualify at a younger (and hopefully healthier) rate if you may have dependents in the future. Some doctors and their families also like the idea of providing a benefit to a charitable cause if they are not able to donate later in life.

**Chapter Summary**

As we have seen with Erin and Mark, life insurance can be used for several purposes in a financial plan outside of protection for dependents. This versatility can lead to confusion with the many possible applications, though it does not have to. Remembering that life insurance is first and foremost just that—insurance—should help simplify what can become a complicated topic. We have seen the beneficial impact life insurance can have on a family when they are covered and the strain it can create when they are not. If an unexpected passing could cause a financial difficulty on a business partner, family member, or another loved one, this indicates it is time to consider life insurance in your plan.

## Key Takeaways

Life insurance can be used for a number of purposes, including *protection, estate planning, as an accumulation vehicle,* and for *business planning.*

*Term life insurance* exists for a specified period of time before expiring and is usually the least expensive way to purchase a large death benefit.

*Permanent life insurance* is designed to last for the insured's entire life and, because of this, has a higher cost of insurance than term life insurance. In addition to their death benefit, these policies have a *cash value,* which can go up or down in value depending on the type of policy. The four main type of permanent life insurance are *whole life, universal life, variable universal life,* and *indexed universal life.*

Business planning with life insurance can take the form of *collateral for business loans, key employee protection, executive compensation plans,* and *funding business succession plans.*

# CHAPTER 12

# ESTATE PLANNING

TIM AND LAUREN began their financial plan during Tim's first year of family medicine residency but had not met for a review session in over three years. In that time, they welcomed two daughters, and Tim had joined a local neighborhood clinic. Lauren decided to take time off work to raise their daughters, ages three and one, and was unsure whether she would return to her previous job.

"We're sorry it's taken us so long to get back in touch," said Tim. "Honestly, these last three years have been a blur with the arrival of our girls and my transition."

"We know that there's more planning we should do, like get a will drafted," admitted Lauren. "We felt like we haven't had time to catch up on much, let alone meet with an attorney for a will …"

This is understandable with everything Tim and Lauren have going on. Estate planning is one of the last topics doctors and their families usually address, not because they do not value it but because it may seem too daunting or morbid to place at the top of one's to-do list. Nevertheless, if you have a family or plan to start one soon, we would encourage you to consider these items to ease the burden on your loved ones in the unfortunate event they are needed. For many people, the term "estate planning" quickly turns to thoughts of who will be providing care for minor children if both parents have died. Designating a contingent guardian for children is one of the most important estate planning steps parents can take. For our purposes, we will define estate planning as:

*Proactively planning and implementing steps to prepare for death or incapacity, including care for dependents and transfer of assets.*

We have purposely left our definition broad to illustrate the range of areas we will cover, including:

- basic estate planning documents
- how assets are transferred upon death
- planning for estate taxes
- dealing with an inherited IRA

As you read this chapter, keep in mind the authors are not attorneys and this should not be considered legal advice or recommendations. This is meant to provide an educational overview of various areas within estate planning. You should consult with an attorney familiar with estate planning for specific recommendations and to draft documents.

**Basic Estate Planning Documents**

Estate planning can become complicated when distributing a large amount of assets to many heirs or when planning around the future of a business. Fortunately, this is where an estate planning attorney will provide assistance evaluating and explaining all of the "what ifs" that may occur. A will, living will, HIPAA release, and power of attorney are common documents individuals and families should consider even if their financial situation is relatively simple.

*Will*

A will conveys the wishes of the deceased with regard to how they would like their assets distributed upon death. Most people have an idea of who they would like to receive their property. However, property may pass to unintended parties if this is not clearly outlined in a will. For example, if one dies without a will (having died "intestate"), then the state will decide which of your relatives receive each asset, and this may cause discord among family members. Assets that pass from instructions in a will go through the probate process, so selecting a different method of transferring assets may be preferable due to the cost and inconvenience of probate.

Another benefit of creating a will is the ability to name a contingent guardian to care for your minor child or children in the event both parents have passed away. Without a will naming a contingent guardian, the state will make this decision for you. Most people desire to not have this happen, so having a will in force and periodically revising this will help avoid this scenario. You will also want to discuss this with the family member or close friend in advance of executing your will so the contingent guardian is aware of their potential responsibility.

*Living Will*

A living will is a type of medical directive that declares what medical treatment, if any, may be used in the case of terminal illness or other life-threatening conditions in which the patient becomes incapacitated or unconscious. This document may also be referred to as advance medical directive, advance health care directive, or simply advance directive.

*HIPAA Release*

A HIPAA release form allows your health information to be shared with people who are not directly involved in your care, such as family members. Estate planning attorneys should be able to add a HIPAA release form to your basic estate planning documents without much additional effort or cost.

*Power of Attorney*

A power of attorney authorizes someone else to act on your behalf, often used if you are incapacitated and cannot make decisions on your own. The principal is the person whose decision-making ability will be given up. The agent is the person who will now be making decisions for the principal. An auto accident resulting in the principal being in a coma is one example of incapacity. Another type of incapacity is the loss of cognitive function due to Alzheimer's disease or another form of dementia. As this condition is more popular with seniors, you may want to consider talking with parents or grandparents about a power of attorney if you notice early signs or have a family history of dementia.

You may see powers of attorney used in the plural because there are multiple forms of this document. For example, a principal may have separate powers of attorney for health care and property, so the agent who is making health care decisions does not also have access to the principal's assets. For a power of attorney to be an effective incapacity planning document, it will need to be a drafted as a durable power of attorney, which allows the agent to act on the principal's behalf after incapacity. This contrasts with a nondurable power of attorney, which can only be used when the principal is competent and not incapacitated. All powers of attorney cease at death, so it will be important to have a will in place to guide planning after the principal has died.

**How Assets Are Transferred upon Death**

"Okay, so just to clarify my understanding, powers of attorney deal with being unable to function while alive but don't have any use after death. Whereas a will is activated once someone has died to outline care for minor children if the other parent isn't alive and to provide instructions for distributing the deceased's assets. Is that right?" asked Tim.

Tim is correct. One point to add is that there are four ways in which property is transferred at death, so a will is not the only option. Assets passed through a will go through the probate process, but transferring assets by operation of law, by contract, or through a trust are alternatives.

*Probate*

Probate is the process of distributing the deceased's assets that fall within their probate estate, which includes assets passing by a will. If the deceased did not have a will when they died, then their assets will also go through probate if they do not pass by operation of law or contract. In this case, the state's intestacy laws will dictate how assets are passed to the deceased's family. Assets passing through certain types of trusts avoid probate, while other types of trusts have assets included in probate.

The probate process has numerous downsides, including a delayed distribution of assets, increased estate administrative costs, and all information is available to the public. Probate will generally take a minimum of four to nine months, but can take two years or longer depending on the complexity of the estate and the court's waiting time. Estate administrative costs include fees paid to the court, executor, and lawyer. An executor is the person appointed to carry out the instructions listed in a will. As probate is open to the public, your family will not have privacy over the proceedings. Due to these reasons, many people choose to pass their assets in other ways.

## Operation of Law

Assets that pass by operation of law avoid probate without additional instructions needed. For example, property held in joint tenancy with right of survivorship automatically passes to surviving joint tenants. Joint investment accounts co-owned by spouses are commonly titled this way to facilitate a smooth transfer at the death of the first spouse. You may see the acronym "JTWROS" in front of the investment account registration, indicating this type of asset title is being used.

## Contract

Life insurance proceeds and retirement plans avoid probate by designating beneficiaries when they are established. This is known as transferring assets by contract. Applications for life insurance include a beneficiary designation form to specify who will receive the death benefit proceeds when the insured passes away, known as the primary beneficiary. If the insured outlives all primary beneficiaries, then the life insurance proceeds will be distributed to the contingent beneficiaries. Similarly, retirement plans name one or more beneficiaries to receive the balance when the account owner dies. In addition to natural people, trusts and charities can also be named beneficiaries. Keep in mind that if a beneficiary is not listed, then the death benefit or account balance may transfer to the deceased's estate and be subject to probate.

"Okay, this reminds me of a question I have been meaning to bring up," mentioned Lauren. "Our life insurance policies name each other as our primary beneficiaries. Now that our girls are in the picture, we want them to have our life insurance proceeds if we have both died. Do we name them as the contingent beneficiaries? Or would this create a problem because they are minors?"

Lauren brings up a good point. While she could name her daughters as contingent beneficiaries, this is generally not recommended because minors are not considered valid beneficiaries for life insurance. Until Lauren and Tim's daughters are adults, they may not be allowed to benefit from their life insurance as Tim and Lauren wish. Their daughters will then inherit a large sum of money with no restrictions when they reach adulthood, even though they will still be fairly young. There are several options to avoid this scenario. One of the most common is to establish a trust to receive, manage, and distribute the insurance proceeds for the benefit of minor children according to the parents' wishes established in the trust document.

*Trust*

A trust is a fairly common estate planning document. More specifically, a trust is a separate legal entity that holds assets, manages them, and distributes them to beneficiaries according to instructions outlined within the trust document. There are three parties involved with a trust:

1. The grantor creates and gifts assets to the trust.
2. The trustee manages the assets, pays taxes, and facilitates distributions to trust beneficiaries.
3. The beneficiaries are entitled to the assets or income generated from the assets according to instructions outlined in the trust document.

There are many types of trusts—revocable and irrevocable trusts, living and testamentary trusts (created by instructions set forth within a will upon death), and trusts designed for specific purposes, such as special needs trusts to provide care for a dependent with special needs. The trust document allows the grantor to convey more detailed instructions than a will for how and when beneficiaries receive assets. As a separate legal entity, a trust may be required to pay taxes on income earned on the assets held or may pass the tax burden to the grantor or beneficiaries.

Trusts can be named the contingent beneficiary on a life insurance policy to receive and manage the death benefit on behalf of minor children, as we are discussing with Tim and Lauren. They will need to consult with an attorney to draft the trust document detailing how they would like the trust to operate. One advantage is that the trust does not have to end when minor beneficiaries reach adulthood. Parents can instead provide instructions for the trust to distribute portions of the trust assets at various times or ages of their children, allowing them to convey their values for many years. For example, parents may wish to fully pay for their children's college expenses and may require the trust to disburse assets to pay for higher education costs as needed. Another example is to allow beneficiaries to use trust assets for a wedding or home down payment. When used in this manner, the trust is often structured as a revocable living trust.

Living, or inter vivos, trusts are established while the grantor is alive, and trust assets avoid probate. In contrast, testamentary trusts are created at the grantor's death through instructions listed in their will. As assets included in a will pass through probate, using a testamentary trust to receive life insurance proceeds may not be the most efficient way to accomplish Tim and Lauren's goal because the death benefit would now be subject to the probate process and related costs involved. A revocable trust may be preferred to allow the grantor to revoke or change the trust document while alive. This is not possible with an irrevocable trust, which cannot be modified once established, causing the grantor to permanently give up control of the trust document and property it holds. At the grantor's death, a revocable trust becomes irrevocable and is then managed by the trustee on behalf of the beneficiaries.

## Planning for Estate Taxes

"That is helpful to know. We should probably schedule a time with an attorney to do this," said Lauren, looking at Tim.

"Yeah, definitely," agreed Tim. "In addition to talking with an attorney about these documents, are there other topics we should bring up, like planning for estate taxes?"

Those documents are a great starting point, and we would defer to the attorney on other areas to consider. Planning ahead for possible estate taxes is better than not addressing this, though it may be a few years before you accumulate enough assets to be concerned about estate taxes. As we touched on during the Life Insurance chapter, the government has established a system to tax assets transferred from one person to another. This is called the unified transfer tax system and includes gift taxes for assets gifted while alive and estate taxes for property transferred upon death. Combining gift and estate taxes into one system prevents people from gifting substantial assets prior to death to avoid paying estate taxes. There are several terms we will define shortly, but here is a much-abbreviated explanation of how the transfer tax system works: If the combined value of your lifetime taxable gifts and taxable estate is greater than the lifetime transfer tax exemption, then any additional taxable gifts or amount of taxable estate over the lifetime exemption will result in taxes owed.

Why is this important to consider? Because the tax rate that applies to this is 40 percent, so being over the lifetime exemption by only $100,000 could result in an additional $40,000 in taxes owed. Proactive planning can reduce or even eliminate this tax bill.

The reason estate taxes may not be applicable to Tim and Lauren at the present is due the lifetime exemption of $11.2 million per person. This means no gift taxes are owed to the IRS unless you have made over $11.2 million of taxable gifts. Estate taxes would not be owed unless the size of your taxable estate plus lifetime taxable gifts exceeds

$11.2 million. Married couples can use strategies to avoid paying taxes on up to $22.4 million of taxable assets transferred. While the size of the current exemption allows most people to avoid paying gift or estate taxes, the lifetime exemption has been smaller in the past—even as low as $2 million as recently as 2008. Remember, Congress keeps us on our toes with future tax legislation, and the lifetime exemption during your later years may be lower than it is today.

Upon first thought, a $11.2 million estate may seem like an incredibly large number that you may not reach for decades, if ever. However, your estate may already be larger than you think. Life insurance is included in your gross estate if you have any incidents of ownership at death. For example, if Tim has $5 million of life insurance, he may already be close to the lifetime exemption if the amount reverts back to its base of $5 million set in 2011 dollars. In addition, several states have their own estate or inheritance tax and may have a much lower lifetime exemption amount. Tim and Lauren may owe state estate taxes even if they do not owe at the federal level.

### Gifting Assets

We have mentioned the term "taxable gifts" several times, so it will be helpful to understand whether a gift may be taxable or not. First, a gift is made when money or an asset is transferred to someone else for less than the full value of consideration received by the giver, or donor. Each donor is allowed a $15,000 annual gift tax exclusion per recipient, also called the donee.[1] Next, there are two unlimited deductions that automatically result in a nontaxable gift for the entire amount—the marital and charitable deductions.[2] A donor can claim an unlimited marital gift tax deduction

---

[1] A married couple may elect to split gifts made in a year, which causes all gifts to be considered to be gifted 50 percent from each spouse, independent of which spouse actually made the gift. This allows a couple to gift up to $30,000 to a single donee without creating a taxable gift.

[2] Keep in mind the marital and charitable deductions are unlimited for gift tax purposes, not when calculating income taxes.

for qualifying gifts made to a spouse.[1] A donor can also deduct the entire amount gifted to a qualified charity with the unlimited charitable gift tax deduction.

The amount of a gift that exceeds the annual exclusion and does not qualify for the unlimited marital or charitable deductions is now a taxable gift. Here are four examples to illustrate these concepts.

Tim and Lauren's oldest daughter, Anna, wins first place in her preschool's painting contest. Convinced Anna is destined for greatness, Tim gifts $25,000 to Anna's college fund, with her listed as the beneficiary.

> Result: Taxable gift of $10,000. The $25,000 gift is reduced by the $15,000 annual gift tax exclusion, but the remaining $10,000 does not qualify for the marital or charitable deduction.

The following year, Anna again wins her preschool's painting contest. Tim makes another $25,000 gift to Anna's college fund. However, Tim and Lauren agree to split their gifts this year, having learned their lesson from last year.

> Result: Not a taxable gift. The $25,000 gift is first split equally between Tim and Lauren, and therefore each parent is deemed to have gifted $12,500. Tim and Lauren can then reduce their $12,500 gifts to $0 with the $15,000 annual gift tax exclusion per recipient.

Tim is inspired by a holiday commercial and surprises Lauren with a brand-new luxury car worth $60,000.

> Result: Not a taxable gift. This gift qualifies for the unlimited marital deduction.

---

[1] For a spousal gift to qualify for the unlimited marital gift tax deduction, the recipient spouse must be a US citizen and the gift must not be a terminable interest. A terminable interest in an asset ends at a certain event.

Lauren is moved by the plight of thousands of people in a developing country who were displaced by a massive earthquake and makes a $50,000 donation to Doctors Without Borders.

> Result: Not a taxable gift. This gift qualifies for the unlimited charitable deduction.

Once a taxable gift is made, it does not automatically trigger a tax bill owed to the IRS. You have a $11.2 million lifetime transfer tax exemption that must be fully used before you actually pay gift or estate taxes. In the previous example, Tim's $10,000 taxable gift would reduce his lifetime exemption to $11.19 million. By taking advantage of gift splitting, the annual gift tax exclusion, marital deduction, and charitable deduction, donors can reduce the size of their estate while limiting the taxable effect of their donations. One item to note is that even though Tim will not owe taxes for his taxable gift, he will still need to report this with the IRS by filing Form 709 (Gift Tax Return) with his annual tax return.

*Methods to Reduce Estate Taxes*

"Let's say that many years from now, Lauren and I are fortunate enough to have a substantial amount of assets, and paying estate taxes is a real concern. In addition to giving assets to our family and charities while alive, are there other ways in which we can reduce our estate tax bill?" asked Tim.

Yes, there are a few strategies Tim and Lauren can implement to further reduce the amount of estate taxes. These include the portability feature of the unused lifetime exemption, charitable estate tax deduction, marital estate tax deduction, and trusts.

Using the portability feature of an unused exemption amount can be an effective way to reduce estate taxes if the surviving spouse has a greater amount of assets than the deceased spouse. For example, let's say that Tim had a large 401(k) balance later in life, and Lauren's estate value did not use her entire lifetime exemption when she passes away first. Tim could elect to use Lauren's unused exemption—whatever is remaining of her $11.2 million. The unused exemption amount can now be used to offset an equivalent amount of Tim's taxable estate when he dies.

As with gift taxes, the estate tax calculation allows an unlimited deduction for assets transferred to a charity. This can be done as an outright gift or in conjunction with trusts, as well as other methods. Charitable trusts allow the grantor flexibility in designing how trust assets and income are distributed. For example, the grantor can give shares of stock to the trust to remove them from his estate and maintain the right to receive dividends from the shares as an income stream. The trust may then be instructed to donate the stock holdings to the specified charity at the grantor's death.

You are also allowed an unlimited marital estate tax deduction for assets passed to the surviving spouse.[1] While this may reduce the estate tax liability of the first spouse to die, it may burden the surviving spouse with additional taxes owed if the couple has a large estate between them. Another caveat of this strategy is that assets transferred to the surviving spouse may continue to rise in value, such as shares of stock or private business ownership interest, increasing the surviving spouse's estate. To counter this, a bypass trust, also known as a B trust or credit shelter trust, may be established to accept appreciating assets so they are removed from the grantor's estate, and subsequent appreciation occurs outside the estates of both the grantor and surviving spouse. By placing these assets in a bypass trust, a grantor can pass significant amounts of appreciation to subsequent generations without increasing estate taxes owed upon the surviving spouse's death. B trusts may be set up concurrently with A and C trusts for additional planning strategies with regard to transferring assets to a spouse.[2] A detailed explanation of this strategy is beyond the scope of this book and best left to an estate planning attorney.

---

[1] As with gift taxes, for a transfer to qualify for the unlimited marital estate tax deduction, the surviving recipient spouse must be a US citizen and the gift must not be a terminable interest. A terminable interest in an asset ends at a certain event.

[2] A, B, and C trusts are also referred to as marital, bypass or credit-shelter, and qualified terminable interest property (QTIP) trusts, respectively.

## Dealing with an Inherited IRA

"Changing the subject to our parents," said Lauren, "my mom passed a few years ago and left her possessions to my dad, George. I don't have any siblings, and my dad has already told me he will leave all of his assets to me. These are valued well below $5 million, so he should not owe any estate taxes, but is there anything that could adversely affect us? I think his largest assets are his home and an IRA that was rolled over from his old 401(k) plan when he retired."

Yes, there are special rules with inherited IRAs that cannot be ignored as our parents and other family members approach retirement and eventually leave their assets to younger generations. Many people have heard of the baby boomer generation, those born between 1946 and 1964. Fewer people may be familiar with the amount of assets baby boomers will pass to their children and grandchildren over the next few decades. The consulting firm Accenture estimates $30 trillion in financial and nonfinancial assets will be transferred from baby boomers to their heirs over the next thirty to forty years. George's IRA balance invested in mutual funds is an example of a financial asset, whereas his home is an example of a nonfinancial asset. Proactive planning and open communication between generations can allow them to achieve a seamless transition of wealth.

Returning to George's IRA that will pass to Lauren, certain rules regarding inherited IRAs must be followed; otherwise, beneficiaries may be forced to take distributions faster than desired. The two main factors that determine how withdrawals will be taken from inherited IRAs are:

- whether the beneficiary was the surviving spouse or a non-spousal beneficiary
- whether the deceased account owner had started taking required minimum distributions (RMDs)

IRA owners must begin taking required minimum distributions (RMDs) from their accounts by April 1 of the year following the year of their seventy and a half birthday.[1] Withdrawal amounts are determined by the account owner's age and life expectancy table. Once George has passed and Lauren is taking distributions from the inherited IRA, the amount withdrawn is taxable as income. However, the 10 percent early distribution penalty for withdrawals when the account owner is under age fifty-nine and a half does not apply because death of a previous account owner is an exception for inherited IRAs and qualified retirement plans.

*Scenario 1: Lauren as beneficiary, and George had not yet started taking his required minimum distributions*

*Stretch over beneficiary's life expectancy.* If Lauren were to inherit George's IRA before he began his required minimum distributions, she has the option to stretch the distributions she must take over her life expectancy (as opposed to a full distribution within five years). This can be preferable to the other withdrawal option for greater flexibility. Two things must be accomplished for Lauren to stretch distributions based on her life. First, the inherited IRA account title must include the names of both the deceased previous owner and beneficiary. For example, it could be titled "George Smith's IRA FBO Lauren Smith." Second, Lauren will need to take her first distribution by December 31 of the year following George's year of death.

*Five-year rule.* If either of the previous two requirements are not completed, the five-year rule will apply. This requires Lauren to withdraw the entire amount of the IRA by December 31 of the year of George's fifth anniversary of his death. Accelerating the account withdrawal under the five-year rule is generally not desirable for a couple of reasons. First, Lauren may not need the entire balance within five years, so a mandatory full withdrawal eliminates her ability to leave investments in a tax-deferred account to grow. Second, distributions are taxable as income, so withdrawing the entire balance in a short period of time may create a large tax bill due to income taxed at higher marginal rates.

---

[1] Failure to take the full amount of the RMD will result in a tax penalty of 50 percent of the RMD amount not taken.

Lauren would not need to take a distribution every year, but the IRA is required to be emptied by the end of year five. The five-year rule also applies if George did not name a beneficiary or if he had a trust or his estate listed as the beneficiary.

*Scenario 2: Lauren as beneficiary and George had already started taking his required minimum distributions*

If George was over seventy and a half when he died, then the option to delay distributions and withdraw the entire balance by the end of the fifth year is no longer available. Lauren would use her life expectancy to calculate the percentage of the IRA balance she must withdraw each year. However, if Lauren was not listed as the IRA beneficiary, then she would not be able to stretch distributions over her life. The distribution schedule would instead remain based on George's life expectancy, requiring Lauren to compress her withdrawals into fewer years and claim more income each year.

Independent of whether George had started his required minimum distributions, these examples illustrate that planning ahead by naming Lauren the beneficiary provides her with more options of when to take withdrawals. Additional options would be available if George's wife were still alive to inherit his IRA. If Lauren's father would like to transfer his IRA to her and he has not yet named her as the primary beneficiary on his IRA, he should do this soon. Remember, assets in a retirement plan are transferred by contract, so the IRA beneficiary designation document must list Lauren as the primary beneficiary, even if his will states this too.

"That's great to know about my dad's IRA. Is there anything we should be aware of with his home? He may need to move into an assisted living facility soon and is thinking about either selling his house or renting it out until he passes so I can inherit it. He bought it over forty years ago for $100,000, and it is now valued around $850,000 with the mortgage fully paid off. Do you have any thoughts about whether he should sell it while alive or retain ownership so I receive it when he passes?"

Yes, some choices could be quite costly. For the following examples of basis treatment with George's home, we are ignoring any adjustment to basis that would have occurred at the death of George's wife. This would have been affected by how the home was titled as an asset and whether Lauren's parents lived in a community property state.

*Step-Up in Basis*

In simple terms, an asset's initial cost basis is its purchase price plus certain acquisition costs paid. Capital improvements made to a home will be added to the home's basis because the homeowner is paying for the improvements with after-tax money. Similarly, investments held in a taxable brokerage account will have their basis increased by the amount of dividends, interest, or capital gains if these were reinvested to buy additional shares. Dividends, interest, and capital gains in a brokerage account are taxed when realized, so the additional shares are purchased with after-tax money. This is important because an asset's basis is not taxed when sold, whereas any unrealized gain—the difference between the asset's fair market value and cost basis—has not yet been taxed and will be realized and taxed when sold.

Some assets receive a step-up in basis at the owner's death to the asset's fair market value if they pass through the deceased's gross estate. Homes and non-retirement brokerage accounts are two examples of assets that qualify to receive a stepped-up basis. This is applicable to George's home, so let's walk through a few scenarios showing the possible tax effects. We will assume that George has not made any capital improvements to his home, so the basis remains at $100,000 (ignoring the basis adjustment at his wife's passing). With a fair market value of $850,000, it carries a $750,000 unrealized long-term capital gain.

*Scenario 1: George gifts his home to Lauren*

If George gifts his home to Lauren while he is alive, then the home's basis does not change because the basis of gifted assets is carried over and becomes the recipient's basis in the asset. Lauren's $100,000 basis in the home would cause her to realize a $750,000 long-term capital gain if she were to then sell the home. The applicable capital gain tax rate would range from 15 percent to 20 percent, depending on Lauren and Tim's income. This may also be subject to the 3.8 percent net investment income tax, causing 15 percent to 23.8 percent of the $750,000 capital gain to be owed in taxes. While this is a generous gift by George, the $112,500 to $178,500 tax bill that comes with it can be avoided with other options.

In addition, this would count as a taxable gift to George because it does not qualify for the marital and charitable deductions. Any amount over the $15,000 annual exclusion would be a taxable gift and reduce George's $11.2 million lifetime transfer tax exemption.

*Scenario 2: George sells his home*

If George decides to sell his home, he will realize the $750,000 capital gain and owe taxes on it but not on the entire amount. The IRS allows a $250,000 exclusion on the gain from the sale of your home. If Lauren's mom were alive, she would also be eligible to claim a $250,000 exclusion, allowing $500,000 of the gain to not be taxed. For George to qualify for his $250,000 exclusion, he will need to have lived in his home as his primary residence for at least two out of the last five years, which he has. This will decrease the amount of capital gain from $750,000 to $500,000 but will still result in a substantial amount of taxes owed. Assuming George's income (from his IRA distributions) places him in the 15 percent long-term capital gain tax rate bracket, the $500,000 gain would cause him to owe $75,000 of capital gain taxes. George has saved Lauren and Tim a six-figure tax bill, though he has still taken quite a tax hit himself.

*Scenario 3: George retains ownership of his home and passes it to Lauren at death*

If George instead retains ownership of his home until his death and passes it to Lauren so it is included in his gross estate, his home will receive a stepped-up basis to $850,000. Lauren will inherit the home and can then sell it at its fair market value of $850,000 without realizing any gain and therefore owing no taxes.

The analysis of whether to gift George's home while alive, sell it, or retain ownership until death shows that, in some situations, it can be advantageous to not get fancy with estate planning. Simply allowing his home to pass through his gross estate to receive a step-up in basis could save George and Lauren from paying a substantial amount of taxes.

While we are on the topic of stepped-up basis, it is worth mentioning that some assets do not qualify for this favorable tax treatment, such as annuities. These financial products are sold by insurance companies with the option to structure them for guaranteed income for life. In this regard, annuities can be viewed as insurance against the risk of outliving your retirement income. However, annuities come with hefty expenses to provide this guarantee. Another catch is that if the annuitant (the person who was receiving the annuity's income stream) dies, any remaining assets in the annuity may become the property of the insurance company rather than pass to the annuity's beneficiaries. If the annuity is structured to leave a benefit to beneficiaries, then the benefit will be treated as "income in respect of a decedent" (IRD) and will not receive a stepped-up basis. We will refrain from getting long-winded here and summarize by saying annuities are not very estate planning friendly. If you or someone you know is considering buying an annuity and funding it with investments held in a non-retirement account, you will want to consider the long-term effects of missing out on the step-up in basis.

## Estate Planning as a Business Owner

Estate planning with regard to the transfer of a business ownership interest adds another layer of complexity. The deceased owner likely wanted the ownership value to be passed to family members, while the surviving partners desire to maintain full control of the company. Planning in advance can help all parties achieve their goals through a properly drafted and funded buy-sell agreement, as explained in the life insurance chapter.

## Chapter Summary

"Wow, that was a lot to learn in one sitting. It looks like we have a few action items to work on," said Tim, looking at Lauren.

"We certainly do. I need to call my dad …"

Establishing your estate plan does not need to be complicated. A will, living will, HIPAA release, and powers of attorney provide a good place to begin. If you have children or other dependents who could experience a financial hardship from your passing, then considering life insurance should also be part of your planning. Properly setting up these documents, including any trusts, may require the expertise of an estate planning attorney. Intergenerational planning can be particularly difficult to get started. Family members may not be ready to address end-of-life plans or comfortable discussing these with their children or parents. Despite these challenges, adequately planning for end-of-life care, care for children, death, and transfer of assets can help when going through these emotional situations.

---

### Key Takeaways

*Estate planning* involves proactively planning and implementing steps to prepare for death or incapacity, including care for dependents and transfer of assets.

Basic estate planning documents include a *will, living will, HIPAA release,* and *powers of attorney.* This can extend to *trusts,* commonly to act as the beneficiary on a life insurance policy for the benefit of minor children or for strategies to reduce estate taxes.

Assets transfer at death by *probate, operation of law, contract,* or *trust.*

To plan for possible *estate taxes*, you will consider the rules of the unified transfer tax system to best coordinate the transfer of assets while alive and after death.

One strategy to reduce estate taxes is to gift assets while alive to remove them from your estate. Current *gift tax* laws allow donors to exclude $15,000 of gifts each year to each recipient. Donors can also take advantage of the *unlimited marital and charitable exclusions* to further transfer assets.

The large federal *lifetime estate tax exemption of $11.2 million* in 2018 allows most people to avoid paying estate taxes. The Tax Cuts and Jobs Act of 2017 temporarily increased the lifetime exemption to this amount, but this increase is scheduled to expire in 2026, after which it may be cut roughly in half. States may have their own estate tax laws, which may have lower exemption amounts. Even if you avoid the federal estate tax, *your estate may be subject to state estate taxes.*

In general, assets included in the gross estate of a decedent receive a *step-up in basis* upon death of the owner, allowing the beneficiary to avoid paying capital gains tax on any untaxed appreciation of the asset that occurred while the former owner was alive. Assets classified as *income in respect of a decedent (IRD)* do not receive a step-up in basis, including IRAs, qualified retirement plans (but excluding Roth accounts), and annuities.

*Inherited IRAs* have special transfer rules of their own, depending on whether the beneficiary was the decedent's spouse and whether the deceased account owner had started taking required minimum distributions (RMDs).

*Annuities* are financial products sold by insurance companies that provide an income stream, potentially guaranteed for life. However, they have higher expenses than investment accounts due to this guarantee. They are also not the most tax-efficient with estate planning because they do not receive a stepped-up basis and instead shift an income tax burden to the recipient.

**Additional Resources**

*Estate Planning Smarts* by Deborah Jacobs

*Last Wishes: A Family Guidebook* by Robert Kabacy

www.avvo.com (attorney search and review website)

# CHAPTER 13

# COLLEGE EDUCATION FUNDING

AFTER MANY LONG nights and countless babies delivered, Rachel completed her residency in obstetrics and gynecology last year and stayed on as faculty at the local teaching hospital. Her wife, Ashley, recently joined a small dermatology practice upon finishing her residency and was carrying their first child, due in a few months. Their financial plan was taking shape, and one of their next priorities was to begin saving for their future son's college.

"We were both raised in families that place a lot of value on higher education," Rachel explained. "Once this little guy arrives, we would like to pass these values on to him."

"We don't want to be overbearing with his schoolwork," continued Ashley. "More like very supportive of his academic pursuits and be able to reassure him that he won't have to worry about paying for college."

It sounds like Rachel and Ashley would like to be able to fully cover four years of undergraduate education at a public or private university. Some students will take a fifth year of undergraduate to complete their degree or may go to graduate school. These possibilities must also be considered when planning for higher education.

"Yes, certainly four years of college," confirmed Ashley. "I think we're still deciding whether to plan for a fifth year or grad school. What do you think, Rachel?"

"Yeah, I agree. If he needs a fifth year to complete a double major, then I would like to support that, but if his second major is partying, then we'll see!" Rachel said, laughing. "It would be nice to provide some financial help if he goes to grad school, but we're not sure how possible that may be, depending on whether we have more kids. It's many years away, but we would like to start learning about how to save for college well in advance ..."

Like several areas of financial planning, saving for a child's higher education often gets put on hold as doctors and their families go through their final years of training. Paying off credit card balances, replenishing emergency reserve accounts, and home purchases are common priorities shortly after incomes increase over the summer. Once the dust settles from these, one of the next questions parents reflect on is "How do we want to plan for our children's education?" Many parents would like to provide their children with a similar amount of financial assistance they received through their own schooling. Some, like Rachel and Ashley, prefer to give as much financial support as reasonably possible. Other parents may feel paying for college should be the child's responsibility, as they have done themselves. Perhaps they worked a part-time job to pay for their degree and felt this enhanced their work ethic and appreciation for college. There is not a right or wrong answer for how you may or may not want to contribute toward higher education costs. Instead, you may choose to provide a level of support that aligns with the values you wish to convey as your child graduates high school and enters the adult world.

This chapter will review the options available for college saving and several other considerations. These may include questions like, How much of the expense should I cover? What if my child pursues graduate education? And how will these savings efforts impact other areas of my financial plan? These questions, coupled with several unknowns, make for a complicated decision. We will address these points with the following outline.

- analyzing the cost of higher education
- overview of college saving accounts
- scholarships
- student loans (relax, only briefly and from the parents' point of view)
- how to balance higher education support with your financial plan

Without further ado, let's dive in and hit the books!

## Analyzing the Cost of Higher Education

"Before we talk about the ways to save for college, we want to know what it may cost to put him through undergrad," mentioned Rachel. "We have no idea how much we may need to save over the next eighteen years ..."

Rachel brings up a good point. While we know how much college costs today, we are unsure of what higher education will cost when your child attends or what preparation is needed until then. According to College Board, the average tuition and fees for a year of undergraduate education for the 2017–2018 academic year was:

- $9,970 at public colleges and universities for in-state students
- $25,620 at public colleges and universities for out-of-state students
- $34,740 at private colleges and universities

It is helpful to know today's tuition rates; however, it is more informative to know what tuition may be in several years when your child attends college. The decade from the 2006–07 to the 2016–17 school years saw tuition and fees increase at an average annual rate of 3.5 percent for public four-year institutions and 2.4 percent for private, nonprofit four-year colleges *above inflation*. Over that period, inflation averaged 1.8 percent per year measured by the Consumer Price Index for all urban consumers (CPI-U, a common gauge of inflation), resulting in annual tuition inflation rates of 5.3 percent for public colleges and 4.2

percent for private colleges. Tuition inflation has historically been higher than the increase in the general cost of living and has outpaced CPI-U inflation in each of the previous three decades.

How does this affect your college savings? Unless we know otherwise, we could assume tuition will continue to inflate at a similar rate over the years to come. This means tuition for Rachel and Ashley's son's first year of college at a public in-state school will have grown from $9,970 to $25,258 after having inflated at 5.3 percent for eighteen years, an increase of 153 percent. Their son's fourth-year tuition will be $29,491 for a total cost of $109,353.

Rachel and Ashley may have room in their budget to pay for tuition as it is due each term, but they can alternatively save in advance to meet the future tuition bills and have expressed interest in doing this. If they put away money each month starting when their child is born until he begins college and this was invested to earn a constant 7 percent return per year in a tax-advantaged account, they will need to save about $234 per month. We can replicate these calculations with tuition for an out-of-state student at a public college and private institutions. Public out-of-state tuition grows from $25,620 per year today to $64,907 in eighteen years, requiring $602 to be saved each month. Tuition for private school inflates from $34,740 to $72,853 with $665 to save each month.

While attending college, students often live in dormitories or off-campus housing and also pay for expenses such as food, books, supplies, and transportation. These can add a significant amount to the total cost of attendance. Averaging about $15,000 per year, they raise the annual cost of higher education for the 2016–17 school year to:

- $25,290 at public colleges and universities for in-state students
- $40,940 at public colleges and universities for out-of-state students
- $50,900 at private colleges and universities

Room and board costs have historically risen at lower rates than tuition inflation, resulting in annual increases in the cost of tuition, fees, room, and board of 4.6 percent at public four-year colleges and

4.1 percent at private schools. If we follow the same process and inflate today's current costs of attendance by the applicable inflation rates, we estimate the total cost of a year of in-state public education to grow from $24,610 to $56,822 after inflating at 4.6 percent for eighteen years. The cost of four years comes to $243,459 and requires $522 to be saved each month earning a constant 7 percent return each year. The first year of a public out-of-state school grows from $40,940 to $91,985 and needs $845 to be saved each month. The average private college will have seen its cost of attendance increase from $50,900 to $104,913 with $957 of monthly savings required.

"Wow, okay. So, it looks like we may be saving almost a thousand dollars a month if we want to cover his undergrad degree," said Rachel.

Potentially, if they wanted to have the full amount of a private four-year degree saved by the time their son begins college. Keep in mind there are scholarships available, and they can pay for costs out of pocket when he is in school. In the meantime, there are several options for saving and investing for their son's education.

**College Savings Accounts**

There are a few common accounts used to save for higher education, including 529 College Savings Plans, Coverdell Education Savings accounts, custodial accounts, and prepaid tuition plans. Each has distinctive characteristics with regard to taxes, contribution amounts, and account ownership.

*529 College Savings Plans*

The government needs our nation's youth to attend college to maintain our educated workforce and replace the millions of workers retiring each year. To encourage families to save for this, the government provides tax incentives for higher education investment accounts. State-sponsored 529 College Savings Plans are accounts offered by an investment company.[1]

---

[1] See the disclosure at the end of the book regarding 529 plans and investment risks.

They are usually established with the child as the beneficiary and an adult as the account owner. This is commonly a parent but can be another adult, and relatives may choose to open and fund accounts for their grandchildren, nieces, and nephews.

Contributions to 529 plans do not receive a tax deduction for federal income taxes, though some states allow a state income tax deduction for in-state residents up to a certain amount.[1] Maximum contribution limits vary by state and are quite high per 529 plan, such as $250,000 to $400,000. With that said, contributions are classified as gifts, so donors usually limit their annual contributions to $15,000 per beneficiary; otherwise, the excess amount is a taxable gift and filing a gift tax return is required. Taxable gifts may not result in gift taxes actually owed due to the lifetime exemption amount but are easily avoided. Married couples can elect to split gifts, allowing $30,000 to be gifted per beneficiary each year without triggering a taxable gift. In addition, donors can choose to make an accelerated gift of up to the next five years' worth of gifts in a single year, amounting to $75,000 per donor or $150,000 per married couple. These accounts provide plenty of room to contribute for higher education costs.

This money is invested in mutual funds and grows tax-deferred with the goal of outpacing tuition inflation. Investment options typically include mutual funds that cover a single asset class and age-based funds for a one-stop choice. These age-based funds are usually comprised of underlying mutual funds and managed to be more aggressive when your child is younger with a longer time horizon until college. They become more conservative as your student approaches high school graduation due to a shorter time horizon until the funds are needed.

When the funds are needed, they can be withdrawn from the 529 plan tax-free if used for qualified education expenses, including tuition, books, room and board, a computer, and certain other costs. Recent legislation now allows up to $10,000 per beneficiary each year to be withdrawn from a 529 plan to pay for tuition from kindergarten

[1] The website SavingForCollege.com is a good resource to check whether your state's 529 plan offers a state income tax deduction for contributions.

through high school. However, if a distribution is taken from a 529 and not applied toward qualified expenses, then the earnings above the amount contributed will be taxed as income and charged a 10 percent penalty. Buying a car for your child would be an example of a nonqualified expense. An exception to this penalty is if your child receives a scholarship. You are allowed to withdraw the amount of the scholarship received from the 529 and avoid paying the penalty, though investment earnings distributed will still be taxed as income.

"Does it matter whether our son goes to college in the same state as the 529 plan is sponsored by?" asked Rachel.

This is a common question, and the answer is no, it does not matter which state their son's college is located in.[1] You can choose any state's 529 plan, and you receive the full 529 tax benefits independent of where your child attends school, as long as it is a qualifying institution. Many international colleges also qualify as eligible schools for 529 tax benefits.[2]

"What if we over-save for college?" inquired Ashley. "Let's say we save enough for a private school education, but he goes to a public in-state school. What are our options for the extra amount saved?"

You have several options with extra money, including:

*Change the beneficiary.* You can change the beneficiary from your child to another family member who may be attending college soon, including another child, nephew, niece, or grandchild.

*Leave funds in account.* You can allow the funds to stay in the 529 plan and continue to grow for a number of years to pay for graduate school or for grandchildren.

*Withdraw for purposes other than education.* This option will incur the 10 percent penalty and income tax on earnings.

---

[1] Asset protection laws vary by state, so the state in which your 529 plan is held will determine how your plan's assets are protected from creditors in the event of a lawsuit.

[2] SavingForCollege.com's 529 institution eligibility search allows you to search whether an international school qualifies for 529 tax benefit purposes.

These accounts allow large contribution amounts independent of your income, tax benefits, and many options among the different states' plans. Because of these features, 529 plans have become the college savings plan of choice for many parents and relatives who want to save for a child's higher education costs.

### Coverdell Education Savings Accounts (ESAs)

Coverdell Education Savings Accounts, commonly referred to as ESAs, are an alternative to 529 plans. ESAs also offer tax incentives but are much more limiting than 529 plans. Contributions are made with after-tax money, so they do not receive a tax deduction at the federal or state level. Unlike 529s, which do not have an annual contribution limit and a high total contribution limit, ESAs restrict contributions to $2,000 per child per year among all donors. So, if a grandparent contributed $1,200 to an ESA, then all other donors could only contribute another $800 for the year. There is also an income phase-out range for the ability to make contributions. Depending on your filing status and earnings, you may not always be able to make contributions. The adjusted gross income (AGI) phase-out range for a married couple filing their taxes jointly in 2018 was $190,000 to $220,000. Contributions also cannot be made after the child turns eighteen.

ESA plan balances grow tax-deferred and are available tax-free for qualified educational expenses even if you eventually become income disqualified for ongoing contributions. Qualified expenses include costs for primary education, such as private elementary or high school tuition. Unlike 529s, ESA balances must be spent by the time the plan beneficiary is thirty years old. If there is still a balance in the Coverdell account when the beneficiary turns thirty, then the account must change the beneficiary to a younger relative of the original beneficiary. Due to the contribution limits, income phase-out, and strict distribution rules, Coverdell ESAs are not as popular as 529 plans.

*Custodial Accounts—UGMAs and UTMAs*

If you are concerned that funding only 529s or ESAs may create limitations years down the line, then a custodial account may be appropriate to consider. With the Uniform Gift to Minor Act (UGMA) or Uniform Transfer to Minor Act (UTMA), UGMA and UTMA accounts allow you to gift money to your child without the distribution restrictions associated with 529 or ESA plans. They are established as custodial accounts with an adult, usually a parent, acting as the custodian to manage the account and oversee the investments while the child is a minor. Once the child reaches the age of majority in their state, commonly eighteen to twenty-one, they assume control of the account and can use the balance as they like. For some parents, the prospect of their child having access to a large sum of money at eighteen without restriction raises some concern. On the other hand, knowing their child will have a start on a home down payment or the ability to experience travel can make these accounts attractive.

An important item to note with custodial accounts is that the tax benefits of 529s and ESAs do not apply. Instead, if the custodial account's investments generate over $2,100 of unearned income in a year, the excess amount of income will be taxed at the parents' highest marginal income tax bracket. This rule is known as the Kiddie Tax, and most doctors will have a federal marginal tax rate of 24 percent or higher. Due to the tax consequences and lack of parental control once the child reaches adulthood, custodial accounts are often kept to small balances, if used at all.

Another point of consideration with custodial accounts relates to how they are treated for financial aid purposes. If you think your child may qualify for federal aid, be aware that having assets in a custodial account can significantly reduce your child's eligibility for need-based programs. The reason behind this is that your student is deemed to be the owner of a custodial account, which has a greater impact on financial aid calculations than assets held in a parent's name.

*Prepaid Tuition Plans*

Prepaid tuition plans are what their name implies; they allow you to buy credits today to be applied to future tuition costs. With traditional 529 plans, you control the amount contributed, money is invested and earns a return based on the mutual funds' performance, and the specific amount available for future use is unknown until withdrawn. Prepaid tuition plans work in the opposite manner. Tuition credits are purchased in today's dollars and guaranteed to appreciate at a rate consistent with the rising cost of tuition. When your child needs the funds to go to school, you will have exactly what you purchased to cover tuition expenses in the same proportion. For example, if you purchase credits to cover one term worth of tuition cost, you have enough to cover the cost of one term at distribution, regardless of what the tuition price is at that point.

Once tuition credits are purchased, the responsibility for these funds to meet future tuition costs lies exclusively with the state. If the state does not invest the funds appropriately to meet anticipated costs, then the prepaid tuition plan may become underfunded (like many state and company pension plans), and state resources may be used to make up the difference. States may also raise the cost of new tuition credits purchased, causing new enrollees to buy credits at a higher cost than earlier participants. Because of this, some prepaid tuition plans have started to limit new enrollment or have even shut down over the past several years. The ability to use prepaid tuition credits for an out-of-state school is not as clear as with 529 plans, as each state may have a different conversion factor for how much a tuition credit purchased in one state may buy in another state. The result of these factors is that prepaid tuition plans are not as popular as 529 plans.

*Non-Retirement Brokerage Accounts*

Brokerage accounts do not provide tax benefits, but they also do not have restrictions or penalties with regard to what distributions are used for. They can be a helpful complement to other college savings accounts if you are unsure of the future cost and want to maintain flexibility. For example, Rachel and Ashley may choose to fully fund the estimated cost of an in-state public school in a 529 plan but also want to have extra funds on hand if their son attends a private university. If he does indeed go to a private school, then the brokerage account has funds readily available for the higher expenses. If he doesn't, then the 529 balance may be sufficient, and the brokerage account can be used for retirement savings or another goal.

## Scholarships

"So, it sounds like 529 plans are the most common way to go," said Rachel. "Apart from saving in advance, what other options do we have to pay for our son's education?"

Student loans are the main alternative, and we will touch on that in a moment. Before we do, let's discuss the possibility of scholarships.

Scholarships are awarded by the college or an outside entity and generally fall within two categories—need based and merit based. There is a good chance that children of doctors will not qualify for need-based scholarships or financial aid, allowing these programs to benefit students from lower-income families. Your child may still be able to qualify for merit-based scholarships if they are a competitive applicant. Universities understand there is a finite pool of top students in the state or country and may offer scholarships to better recruit students (and their parents). Once your student has enrolled at a college with a scholarship, they will usually be required to maintain a minimum grade point average to continue receiving this benefit. Colleges may also provide an athletic scholarship if your child will be participating on one of their sports teams.

There are many merit-based scholarships offered by outside entities not affiliated with educational institutions. These require a separate application and frequently include a writing component, such as an essay on a specific topic related to the entity's purpose or values. Online resources to search for outside merit-based scholarships include:

- www.collegeboard.org
- www.fastweb.com

- www.niche.com
- www.scholarships.com
- www.studentscholarships.org

## Student Loans

What would a college-funding chapter be without student loans? You should have a basic understanding of student loans after the earlier chapter dedicated to them. If your child will need student loans to finance their education, then the first step is to complete the Free Application for Federal Student Aid (FAFSA). The FAFSA reports the assets and income of parents and the student to arrive at the expected family contribution, which is then compared to the school's cost of attendance to determine whether your student qualifies for need-based loans or other financial aid. If so, these programs are usually more favorable than non-need-based options. Examples of need-based student loans include Perkins and subsidized Stafford loans.

Your income may disqualify your child from need-based student loan programs. If so, then unsubsidized Stafford loans and Parent Loans for Undergraduate Students (PLUS loans) become your remaining federal student loan options. Stafford loans are taken out by your student and become their responsibility, though you can help pay these off if you wish. PLUS loans are available to graduate students and parents of undergraduate students and generally have a higher interest rate than Stafford loans.

## Balance with the Rest of Your Financial Plan

"We're starting to get a good understanding of how we will pay for his college among all of our options. This is an important goal of ours, so my next question is how we should balance college saving with the rest of our financial plan, like adequately funding our retirement?"

This relates to the idea of opportunity cost; any resources applied to one area of your plan cannot be applied to another part. Education saving and retirement planning provide an example of trade-offs with limited funds. Both objectives may invest their balances in mutual funds to earn comparable rates of return. If there is no clear winner for which objective may provide a larger financial benefit, a second criteria to look at is the possible downside of not sufficiently funding each goal: does failing to achieve one objective result in a more severe problem than the other?

When looking through this lens, we can reason that the risks of failing to save enough for college or retirement are not equal. If you do not have enough saved to fully pay for your child's education, you have several alternatives that may not result in much of a financial strain. For example, you can pay for college expenses out of your monthly cash flow as another expense while your child is in college, take out PLUS loans, or your child can take out student loans of their own. In comparison, failing to save enough to retire at your desired age and standard of living could have greater consequences. Remedies here include delaying retirement, significantly cutting back from your preretirement lifestyle, or, in a worst-case scenario, outliving your savings and relying on family or government assistance. We understand and appreciate supporting your children in their academic endeavors; however, we would encourage a balanced approach so your retirement plan is not neglected.

**Chapter Summary**

"Whew, great power session!" exclaimed Ashley. "You've certainly done your homework."

We definitely give it plenty of effort. The decisions around higher education are important and can be challenging. Before you commit significant resources, we suggest reflecting on what amount of costs you would like to cover. You can then decide which options best align with your goals and how you would like this to fit within your financial plan as a whole.

Parents want to give their children the best possible opportunity for success in the adult world. For many, particularly doctors and their spouses, this means providing financial support through your children's undergraduate education so they can begin a promising career or go on to graduate school without a large student loan burden. The career of a doctor requires you to hold yourself to a high standard academically and professionally. While living at this standard has many benefits, we have seen this cause stress when parents feel they are not adequately funding their children's education. If you notice yourself feeling guilty about this, remember that you have given them much more than simply paying for some of their college expenses. Your love, care, and guidance have given them an invaluable example to follow as they find their own way in the world.

---

### Key Takeaways

*The cost of attending college has historically risen at a faster pace than general inflation*, causing the estimated cost of an undergraduate degree to potentially more than double from the time a child is born to when they begin college. Because of this, many parents will choose to save in advance for the future cost of their child's education.

*State-sponsored 529 plans* are popular investment accounts because of their tax advantages and large contribution limits. Alternatives include *Coverdell ESAs, custodial accounts, prepaid tuition plans*, and *non-retirement brokerage accounts*.

*Scholarships* fall into need-based and merit-based programs, though the high incomes of doctors will likely cause your student to become ineligible for need-based scholarships.

*Student loans* remain another way to pay for college.

*Saving for higher education and retirement are competing goals*, so finding a balanced approach will help ensure neither priority is neglected.

# CHAPTER 14

# INTRODUCTION TO INVESTING

MOST DOCTORS WOULD like to have the option to retire from medicine and not be concerned about outliving their money. To achieve this, it takes careful preparation along with an understanding of investments and the retirement landscape. The goal of the next several chapters is to provide an overview of these topics. Saving for retirement will likely be your biggest investment challenge, so we will generally use retirement planning when going through examples. However, the ideas that follow can be applied to other goals, such as investing for a child's college education. After a short introduction to the basics, we will review the traditional model retirees have relied on for their income, as well as reasons why this model may no longer apply to young families today. We will then look at retirement planning for doctors and their families, specifically overcoming the delayed start to saving due to your training. The remaining pages are devoted to three forms of diversification that serve as a conceptual framework when investing.

**What Is Investing?**

The term "investing" is often used but not always clearly explained. So, what are you actually doing when you invest? *Merriam-Webster's*

*Dictionary* defines investing as "the act of putting out money in order to gain a profit."

In other words, investing is using your current resources in a certain manner with the expectation that you will have more resources at some future time than you began with. We will focus on investing in the form of using your money to purchase securities with the goal of selling them at a later date for more than you originally bought them for, or to receive payment from the securities while you own them. A "security" is a general term to describe a tradeable financial asset, such as a stock, bond, or mutual fund. Some investments may both appreciate in value and provide income along the way, as stocks do when they declare a dividend.

One of the most appealing features of investing is the ability to passively grow your wealth without additional time. When you work, you are essentially trading your time, effort, and skills for a paycheck. You can earn more through your occupation, but this would require you to work more, and time is a limited resource. Investing allows you to leverage your time by letting your stocks, bonds, and mutual funds appreciate without extra involvement on your end. While this is useful, leveraging your time becomes much more powerful when combined with the compounding of growth on your investments.

**Compound Growth: It's Not That Simple**

When your investments grow in value from one period to the next, this rate of return may be applied in one of two ways—either as simple or compound growth. Simple growth refers to a rate of return applied to the initial balance only. Compound growth applies a rate of return to both the principal balance and all previously accrued growth. As you may expect, compound returns can greatly outpace simple returns over time, which is fortunate for us because investments exhibit this kind of growth. Your investment return over a year is based on that year's starting balance, which includes all previously earned growth from dividends, interest, and capital gains from prior years. We will use interest earned from a fixed savings account in the following example, but the math works the same way for compound growth on investments from a return perspective.

*Simple Interest*

Simple interest is interest you earn on the principal balance only. For example, if you deposit $100 at the bank, and their savings account was providing an 8 percent annual interest rate, you would earn eight dollars in interest after a year (we will assume the interest rate does not change in this example). If the bank were crediting simple interest, then the following year you receive another eight dollars in interest, and your balance would have grown to $116. In math notation, the accruing of simple interest can be expressed in this formula:

$$F = P(1+rn)$$

F = future value
P = present value
r = interest rate per period
n = number of periods

After thirty years, your savings account yielding 8 percent simple interest would have grown from $100 to $100 × (1 + (8% × 30)) = $340. This makes sense if you earn eight dollars in interest each year for thirty years, or $240 in interest, plus your original $100 deposit.

*Compound Interest*

Compound interest is applied to both the principal balance and previously accrued interest. After the first year, you would also have $108 in your savings account with compound interest because no prior interest has been earned. The difference begins after the first period. After the second year, your bank account will have $108.64, with eight dollars earned again on the $100 principal and sixty-four cents earned on the eight dollars of interest from year one. This sixty-four cents is compound interest and is expressed in this formula:

$$F = P(1 + r)^n$$

Changing $n$, the number of periods, to an exponent reflects the interest earned on interest from prior periods. After year thirty, your $100 earning 8 percent compound interest would have grown to $100 × $(1 + 8\%)^{30}$ = $1,006.27. That's quite a difference, as seen in the following graph.

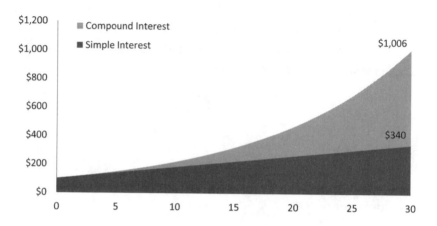

How powerful is compound growth? Let's say you started with one dollar on the first day of a thirty-day month and you were able to double your money each day. At the end of the month, you would have over a billion dollars![1]

## A Brief Introduction to Investment Risk

While you expect to have a positive outcome from an investment, there is always the possibility that your investment will fail to do so, and you may be left with less than you began with. The volatility of your investment's value, particularly downward volatility, is one application of the term "risk." However, risk is too broad to confine to a single definition and is viewed differently depending on the context. We viewed risk in the insurance chapters as an event or change to your situation that could cause an adverse financial impact. In the investment world, risk may take

---

[1]  F = $1 × $(1 + 100\%)^{30}$ = $1,073,741,824.

several shapes, and we will specify which type of risk we are referring to in each case. For example, a loss of purchasing power due to the rising cost of living over time, otherwise known as inflation risk, is different from losing money due to your investment's price decreasing in value. Inflation risk and price volatility are the two main types of investment risk we will be focusing on, and we will point out when we are covering another type of risk. Investments exhibit different risk and return characteristics depending on their asset class, or investment category. Certain traits that cause an asset class to be susceptible to one type of risk may cause that asset class to hold up well against another. Understanding the various risks and structuring your portfolio to weather these will be a key theme throughout our investment chapters.

Now that we know *what* investing is, let's take a look at the *how*. How do you grow your money? There are a few ways to do this. One of the most common methods is to invest within the financial markets by purchasing stocks, bonds, and mutual funds. These fall into the broad category of investments known as "securities," and each have their own characteristics.

**Basic Securities—Stocks, Bonds, and Mutual Funds**

*Stocks*

Stocks are probably the most commonly thought of investment vehicle, but what are they? Stocks are shares of ownership, or equity, in a company. An investor can buy a share, one unit of ownership, and become a partial owner of a company with all the other individuals that own the company's stock. Firms sell pieces of their company to the public to raise money for different strategic goals. At any point in time, there are investors who want to buy a company's stock and other investors who already own shares and would like to sell them. The marketplace that brings these buyers and sellers together is called the stock market and is a commonly referenced part of our society. Movies and television shows have stereotyped the stock market with scenes of frantic traders yelling buy or sell prices across a large computer-filled room at the top of their voices. Today, this is mainly done electronically and with much less drama.

Why do people buy stocks? The short answer is they believe a company will be successful in the future, and they want to benefit from the firm's profitability by owning a piece of the company's equity. As a company's growth prospects, product lines, and overall financial health improve or diminish in the eyes of its shareholders and prospective buyers, the value of the company's stock price will fluctuate based on the supply of shares (how many outstanding shares of stock are available to be owned) and the demand for ownership (how many buyers would like to purchase the stock and the price at which they are willing to pay). If a company's future looks stronger than it has in the past, its stock price will increase because more buyers will be willing to pay a higher price to own a portion of the company than there were previously. If the opposite happens and the company is now viewed as less profitable, the amount someone is willing to pay for a share will decrease, driving the stock price down.

Share price appreciation is one way in which an investor can profit by owning a share of stock. Perhaps you buy a pharmaceutical company's stock at forty dollars per share, and due to a promising drug passing FDA approval, the share price increases to eighty dollars. You can now sell your shares at the current market price, doubling your money. Mature companies or those in industries with limited growth prospects may be profitable but may not have many new opportunities to pursue within the market they operate in. If a company feels they are unable to use their excess cash effectively, they will distribute this cash to their shareholders in the form of a dividend. Shareholders can reinvest this dividend by buying additional shares of the company's stock or another company's stock. They may alternatively spend their dividend payment, as many retirees do to fund their living expenses.

Stocks can be classified in many ways, such as by geographic location (domestic versus international), company size (large, medium, and small), and sector (health care, financial companies, etc.). We will address stock classification in more detail in the Asset Class Diversification chapter.

In the meantime, we can focus on a couple of characteristics that equity, as a broad asset class, exhibits across its sub-asset classes. One trait is greater price volatility than other investment categories, especially over short time periods. It is not uncommon for a company's stock price to decrease significantly within weeks, days, or even minutes of announcing unfavorable news. On the other hand, investment returns of stock of successful companies, and the stock market as a whole, have generally outpaced inflation over long time periods despite occasional dips. Combining these characteristics leads us to view stock as having considerable uncertainty with short-term returns while also serving as a long-term hedge against inflation.

*Bonds*

Bonds are another common type of investment and are a form of debt issued by a company or government entity. When you purchase a bond, you are lending your money to the entity issuing the bond. The issuer makes payments to you as the bond owner based on the bond's stated interest rate until the maturity date, the date at which the company returns your original money, or principal, you lent. Companies will issue bonds as a method of financing their operations when they need capital and would prefer to pay interest on their bonds rather than dilute shareholder ownership by selling new shares of stock. Government entities will issue bonds to supplement their tax revenue or to pay for a specific public project, like a bridge.

Why do investors buy bonds? One appealing feature is their regular interest payment, which many retirees rely on for part of their income. Unlike a stock's dividends, which are paid at the company's discretion, bond interest payments are required to be made, usually semiannually. Many years ago, before electronic systems became the accepted method of tracking investments, bonds were issued as physical certificates. Coupons that represented the interest payments to be received were attached to the bond certificate, looking similar to coupons you might find in your local newspaper. When each coupon payment was due, the owner would clip the coupon from the bond certificate and present it to receive the interest payment. Even though the system has changed, the name has stuck, and bond interest payments are still referred to as coupon payments. Bonds are normally issued at a par value of $1,000, and their semiannual coupon payments are based on this value. For example, a bond with a 5 percent stated interest rate would pay fifty dollars in interest throughout the year as two twenty-five-dollar semiannual coupon payments to the bondholder until the bond matures. For this reason, bonds are also referred to as "fixed income" because the income payments they provide are a flat dollar amount based on the bond's coupon rate and par value. At the end of the bond's term, it matures, and the investor receives the final coupon payment and the return of their principal. If the issuing company runs into financial troubles and is unable to continue operating, bondholders have priority over shareholders for the company's remaining cash and assets. The company must pay off all debts before its owners receive anything in the event of a bankruptcy.

Like stock, there is an active secondary market for bonds in which bondholders can sell their bonds to other investors if they do not wish to hold their bond to maturity. However, a bond may sell in the secondary market for a price other than what you initially purchased it for, particularly if the bond issuer's creditworthiness or interest rates have changed since it was issued.

Let's say you purchased a bond issued by the city of Detroit for $1,000 in 2010. The city's finances then took a turn for the worse over the next couple of years. Murmurs emerge about possibly declaring bankruptcy. Detroit's solvency directly impacts its ability to meet its financial obligations, including your bond's interest payments and return of principal. After months of concerning news headlines, you have had enough and decide to sell your bond. Unfortunately, a buyer in the bond market will no longer be willing to pay $1,000 for your bond because Detroit's financial health has deteriorated since your purchase. You will have to sell your bond for less than $1,000 and take a loss.[1] Default rates for bonds issued by high-credit quality government entities and companies have historically been low in the United States. With that in mind, bond prices in the secondary market can fluctuate daily if the issuer's creditworthiness has been improved or downgraded.

Bond prices are also susceptible to changes in the interest rate environment. Let's say you purchase a $1,000 bond yielding a 5 percent coupon rate. A few years go by, and interest rates throughout the economy are higher than they were when you purchased your bond. The same company with an unchanged credit rating now issues another round of bonds. However, due to interest rates being higher than they were previously, the company's new bonds are issued with an 8 percent coupon rate, making your 5 percent bond relatively less desirable. To find a buyer for your 5 percent bond in the secondary market in which similar bonds are yielding 8 percent, you will need to make your bond appear as attractive as the 8 percent bonds by lowering its price. Instead of selling your bond for the $1,000 par value you purchased it for, you will have to price it below $1,000 and sell it at a discount, taking a loss on the bond's principal. In finance lingo, the 5 percent bond selling at a discount and 8 percent bond selling at par need to have equal yields to maturity so a buyer is indifferent between the two.[2] Conversely, if interest rates had gone down since your purchase, your 5 percent bond would now sell at a premium, and you would price it above $1,000 in the secondary market, receiving a gain on the bond's principal.

Bonds can be classified in many ways, including by issuer (federal government, municipality, corporation, or foreign entity), credit quality (high to low), maturity (how long until the bond matures), and duration (limited, moderate, or extended duration; duration is a measure of how

---

[1] Detroit filed for bankruptcy in 2013, resulting in holders of Detroit's bonds receiving less than the full amount owed to them, as well as reduced pension benefits for state workers.

[2] The yield to maturity (YTM) is the internal rate of return an investor will earn if they buy a bond at the current market price and hold it until maturity with all coupon and principal payments made on time.

sensitive a bond's price is to changes in interest rates). As an asset class, bonds tend to exhibit much lower price volatility than stocks, as well as lower historical returns, and have been stereotyped as a "slow and steady" investment. Bondholders have a fairly accurate idea of their investment return, barring an inability of the issuer to pay its debts or any unexpected change in credit rating or interest rates. Even these changes may not impact your return if you hold the bond until maturity. Your return will be exactly as you expect it to be, the yield to maturity, as long as the issuer continues to make the coupon payments and final principal reimbursement.

While bond prices are usually not that volatile, bonds are viewed as being susceptible to inflation due to their fixed income payments. Let's revisit your 5 percent coupon bond as an example and say it has a term of thirty years. You will receive fifty dollars in coupon payments from this bond every year, but we expect the amount of goods and services you are able to buy with your fifty dollars to gradually decrease as inflation increases the cost of living (but not your coupon payments) over the next three decades. Put another way, you are able to buy more goods and services with the fifty-dollar coupon payment you receive in year one compared to the amount you can buy in year thirty. We will revisit bonds in more detail in the Asset Class Diversification chapter and the concept of inflation affecting your buying power in the Time Horizon Diversification chapter.

*Mutual Funds*

Until now, we have focused on single securities—a stock or a bond. This changes with mutual funds. A mutual fund is a collection of individual securities pooled together and managed as a portfolio by the portfolio manager and his or her team of analysts and traders. They can contain shares of stock from dozens, hundreds, or even thousands of different companies. Other mutual funds may hold bonds from many different issuers. Some focus on alternative investments, such as real estate or precious metals, like gold. Mutual funds can be incredibly varied and are a popular choice for today's investors.

Why are they so appealing? Mutual funds allow investors to conveniently buy into a diversified portfolio of stocks, bonds, or other securities. Go ahead and read that last sentence again. The key word is one you have likely heard of before—diversification. You may know this from the adage "don't hold all of your eggs in one basket." While a literal dropped basket means a frustrating second trip back to the store, it can have more severe consequences in the investment world. Enron was a large energy company before declaring bankruptcy in 2001 due to accounting fraud. Unfortunately, many of Enron's former employees had invested their retirement savings heavily in Enron stock. Upon Enron's demise, they lost both their jobs and much of their life's savings. This is an extreme example but highlights how investors may be unaware of a company's internal operations and future stock performance. Even financial analysts who track a company's financial status for a living are not certain about what its stock price may be next quarter or next year, let alone in thirty years. The price of an individual stock at some point in the future is unknown, and it can be a bumpy ride getting there, particularly due to unforeseen events such as a CEO leaving or failing to receive FDA approval on a new pharmaceutical drug. These are unwelcome surprises if this stock represents a decent portion of your portfolio. Even without a significant event, a stock's return may be lower than expected. Perhaps a new competitor enters the industry and takes market share from your company. Investors acknowledge their uncertainty and hedge against this by spreading their money among many companies. Mutual funds are a common tool that allow investors to do this efficiently. Exchange-traded funds, or ETFs, are a similar product that has become popular in recent years. We will go into more detail on ETFs in the Tax Treatment Diversification chapter.

*Don't Hold All of Your Eggs in One*
*Basket: A Further Explanation*

An individual security contains two forms of risk—one that is specific to that company or bond issuer and another that is inherent across all companies or bond issuers. We will focus on a stock in our example, but the same principle applies to bonds. Company-specific risk is known as unsystematic risk and can be diversified away by holding stocks in other companies. In contrast, risk that is found across all companies that operate in the same market is known as systematic risk and cannot be eliminated by holding other stocks.

Let's use Tesla as an example.[1] The innovative carmaker has challenged the auto industry with its ambitious pursuit of mass producing electric vehicles. Central to its plans is its Gigafactory, the colossal manufacturing plant outside of Reno, Nevada. The Gigafactory's rapid production of lithium-ion batteries will lower the manufacturing cost of this key component and allow vehicles to be affordable for the middle class. A fire at the aptly named plant could cause the assembly line to grind to a halt, delaying deliveries and causing would-be customers to turn to a competitor.[2] This negative outlook would cause Tesla's stock price to fall as investors downgrade their estimates of Tesla's future profits. How would this impact the stock prices of other automakers? Likely not very much, if at all. This is a Tesla-specific risk and can be reduced by owning stock in other companies.

---

[1] Examples are for illustrative purposes only and are not intended as a recommendation or comprehensive analysis.

[2] Tesla is aware of the risk posed by impaired production at the Gigafactory. Because of this, Tesla has spent millions fireproofing the factory and designing it to withstand earthquakes on its four foundations.

On the other hand, systematic risk affects all companies that operate in the same industry or market. If the United States were to enter into a recession, we would expect consumers to cut back on their spending and buy not only fewer Tesla vehicles but also fewer Ford autos, Dell computers, and Apple products. Falling sales should be taken as negative news for any company that derives a significant amount of their revenue from the domestic market. We would therefore expect the stock prices of these companies to decline because of their exposure to a slowing economy. This example of systematic risk is not isolated to Tesla. We cannot simply diversify away this risk by holding stock in other companies because their prices will have also fallen. To mitigate the effect of this systematic risk, we must hold other asset classes than stocks.

Why does this matter? It is generally accepted that you need to take on more risk to expect to earn a higher rate of return, but not all types of risk are equal. Investors are not rewarded for accepting more unsystematic risk because this can easily be reduced for free by holding other securities. Mutual funds exhibit similar risk and return characteristics as their underlying holdings, but they are able to diversify away a large portion of unsystematic risk found in individual stocks and bonds due to their numerous holdings.

Mutual funds charge a fee, called their expense ratio, for the benefit of providing instant diversification, as well as handling investment research and trading their underlying holdings. This cost varies depending on the type of fund and how it is managed. Funds that are passively managed are known as index funds, whereas active funds take a more proactive approach. There are thousands of publicly traded stocks, so investors categorize them based on shared characteristics. An index is a formal grouping of similar stocks, bonds, or securities in another asset class that serves as a benchmark for how an investment category is performing. For example, Standard and Poor's created the S&P 500 Index to track about five hundred of the largest US companies. Other indices track different asset classes, such as international stocks, small US companies, and bonds.

Index mutual funds aim to mirror the performance of the benchmark they follow and often base their holdings on the index itself. Some use a market-capitalization weighting strategy, directly replicating the stocks and their respective weights in the index within the mutual fund. For example, if the S&P 500 weights Apple stock as 3.7 percent of its composition, an S&P 500 Index fund will hold 3.7 percent of its portfolio in Apple stock. Because of this, investors should expect to receive the full positive and negative performance of the underlying index they track, less the expense the fund charges. Index funds provide broad exposure to an asset class and, due to their modest level of research and analysis, tend to have much lower expenses than actively managed funds.

Active mutual funds typically have a benchmark index in mind, but instead of aiming to mimic the index's performance, they aim to outperform the benchmark's return. This may be on the upside, earning a greater positive return when the index is up, or on the downside, losing less than the index when it declines. Because of this goal, active funds have higher operating costs to support their research analysts and overall structure. They pass these costs to their shareholders in the form of higher expenses. Investors in active funds pay more for the potential of returns that outpace benchmark returns or for better risk-adjusted returns relative to the benchmark.[1]

---

[1] Risk-adjusted returns means quantifying returns based on how much risk the investment has exhibited. Risk expressed as price volatility may be quantified by the investment's standard deviation.

## Chapter Summary

We now understand the investment basics, beginning with how simple and compound interest differ. Throughout the sections that follow, we will consider price volatility and inflation risk and how they influence our investment divisions. Stocks, bonds, and mutual funds are three common tradeable investments, or securities, and each have different characteristics. Mutual funds can be classified not only by their investment category but also by how they are managed, with index funds generally having lower fund expenses than active funds. With this knowledge in hand, we will turn to the macro picture of where your retirement income may, or may not, come from.

---

### Key Takeaways

*Investing* is the act of putting out money in order to gain a profit.

*Simple growth* is earned on the principal balance only and results in linear growth. *Compound growth* is earned on the principal balance as well as all appreciation from past periods and results in exponential growth.

Two types of investment risk are *price volatility*, which is more apparent over short time periods, and *inflation risk*, which reduces your purchasing power over time due to the increased cost of living.

A *security* is a general term for a tradeable financial asset. Stocks, bonds, and mutual funds are the main types of securities we will cover.

*Stocks*, or *equities*, are units of ownership in a company. They allow investors to benefit from a company's success by representing a proportionate share in the company's future profits. Stocks may exhibit considerable price volatility. The long-term returns of the stock market have historically outpaced inflation, causing equities to be considered an inflation hedge over long periods of time.

*Bonds*, also called *fixed income*, are debt securities. Investors who purchase bonds receive interest from the bond issuer throughout the bond's term. At the end of the term, the bond matures, and the bondholder receives the principal and final coupon payment. Bonds generally exhibit a low level of price volatility. Their fixed coupon payments do not increase over time, causing bonds to be susceptible to inflation risk.

*Mutual funds* are collections of individual securities and provide investors with a convenient way to buy into a diversified portfolio. *Index mutual funds* aim to mirror the performance of their benchmark index and have low fees. *Actively managed mutual funds* aim to outperform their benchmark index and typically charge higher fees than index funds.

# CHAPTER 15

# SOURCES OF RETIREMENT INCOME

KATE, A FIRST-YEAR cardiology fellow, and Connor, an accountant, arrived for a review meeting to discuss their financial plan, as well as a major lifestyle change. Kate's mother, Jane, recently moved in with them due to financial difficulties, and they were interested in learning about how their own retirement may look.

"Thanks for making time for us on such short notice," began Kate. "It's been difficult to find a free moment with the start of my fellowship and the kids, especially since my mom moved in with us."

"On the positive side, the kids really enjoy having Grandma around," said Connor. "And we're all benefitting from her cooking."

"You always see the silver lining, hon. I love my mother dearly, but we have noticed both of us becoming a little more on edge with another body in our already crowded home. Despite how many times Connor calls it 'cozy,' it's simply a small house with five of us. Once my father passed, we became more involved in my mom's finances and noticed she was just getting by each month. After her mortgage payments, she was struggling to keep up with her medical bills and other living expenses. She's getting up there in years, and we didn't like the idea of her continuing to live alone. We talked it over between us, and then with my mom, and the three of us agreed to make this change."

"I think she didn't want to ask for help, but she was very agreeable with our plan and accepted right away," explained Connor. "We noticed Jane felt a big sense of relief once she sold her home too."

"We moved our sons into the same bedroom to free up the third for Grandma. Connor has cut back on his accounting practice to take care of the kids and be around for my mom more often. I'm going to start moonlighting soon too. We could use the extra income. We're all making sacrifices, and to be frank, it's causing some stress."

"One thing this experience has taught us so far is the importance of planning ahead. Kate and I are unfamiliar with the retirement landscape and need to know what to expect so we don't have to move in with our kids …"

As the baby boomer generation leaves the workforce, millions of retirees will face a retirement landscape unlike any seen before.[1] While some have adequately prepared, many, like Jane, have not. Improved longevity coupled with reduced government and employer support places an increased burden on retirees. For a sixty-five-year-old couple retiring today, studies estimate a 50 percent probability of at least one of them living to ninety. Employers are shifting the responsibility of retirement income to their employees, and uncertainty remains around the future of government entitlement programs, like Social Security. If your retirement may span decades, it's only logical to ask, "Where will this money come from?"

**Traditional Model of Retirement Income**

The traditional model of retirement income is known as the three-legged stool. Social Security, employer pensions, and personal savings have been the bedrock for retirees for much of the twentieth century. However, the current outlook for the three pillars suggests this model will not be reliable in the years to come. Social Security is a government program

---

[1] The baby boomer generation includes people born from 1946 to 1964 during the post-World War II era. Starting in 2011, roughly 10,000 baby boomers will turn sixty-five each day for the next two decades.

and was never supposed to provide the majority of retirees' income. It was designed to supplement personal savings and act as a safety net if other income sources were depleted. During much of the 1900s, employers rewarded workers for their loyalty by providing them with a pension, an income stream promised throughout retirement. Today, pensions have largely been replaced by other retirement plans, such as 401(k) and 403(b) plans. Saving on your own remains the option you have full control over. This freedom comes with the responsibility of saving enough and investing it appropriately. The rest of this section will analyze the present state of each pillar to give Kate and Connor the understanding they are looking for.

*Social Security*

Social Security's roots can be traced back to the Great Depression of the 1930s. From the stock market's peak in September 1929 to its bottom three years later, the S&P 500 declined 86 percent, and many investors lost their life's savings.[1] The world spiraled into an economic depression, and unemployment reached a high of 25 percent in the United States. With millions of citizens out of work and out of money, the government realized the need for a social insurance program, and in 1935, President Franklin D. Roosevelt signed the Social Security Act. Numerous revisions have been made since then, but Social Security's core intent has remained the same—act as a safety net by providing a basic amount of income to those who do not have much else.

When people refer to Social Security, they are usually thinking of the monthly income they expect to receive in retirement. There are other components to the Social Security program, such as Medicare, but we will limit our focus to the retirement benefit side.[2] Social Security is funded by a tax on income, called the FICA tax after the Federal Insurance Contributions Act. For 2018, the FICA rate is 7.65 percent

---

[1] Source: J.P. Morgan Asset Management.
[2] Specifically, the Social Security benefit retirees expect to receive is the "old-age" part of "old-age, survivors, and disability insurance" (OASDI).

on income up to $128,400 imposed on both employees and employers.[1] Self-employed individuals pay both sides of this at 15.30 percent, referred to as "self-employment tax." Each year, actuaries review Social Security's funding level and project how well the system will be able to meet its obligations over the next seventy-five years. How do recent findings look? The 2016 report estimates the Social Security trust fund will be able to continue paying full benefits through 2034, after which recipients can expect to receive only about 75 percent of the benefits listed. The demographic shift of lower birth rates and increased life expectancy is partially to blame. In 1960, Social Security had 5.1 workers paying into the system to support one retiree receiving benefits. By 2014, the worker-to-beneficiary ratio had fallen to 2.8 and is projected to be 2.1 in 2034. Remedies include higher tax revenue or reduced benefits, neither of which are popular legislative proposals. For young investors today, there may be a variety of changes that impact the program and cause a wide range of possible benefit payouts.

The amount of Social Security retirement benefits received depends on several factors, including the number of credits earned, your income while working, and age at which you begin taking benefits. You qualify for Social Security once you have forty credits, at which point you are considered fully insured. Credits are received by earning a small amount of income. Only $1,300 of income was needed for one credit in 2017, and up to four credits can be earned each year. For workers who do not have forty credits, your benefit is based on your spouse's benefit if he or she is fully insured. The amount of your benefit is also based on the average of your highest thirty-five years of income that was subject to FICA tax. You can elect to begin benefits as early as sixty-two, but the amount you receive is permanently higher each year you delay until seventy. Full retirement age is at sixty-seven if you were born in 1960 or later; however, this is somewhat of an arbitrary age because your

---

[1] The Social Security maximum wage base of $128,400 in 2018 is adjusted each year. The 7.65 percent rate is made of the 6.2 percent Social Security tax rate up to $128,400 and the 1.45 percent Medicare tax rate, which does not have an income limit.

benefit continues to increase each year not taken up to age seventy. Inflation also impacts the amount you receive because your benefits adjust annually based on increases in the cost of living. Finally, the IRS may tax as much as 85 percent of your Social Security benefit, depending on the amount of income reported each year in retirement. This is more meaningful if we put it in context, which leads us to a metric called the income replacement ratio. The Social Security income replacement ratio is calculated as the gross (before tax) income received from Social Security divided by gross preretirement income.

Social Security is a progressive system, meaning low-income earners receive greater benefits relative to their income than high earners. A family earning $40,000 heading into retirement will see Social Security replacing a higher percentage of their preretirement earnings than a family earning $250,000. Doctors and their families can expect a low income replacement ratio, as benefits should account for only a small portion of their preretirement earnings. Let's take a look at the numbers to see how this could play out. An individual retiring at age sixty-five in 2015 who has earned above the Social Security maximum wage base each of the thirty-five years used in the income calculation would receive $30,504 in benefits that year, or $2,542 per month. If this individual's preretirement earnings were $250,000, then $30,504 of Social Security income results in an income replacement ratio of 12.2 percent. We then remember that young workers today can only expect to receive about 75 percent of their scheduled benefits. Keeping dollar amounts in 2015 terms, this adjustment reduces our monthly benefit from $2,542 to $1,907 for a replacement ratio of 9.2 percent. That's it. Less than 10 percent of this individual's income was replaced by Social Security. Then the IRS comes knocking. If you have modest income from a pension or retirement account withdrawals, then up to 85 percent of your benefit is subject to income tax.[1] Assuming a marginal income tax rate of 25 percent is applied to 85 percent of benefits received, then your after-tax

---

[1] In 2017, 85 percent of Social Security benefits become subject to income tax once modified adjusted gross income (MAGI) is above $44,000 for a married couple filing their taxes jointly.

benefit falls to $1,501 per month, or about fifty dollars a day. Hardly something to get excited about if you were earning $250,000 before retirement.

"We suspected we would not be relying on Social Security for our retirement but didn't know it would be so little," remarked Kate.

"No kidding," Connor added. "We're pretty frugal, but cutting back our spending by 90 percent from our working years doesn't really appeal to me. What are our other options?"

*Employer Pensions*

Employer pensions have been a retirement staple for much of the twentieth century. These have largely been as defined benefit plans that promise employees a stipend throughout retirement, based on their length of service and income level. The longer an employee's tenure and higher their income, the more they could expect to receive upon retirement. Unfortunately for employees, pension plans are becoming less common today with 401(k) defined contribution plans appearing in their place. Nonprofit employers usually offer 403(b) plans, which are similar to 401(k) plans. This is a result of employers shifting the responsibility of providing retirement income to their employees. In 1983, 88 percent of workers were covered by a pension plan, but by 2013 this had fallen to only 30 percent. The same period saw the rise of defined contribution plans with employee 401(k) coverage increasing from 38 percent to 84 percent. Several factors prompted this transition, including increased life expectancy and the burden of unfunded pension liabilities on employers.

With defined benefit pension plans, employers assume the risk of employees' longevity. Employers agree to make pension payments as long as their former employees live, so advances in health care increasing life expectancy have caused retirements to lengthen. A study by the Center for Retirement Research at Boston College found the average retirement for males grew from thirteen years in 1962 to 17.9 years in 2010. This may not seem like much, but to employers it means a 38 percent increase in the number of required pension payments. Having a ghost workforce on the payroll for a longer period of time has made defined benefit plans costlier to administer. With 401(k) plans, employers will usually make a matching contribution to workers' accounts during employment but offer no support once employees move on from service.

Employers are also responsible for the investment performance of the assets earmarked for pension payments. While some of these funds are allocated to bonds and cash, a portion is invested in equities with the goal of earning a greater return for payments due in many years. This works fine when the stock market is rising but can be problematic during market declines. We saw this with the recession in the early 2000s following the technology bubble in the stock market. Three consecutive years of negative returns caused the S&P 500 to lose nearly half of its value. In addition, the Federal Reserve will often lower interest rates during recessions in an effort to stimulate the economy. The Fed used this technique in 2000 and, in doing so, affected one of the key inputs used in calculating the present value of an employer's pension obligation. Lower interest rates increase the present value of projected future payments, causing pensions to appear a much larger liability than previously calculated. Decreased pension assets combined with higher pension obligations resulted in large unfunded pension liabilities on the balance sheets of many companies. This required employers to increase their pension contributions by nearly three times. In contrast, employees are responsible for funding and investing the assets in their 401(k). If they do not save enough or their investments do not perform well, it is up to the employee to remedy this or face the consequences.

Increased longevity and uncertain investment returns are two factors that have caused defined benefit pension plans to largely fall out of favor. In the world of employer benefits, pensions have become an endangered species. Gone are the days of comfortably retiring on a pension and Social Security. With two of our three pillars in doubt, we turn to personal savings as our last hope for a successful retirement.

*Personal Savings*

It's not a closely held secret that Americans are excellent spenders. We are better known for our Black Friday shopping sprees than our frugality.

In fact, we are so good at spending money that Americans had *negative* savings rates in 2005 and 2006. Not only were we failing to make up for the reduced support from Social Security and pensions, but across the country, we were spending more than we were earning. Yikes!

How do things look lately? The 2016 National Retirement Risk Index estimates 50 percent of households may not have enough saved to continue their preretirement lifestyle through retirement. This is reinforced by the Employee Benefit Research Institute's 2017 Retirement Confidence Survey. According to the EBRI's findings, nearly half of workers surveyed (47 percent) reported having less than $25,000 in savings and investments. Even fewer respondents (41 percent) have ever attempted to calculate how much money they need to save to live comfortably in retirement. These numbers do not improve much as Americans approach the decade before retirement. Only half (51 percent) of workers age fifty-five and older have projected how much they will need at retirement, and 45 percent reported having less than $100,000 in savings and investments. While $100,000 appears to be a large number upon first glance, it becomes far less impressive in the context of a decades-long retirement. A 4 percent annual withdrawal rate from retirement assets has been the traditional rule of thumb, however a lower withdrawal rate can be considered for a greater chance of not outliving your savings. A $100,000 nest egg with ten years of work left paints a pretty meager picture at the traditional withdrawal rate, as this balance will only create about $350 of monthly income. As you can imagine, many workers are not feeling too confident about retirement, and almost one in three (31 percent) admit to feeling stressed when preparing for retirement.

"We're seeing this play out with my mother," Kate said. "We're fortunate to be able to support her, but if we weren't …"

"Yeah, Jane's financial life wasn't looking too rosy before she moved in," Connor added. "What we've talked about so far has been very helpful, though it has been a bit of a downer. Is there any good news?"

Yes! Doctors and their families certainly do not fit the mold of the "average" household. The EBRI survey numbers are consistently more positive for workers with a retirement plan, as most doctors have through their employer. In addition, many doctors will establish individual retirement accounts, or IRAs, to supplement their employer plans. Household incomes for most doctors typically fall within the top 10 percent of Americans, with many in the top 5 percent. You will have the ability to save a significant amount toward your retirement. Done right, it is entirely possible to step away from medicine partially or fully before sixty-five, when most workers expect to retire.

**Chapter Summary**

The retirement landscape has evolved since Social Security's arrival in 1935. Social Security enjoyed several decades of expansion through the middle of the last century. However, the focus has been on maintaining solvency and reining in costs since the 1970s. There is considerable uncertainty around the future of entitlement programs and health care, so Social Security retirement benefits and Medicare may be different during your retirement than they are today. Even in its current state, Social Security's retirement benefit should amount to a low income replacement ratio for doctors. The theme with employer benefits has been to shift responsibility to employees with defined benefit pension plans being replaced by defined contribution 401(k) and 403(b) plans, partly due to changing demographics and investment risk. Most employees will receive employer assistance while working but should not expect this support to continue as a pension payment afterward.

Doctors early in their careers may see these trends continue. With defined benefit pensions becoming less common and doubt around the future of Social Security, Americans are increasingly reliant on their own savings for retirement. Fortunately, your high earnings will allow you to make up for reduced income from other sources. Just because many Americans are not prepared for retirement does not mean you have to be one of them.

**Key Takeaways**

*The traditional model of retirement income consists of three pillars—*
Social Security, employer pensions, and personal savings.

*Social Security* is a government-run social insurance program.
The old-age component provides a small monthly benefit that
can be elected as early as sixty-two, though benefits are higher
the longer they are delayed until seventy. This was designed as
a retirement supplement, and Social Security statements caution
workers that "Social Security benefits are not intended to be your
only source of income when you retire. You will need other savings,
investments, pensions, or retirement accounts to live comfortably
when you retire." Doctors can expect only a small percent of their
preretirement income to be replaced by Social Security.

*Employer pension plans* provide retirees with a monthly stipend,
usually based on the employee's length of service and a calculation
of highest average income. Employers assume all longevity risk
of their former employees and all investment risk of pension plan
assets. Advances in health care improving life expectancy and
periodic declines in the stock market have increased the burden
pensions place on employers. As a result, these plans are becoming
less common, and today only three in ten workers have access to a
traditional defined benefit pension plan.

*Personal savings* round out the traditional retirement income trio. You
have full control, as well as full responsibility, of your contributions
and investment decisions within your 401(k) or 403(b) plan,
individual retirement account (IRA), and nonretirement brokerage
account. Due to the reduced role of Social Security and employer
pensions, personal savings will likely account for a greater portion
of income for current and future retirees than in past decades.

# CHAPTER 16

# PLAYING CATCH-UP

"THAT LAST SESSION was great. It really opened our eyes to the reality of what we're facing leading up to retirement," commented Connor.

"And it impressed on us how much we're on our own," Kate added. "As we've talked about in our previous meetings, we're in survival mode through my fellowship. Once that ends, we know we have to start saving in earnest to avoid becoming my mother. No time to dilly-dally!"

"We have a good grasp on the overall retirement picture, but one thing we talked about after our last appointment is *how much* we need to save. We know Kate's income won't jump for a few years but would love to see what the numbers look like once it does ..."

As we saw in the last chapter, only four out of ten respondents in a recent survey have tried to calculate how much money they need for a comfortable lifestyle through retirement. This is a key step in assessing the long-term viability of your financial plan. It's difficult to create your retirement road map without knowing the destination! While the idea of when retirement should start and what it should look like differs from person to person, a characteristic most doctors share is their delayed start to saving for later in life. Kate is not alone in this regard. Many doctors finish their training in their thirties with little, if any, money invested for retirement. This chapter will identify factors to consider with your long-term savings plan before going through scenarios of how the numbers look for Kate and Connor.

**The Cost of Waiting**

Kate has the right idea with starting their long-term savings plan immediately after her higher income allows. Compound growth taught us that investment values can grow exponentially. While this aids in your catch-up effort, it also shows us that further delaying your savings can have large impact on the end result. The following graph illustrates the growth of a one-time $1,000 investment at a constant 8 percent annual rate of return beginning at ages thirty-five, forty, and forty-five grown to age sixty-five. When given thirty years, this investment appreciated to more than ten times its original value at $10,063. Delaying this by five years causes our age sixty-five value to be about a third lower at $6,848. Waiting a further five years to begin at forty-five causes our final balance to only reach $4,661.

Graph 1: Growth of a lump sum $1,000 investment at an 8 percent annual rate of return beginning at ages thirty-five, forty, and forty-five to age sixty-five

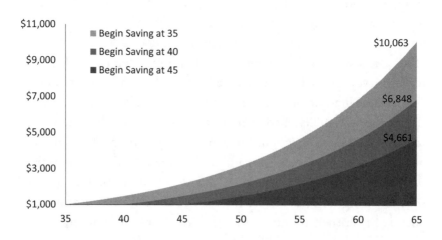

## Factors to Consider

Several factors affect the development of your retirement plan, some of which are within your control, while others are not. The following list identifies the most apparent inputs to your savings plan and the main ones we will be considering with the scenarios that follow.

*Age at which you begin saving.* As we saw in the previous example, it is advantageous to begin your savings soon after training to give your investments the most time possible to benefit from compound growth. It is common to take a few months immediately after graduation to pay off credit card balances and build your emergency reserve account. Once these are completed, ideally you can begin funding your long-term savings plan without further delay.

*Amount you save.* The appropriate amount to save is an output from other factors, such as when you would like to leave the workforce and retirement lifestyle. An earlier and more lavish retirement will require a higher savings rate as a percent of your working income, while postponing retirement with a frugal lifestyle afterward will allow a lower savings rate.

*Rate of return on investments.* How well your investments grow affects when you can retire and how much you are able to withdraw each year. While you have the choice of how to allocate your funds, market forces that affect investment performance are beyond your control. Proper allocation and management of your investments will be the focus of the Asset Class Diversification chapter.

*Age at which you retire.* This is a personal choice and will be a large driver of how much you need to save throughout your career. Workers continue to report an expected retirement age of sixty-five across occupations. Some prefer to work later, though many would like the option to scale back their hours before sixty-five. It is reasonable to plan for an early retirement, as the actual median retirement age of retirees surveyed was sixty-two, with almost half (48 percent) noting they stopped working sooner than they had planned. Of those who retired early, a quarter cited being financially able to do so, while many had to retire due to reasons outside of their control. These include health issues or a disability (41 percent), company changes (such as downsizing, 26 percent), or needing to provide care for a family member (14 percent).

*Length of retirement.* Retirement lengths are projected to continue increasing as life expectancies improve. A sixty-five-year-old in 2018 has an average life expectancy to age eighty-five; however, one in four can expect to live to ninety, and one in ten can expect to live to ninety-five. If your family has a history of longevity, then planning for life into your nineties is recommended.

*Retirement lifestyle.* Your desired lifestyle will affect your long-term plan.

*Inflation.* The rate at which the cost of goods and services increases will be a subtle but important factor in determining whether you outlive your savings. Your buying power diminishes as the cost of living increases, so inflation directly impacts how much you need to withdraw from your savings to maintain your standard of living. Since 1914, inflation has ranged from an annual high of 20.4 percent to a low of negative 10.8 percent, though the hundred-year average is around 3.25 percent.

*Tax rates.* We care about how much goods and services you can purchase in retirement, which are expressed in after-tax dollars. After all, you pay for groceries, coffee, and vacations with money in your bank account, which has already been taxed when earned. However, a sizable amount of your retirement savings will likely be in pretax accounts, such as your 401(k) or 403(b) plans. When you withdraw money from your pretax accounts, which has never been taxed before, to your bank account, you will have to pay income tax on the amount of the distribution. The tax rates themselves are out of your control, but you can choose how much or little to withdraw (while adhering to the required minimum distribution rules once in your seventies). This idea will be a key concept in the Tax Diversification chapter.

*Health care costs.* Most retirees receive their health care through Medicare. Even so, health care costs may remain one of the larger budget items. Certain expenses are not covered by Medicare, and individuals are still responsible for insurance premiums and copayments. In addition, the Medicare system you encounter may be significantly different from the system you know today.

## Playing Catch-Up

"Okay, so how much do we need to save? I've heard 10 percent of our income is a good rule of thumb. Will that be enough?" asked Connor.

"Weren't you listening?" answered Kate. "It depends on the factors we just went over …"

Kate is indeed right. There is no one-size-fits-all set of savings plan recommendations. The retirement plan that best fits your lifestyle, during both your working years and after, will be the output from how you prioritize the factors within your control and deal with the ones that are not. With that said, most doctors share the goal of being able to retire at some point, usually by their early to mid-sixties. Many also do not have much saved by the time they finish training, so there is some catch-up to be done. The general goal we suggest to doctors early in their careers is to save 20 percent of their gross income for retirement.

You were living on a modest resident or fellow income before your transition, so we encourage basing your post-training lifestyle on 80 percent of your income and deferring 20 percent to support your sixty-five-year-old self. One of the keys to doing this successfully is to be mindful of how large expenses, such as a mortgage, affect your overall financial plan. Structuring your new home and its mortgage payment into your cash flow *after* your retirement contributions are accounted for will help you be aware of how much home you can truly afford. As a substantial fixed cost, your mortgage will set the tone for how much you are able to save for years to come.

In the projections that follow, we will adjust some variables while keeping others fixed. Inputs that will not change include Kate and Connor's gross household income at $360,000 (adjusted in line with inflation, so keeping the same purchasing power as today's dollars), annual inflation at 3.25 percent, the annual rate of return on investments during their working years at 8 percent, annual investment rate of return in retirement at 6 percent, and gross (before tax) retirement withdrawals of $12,000 each month. The logic behind reducing the investment rate of return in retirement is due to their time horizon. Specifically, Kate and Connor's retirement investments are more susceptible to stock market volatility with a short-term time horizon in retirement than they were during their accumulation phase with a longer time horizon. We are estimating they will have a greater portion of their investments allocated to stock, which tends to have higher long-term investment returns than bonds, during their accumulation years than in retirement. They will then reallocate some of their stock holdings to bonds to lower their portfolio's volatility as they enter retirement and begin taking withdrawals (more to come here in the Time Horizon Diversification chapter). Gross monthly distributions in retirement of $12,000 may sound high but are only 40 percent of their monthly income while working and are further taxable if taken from their pretax 401(k) or 403(b) plans.

**Common inputs across all scenarios:**

Gross household income:                    $360,000
Annual inflation rate:                      3.25%[1]
Annual rate of return (accumulation):       8%
Annual rate of return (distribution):       6%
Gross monthly distributions in retirement:  $12,000

---

[1] Mean annual inflation rate from 1914 through 2016. Source: Bureau of Labor Statistics.

## Scenario 1: Begin saving 20 percent of gross income at age thirty-five, retire at age sixty

| | |
|---|---|
| Begin saving at age: | 35 |
| Saving rate (percent of income): | 20% |
| Retire at age: | 60 |
| Balance at retirement: | $7,271,612 |
| Savings depleted at age: | 93 |

In our first scenario, Kate and Connor are able to save 20 percent of their income immediately after Kate's training ends at age thirty-five. A portion of this $72,000 saved will be to their employer retirement plans, while the remainder will be held in other accounts. Their investments enjoy compound growth at a steady 8 percent until they retire at sixty when they have almost $7.3 million. The past twenty-five years have not only grown their nest egg but have also increased the cost of living. To retire on today's equivalent of $12,000 inflated at 3.25 percent annually, they will need to withdraw $26,695 each month their first year of retirement. In other words, the cost of living has increased 122 percent since their savings plan began. This is the subtle yet damaging effect inflation has on your purchasing power. Their first decade of retirement sees their balance continue to grow, as the 6 percent annual return on their investments outpaces distributions until they are seventy. At that time, their balance peaks at $7.9 million and begins to decline as withdrawals overtake new growth. Their savings decline at an accelerated pace through their eighties and are depleted at age ninety-three.

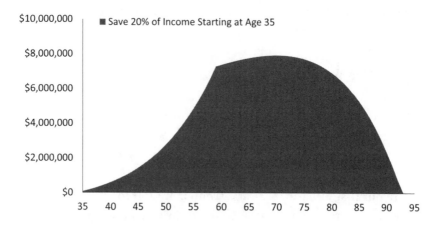

If these dollar amounts seem unrealistically high or low for your situation, we can alternatively explain this scenario in numbers relative to a salary to apply to all income levels. Rephrasing the earlier paragraph into relative terms gives us the following story based on their gross income at age thirty-five when Kate finishes training.

Kate and Connor are able to save 20 percent of their income immediately after Kate's training ends at age thirty-five. A portion of this 20 percent saved will be to their employer retirement plans, while the remainder will be held in other accounts. Their investments enjoy compound growth at a steady 8 percent until they retire at sixty when they have just over twenty times their age-thirty-five combined salaries. The past twenty-five years have not only grown their nest egg but have also increased the cost of living. To retire on the equivalent of 40 percent of their age-thirty-five income inflated at 3.25 percent annually, they will need to withdraw 89 percent of their age-thirty-five income their first year of retirement. In other words, the cost of living has increased 122 percent since their savings plan began. This is the subtle yet damaging effect inflation has on your purchasing power. Their first decade of retirement sees their balance continue to grow, as the 6 percent annual return on their investments outpaces distributions until they are seventy. At that time, their balance peaks at 22 times their age-thirty-five income and begins to decline as withdrawals overtake new growth. Their savings decline at an accelerated pace through their eighties and are depleted at age ninety-three.

Unless Kate and Connor live well into their nineties, they should be in a good position to avoid exhausting their savings and potentially leave a sizable amount of wealth to their children. We have not included Social Security benefits or employer matching retirement contributions, both of which would improve their situation. This projection—saving 20 percent of income for twenty-five years—will be our base case to which we compare the other four scenarios, as indicated by the lighter gray investment balance that shadows the other projections.

**Scenario 2: Begin saving 20 percent of gross income at age forty-five, retire at age sixty**

| | |
|---|---|
| Begin saving at age: | 45 |
| Saving rate (percent of income): | 20% |
| Retire at age: | 60 |
| Balance at retirement: | $2,447,795 |
| Savings depleted at age: | 67 |

In our second scenario, Kate and Connor fall victim to the "why save for later when I can spend now?" mindset and do not begin saving until age forty-five. They again put away 20 percent of their income, but their investment balance reaches only $2.4 million at retirement and immediately starts to decline as they begin withdrawals.

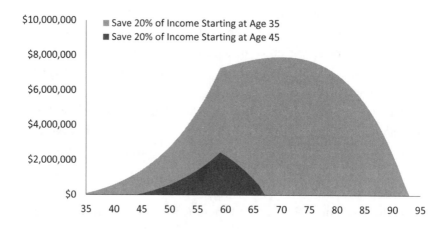

Unfortunately, this does not end well for them. By sixty-seven, their savings have been depleted, and they are polishing their resumes to reenter the workforce. Alternatives include living on only their Social Security benefit, tapping into home equity, moving in with children, or a combination of these. This is likely not the retirement they desire and highlights the tremendous impact a lost decade of compound growth can have.

### Scenario 3: Begin saving 40 percent of gross income at age forty-five, retire at age sixty

| | |
|---|---|
| Begin saving at age: | 45 |
| Saving rate (percent of income): | 40% |
| Retire at age: | 60 |
| Balance at retirement: | $4,895,591 |
| Savings depleted at age: | 78 |

Our third scenario sees Kate and Connor again delay saving until a sense of urgency arises at age forty-five. Frantic, they double their original goal and save 40 percent of their income. Their balance increases quickly until retirement when it crests at $4.9 million.

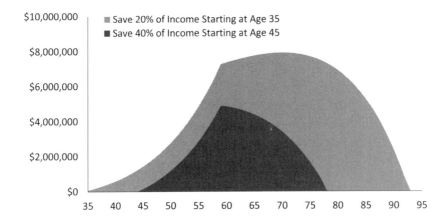

While they have made a valiant effort to catch up, they have also depleted their investments by seventy-eight, well within their life expectancies. Their retirement contributions will also contend with college expenses if they would like to support their children's higher education and have not saved for this ahead of time. We again see the difficulty in making up ten years of stock market appreciation, dividends, and interest earned on their investments.

**Scenario 4: Begin saving 15 percent of gross income at age thirty-five, retire at age sixty**

| | |
|---|---|
| Begin saving at age: | 35 |
| Saving rate (percent of income): | 15% |
| Retire at age: | 60 |
| Balance at retirement: | $5,453,709 |
| Savings depleted at age: | 81 |

In our fourth scenario, Kate and Connor are able to begin their long-term savings plan at age thirty-five, but only at a 15 percent savings rate. Their balance reaches $5.4 million when they retire at sixty and is exhausted by eighty-one.

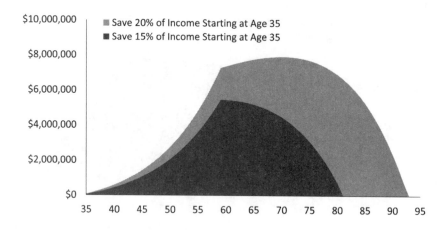

While saving 5 percent less than the target may not seem like much, it translates to outliving their savings twelve years earlier. We again see that less than fully funding their plan raises the risk of a meager retirement.

### Scenario 5: Begin saving 10 percent of gross income at age thirty-five, retire at age sixty-eight

| | |
|---|---|
| Begin saving at age: | 35 |
| Saving rate (percent of income): | 10% |
| Retire at age: | 68 |
| Balance at retirement: | $7,708,058 |
| Savings depleted at age: | 92 |

In our final scenario, Kate and Connor have decided to save only 10 percent of their income and delay their retirement as a result. They want to limit the risk of outliving their investments and would like to see how long they need to work for their balance to last into their early nineties, similar to their first scenario. We see that saving at this level requires them to work until age sixty-eight and retire on $7.7 million.

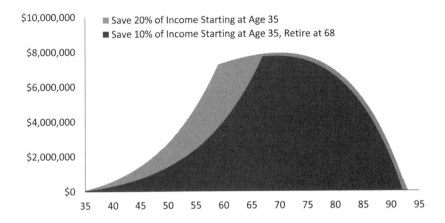

Their nest egg has been fully withdrawn by ninety-two, giving them a decent chance of passing an inheritance to their children. A risk to this plan is that they later decide they do not want to work to sixty-eight, or perhaps they are not able to if a health issue arises. Even if Kate enjoys practicing medicine well into her sixties, she may want this to be her choice rather than mandated by the plans she established at the start of her career.

## A Word on Variables

The goal of the previous examples is to provide a basic idea of the hypothetical growth and draw down of retirement assets. With that said, some of the variables used are just that—variable. We do not expect investment rates of return or inflation to remain constant year after year. In addition, tax rates were not discussed at all. It is likely you will experience presidents from both major political parties throughout your retirement, each with their own tax agendas. Depending on cooperation from Congress, tax legislation may change significantly. Increased tax rates necessitate a larger amount to be withdrawn from savings for an equivalent after-tax distribution, while lower tax rates have the opposite effect. Retirement lifestyles also adjust as people age. Early years of retirement may resemble your preretirement standard of living with an active life and perhaps increased travel. As retirees age, their lifestyles often slow down, and discretionary spending may fall, though health care costs may rise. It is difficult to precisely model how adequate your retirement plans may be when the projection assumes that inputs remain constant and do not account for positive or negative occurrences along the way. We need a different method to account for this uncertainty.

Monte Carlo analysis is a statistical modeling technique that produces a range of how possible outcomes may be distributed based not only on multiple variables but also on the probability of those variables occurring at different values. For example, instead of assuming a constant 8 percent annual investment growth rate, Monte Carlo analysis would use an average annual growth rate of 8 percent with a standard deviation of 6 percent to account for the variability in investment returns from year to year. The computer system will perform many independent "runs" with each run creating a unique outcome based on the randomness of each variable. A single run in a retirement projection may happen to exhibit a large number of years achieving above-average investment returns (13 percent year one, 17 percent year two, 10 percent year three, etc.). This favorable run would have Kate and Connor retiring on more than the $7.3 million from scenario 1, likely resulting in their savings lasting beyond age ninety-three if the other variables returned close to their averages. Conversely, a large number of below-average investment returns or above-average inflation rates would result in savings being depleted before ninety-three.

A Monte Carlo analysis aggregates the results of many independent runs to create a probability distribution. This probability distribution may be expressed as a 95 percent confidence level representing an interval two standard deviations from either side of the mean (Kate and Connor have a 95 percent probability of retiring with savings between $5.2 million and $9.4 million) or as a probability of achieving a specified result (Kate and Connor have an 87 percent chance of having an investment balance remaining at age ninety, with 95 percent confidence). A lengthier explanation of Monte Carlo analysis may fast-track you to sleep sooner than this book is intending, so we will summarize by saying this method provides a more realistic way to model outcomes by incorporating uncertainty and leave it at that.

## Chapter Summary

"I asked to see some numbers, and that session certainly delivered," Connor admitted.

"Our sixty-five-year-old selves appreciate it," Kate said.

Most doctors go into medicine because they are passionate about healing people and like the science behind it. However, the past few decades have seen the rise of insurance companies taking on a more active role in delivering care at the expense of providers' discretion. Since 2010, we have seen the passage of the Affordable Care Act and subsequent efforts to repeal and replace it. Additional health care legislation may further change the landscape you practice in. It is safe to say the future of American health care over the next thirty years is somewhat up in the air. Dealing with insurers, electronic record and billing programs, and other facets of our health care system creates an administrative burden few doctors enjoy. While you may practice well into your sixties, you will want this to be your choice instead of a consequence from inadequate planning.

When it comes to retirement planning, your extensive training places you about a decade behind your undergraduate friends who did not go into medicine. Fortunately, your high income will allow you to catch up and retire when or before they do. The key to making this happen is beginning your savings plan in full soon after training. This allows your investments to work for you at an increasing rate as your growth compounds over the years. Kate and Connor's projections highlighted there is no substitute for this, as further delaying your savings or failing to reach your full savings rate will create consequences down the road. Many factors will affect your retirement plan. While some of these are outside of your control, the ones you can manage will determine when you are able to retire and the lifestyle you can afford. It is important to structure your post-training lifestyle after long-term savings are accounted for, not the other way around.

We know a fair amount of retirement catch-up must be done. Now, how do we implement this?

**Key Takeaways**

Most doctors do not begin saving a significant amount for retirement until after training ends in their thirties but would like the option to step away from medicine by their early sixties. This *delayed start to saving for retirement creates a catch-up aspect* that affects other areas of your financial plan.

As we discussed in a previous chapter, buying a home is a common goal for newly graduated doctors. This must be done with one eye on your retirement plan; otherwise, *too large of a home purchase may impose a long-term handicap on your ability to save.*

*When you begin saving and how much you save are two of the most important factors you control* when developing and implementing your retirement plan.

A broad rule of thumb is to *save at least 20 percent of your gross, post-training income toward retirement for twenty-five years.* This does not include contributions made by your employer, as these are out of your control. Saving this much not only defers a lot of income for later in life but also results in living on a maximum of 80 percent of your earnings. You may need to save more or less than this amount depending on your desired retirement.

Due to the power of compound growth, *further delaying your long-term savings plan or inadequately funding it can create a large retirement shortfall.*

Retirement projections that use static inputs provide a general idea of how retirement assets may be saved and spent, but they fail to account for the variability of investment returns, inflation rates, and other factors that are uncertain each year. *Monte Carlo analysis* incorporates the probability of variables being a value other than their average. The resulting probability distribution gives us a more realistic range of outcomes than a model that does not consider uncertainty.

## CHAPTER 17

# THREE FORMS OF INVESTMENT DIVERSIFICATION

SO FAR, WE have covered how investing in stocks, bonds, and mutual funds can result in compound growth, helping you overcome a late start to saving for retirement. Declining employer and governmental support places more responsibility on doctors to adequately prepare for retirement than in decades past. This is useful to know, but what we really care about is how you apply this. When we approach investing, we can use the three forms of diversification as a framework to structure your long-term savings given the unknown economic and legislative landscape throughout your working years and retirement.

*Time horizon.* The time horizon for when you plan to liquidate your investments should be a large driver of your asset allocation, with longer time horizons allowing for greater stock market exposure, given that there are no expectations of needing to sell investments if the market goes down in the near term. This is because investors face different risks over short and long-term periods. A key risk for short-term money is stock market volatility, while a key concern for long-term investments is the loss of purchasing power due to inflation.

*Tax treatment.* Different investment accounts are treated differently for tax purposes. It is important to spread your money across these accounts so you have flexibility to adjust the source of your retirement withdrawals based on changes in tax rates.

*Asset class.* Investing in multiple asset classes reduces the volatility of your portfolio by diversifying among investment categories that have different risk and return characteristics, which provides rebalancing opportunities.

We have covered a lot already. Go ahead and get comfortable; we have plenty more to go …

# CHAPTER 18

# TIME HORIZON DIVERSIFICATION

TWINS ROBERT AND Luke arrived for their meeting to settle an ongoing debate. The brothers were in their late thirties, and despite both being in medicine, they had vastly different perspectives on investing. Robert, a geriatrician, had his retirement savings split evenly between stock and bond mutual funds. Luke was in surgery and invested solely in equity mutual funds.

"I keep telling Luke that he shouldn't have all of his money in stocks," began Robert. "The stock market is really unpredictable and could tank at any time. He has always been a bit of a daredevil, and this has carried over to his investing."

"I think you've got it all wrong. If the market crashes, I'll buy more!" Luke rebutted. "We shouldn't be worried at all about our investments losing value with our incomes to support us, right?"

Well, this remains to be seen. The brothers each raise valid points, and the answer depends on *what they are investing for*. If we are focusing on retirement assets, which are not needed for many years, then Luke's logic is correct. A decline in the stock market, even a significant one, should raise minimal concerns for younger investors because they have time to wait out the dip and allow the market to recover.

"See, I told you. Just because you work with seniors doesn't mean you have to invest like one."

"Okay, I'll consider adding more stocks to my portfolio, but does that really mean *all* of our investments should be invested in stocks?" asked Robert. "We are both saving money for a home down payment next year. Mine is in my savings account. Luke's is in stocks."

Robert's approach is the more reasonable one in this case. With Luke's home purchase coming up soon, his exposure to the stock market could be problematic if it drops significantly and lowers the value of his home down payment.

Robert and Luke's dialogue highlights how different investment strategies may or may not be appropriate depending on the time horizon for the investment goal. Misaligning your investment allocation with your time horizon is a common mistake if you are not familiar with different types of risk. What do we mean by this? If you are going to invest for the future—retirement, college expenses, or a home down payment—that time from now until the future (when you need to sell your investments for cash to spend) is your time horizon. This is important because your time horizon should be a large driver of your asset allocation, or how you invest your money between stocks, bonds, and other asset classes.

Earlier in the investment section, we mentioned there are many ways in which you may experience risk as an investor. You may hear of *political risk* (government actions affecting investments; Venezuela nationalizing the oil industry), *currency risk* (changes in the relative values of domestic and foreign currencies through exchange rates; devaluation of the Chinese yuan), and *interest-rate risk* (interest rate changes cause a change in the investment landscape; the Federal Reserve unexpectedly increases interest rates, causing the price of existing bonds to decline). In this chapter, we are going to simplify our view of investment risk to two types—price volatility and inflation. We will define price volatility as buying an investment and ending with less than you began with. Perhaps Luke bought shares of a stock mutual fund for $100 per share that falls to seventy dollars by the time he needs to sell them for his home down payment. He would have avoided this loss entirely had he left his down payment in cash. The risk with inflation is that even if your investments have increased in value, the increased cost of living has made it difficult for your investments to achieve their goal. Understanding these risks and how to structure your investments based on them will be this chapter's focus.

### Short-Term Investment Risk

For investment goals with a short-term time horizon, such as funds earmarked for a home down payment, a key risk is price volatility. Having this balance invested in the stock market is concerning because it could experience a sizable decrease in value immediately before your home purchase. We saw this in 2008 when the stock market, defined by the S&P 500 Index, dropped 37 percent during the year. This would send prospective home buyers scrambling for additional funds if they need to use this balance before their investments have fully recovered. How long of a time horizon is considered short-term? It is difficult to know what the next market dip will look like, but since 1926, it has taken the stock market, on average, about 3.3 years to rebound from a bear market after accounting for inflation and dividends (a bear market is typically defined by a decrease of at least 20 percent from the pre-decline high). Because this is an average and some recoveries will be longer, we could say that funds needed within five years or less should be invested in low-volatility asset classes that have little to no chance of losing value in a stock market decline, such as cash held in an FDIC-insured bank savings account.

One notch up on the price volatility spectrum would be a conservative bond mutual fund. We expect to receive a higher return from the bond fund's interest compared to interest earned on cash in a savings account, but we are now taking on the risk that our investment may decrease in value. Remember our example earlier in the bond section with interest rates increasing? If you want to sell your 5 percent bond in the secondary market where similar bonds are yielding 8 percent, you will have to price your bond at a discount and take a loss from your purchase price.

With near-term goals—those occurring within the next few years—inflation is a minor risk, as the cost of living typically does not increase rapidly in most developed countries. Instead, we are guarding against the likelihood that your short-term time horizon forces you to take a loss because you do not have enough time to let your investments recover from their dip. To protect against this, we can choose to give up the potential for higher returns in the stock market for the higher probability your savings will be able to meet your goal when needed.

**Long-Term Investment Risk**

"I completely agree with protecting against marketing declines," acknowledged Robert. "What I don't understand is why we shouldn't take the same approach with retirement savings. We need this money to be there for us, so why shouldn't we have plenty in bonds to be safe?"

"Probably because bonds are boring," Luke answered. "If we can afford to wait out a market dip, is there any risk to our long-term investments we're not thinking about?"

Yes! Long-term investments are not without their own risk; it's just one that rarely makes the news headlines. Inflation can greatly reduce your ability to buy goods and services in retirement if your investments have not kept pace with, and ideally well outpaced, increases in the cost of living along the way. Much of what we have covered so far has been in nominal terms, or simply numbers by themselves. As we transition to discussing long-term time horizons, we care about real, or inflation-adjusted, numbers relative to the cost of living.

*That One Summer Job*

You're sixteen again, fresh out of your junior year of high school, and have just bought your dad's old Honda Civic as your first set of wheels. It's by no means the flashiest car on the block. Far from it. But you don't care; it's all yours! To pay for your newfound freedom, you take a summer job at a local ice-cream parlor earning ten dollars per hour. These ten dollars alone do not mean much to you, but with gas at two dollars a gallon, an hour of work means five gallons of gas. You will be able to save up for that road trip with your friends next year in no time. As the summer comes to an end, your boss gives you a raise to twelve dollars for next summer. Another gallon of gas earned each hour. This 20 percent raise sounds great, but will this actually make you feel wealthier?

This depends on how the cost of living changes. Senior year flies by, and you are back at the ice-cream parlor earning twelve dollars an hour. Then conflict erupts in the Middle East, disrupting the global oil supply and causing gas prices to spike to three dollars a gallon. Now you only earn four gallons of gas an hour instead of six. Your 20 percent *nominal* raise does not make you feel wealthier when your cost of living—measured in how many gallons of gas you can afford—has increased 50 percent. In *real* terms, your earnings have decreased 33 percent relative to the new cost of living.

Life is expressed in nominal numbers, but what we actually care about is your ability to buy goods and services at given price levels, or what economists call your purchasing power. Why is this important? As we saw, even if your income or investments have gone up in nominal terms, you will actually be less well off in real terms if inflation has increased more. You will likely not feel the effects of inflation during your working years because your income will trend up roughly in line with it, but inflation can have a significant impact on your purchasing power in retirement when small increases in the cost of living have compounded over decades.

According to the Bureau of Labor Statistics, inflation has averaged between 2.1 percent to 4.1 percent per year looking back over the past twenty to fifty years measured by annual changes in the Consumer Price Index for all urban consumers (CPI-U). How much of an impact could this have? If inflation were a constant 3 percent per year for the next thirty years, $1,000 of today's money would buy only $412 worth of today's goods and services, causing a loss of almost 60 percent of your purchasing power from today's price level.[1] This is somewhat of an abstract concept, so let's see how this plays out with our friends Kate and Connor. Our base scenario saw them retire at age sixty with $7.3 million of investments being depleted by age ninety-three with inflation a constant 3.25 percent each year. The following graph illustrates how dramatically a 1 percent adjustment to the inflation rate has on their retirement outcome.

**Scenario 1: Kate and Connor begin saving 20 percent of gross income at age thirty-five, retire at age sixty, at various inflation rates**

| | |
|---|---|
| Begin saving at age: | 35 |
| Saving rate (percent of income): | 20% |
| Retire at age: | 60 |
| Annual rate of return: | 8% |
| Balance at retirement: | $7,271,612 |
| Inflation rates: | 2.25% / 3.25% / 4.25% |
| Savings depleted at age: | Not depleted / 93 / 80 |

---

[1] $1,000 / (1.03^{30}) = $411.99

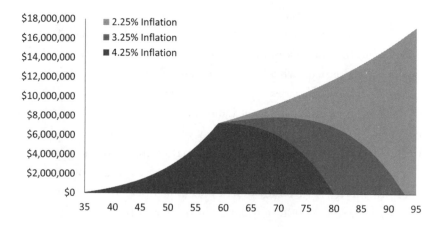

Increasing the inflation rate to 4.25 percent has Kate and Connor exhausting their nest egg by eighty, whereas 2.25 percent inflation sees them not spending enough money. Their savings continue to grow indefinitely because their retirement distributions never exceed the amount their investments earn each year. Inflation will play a big role in how steep your retirement drawdown occurs, as higher inflation rates require more assets to be withdrawn each year to maintain the same standard of living.

"Wow, that's pretty insightful," Robert said. "One thing that bothers me is that inflation is completely out of our control. How do we prepare for this?"

"Not to sound like broken record here, but is the answer to hold more in stocks?" Luke asked.

Yes, Luke is on the right path here. With inflation being a variable we cannot control, we need to adjust the factors we can, like your investment allocation. Our overview on basic securities introduced us to the idea that bonds exhibit low price volatility risk and high inflation risk, whereas stocks have higher price volatility, but their long-term returns have well outpaced inflation. *By holding half of his retirement savings in bonds, Robert is actually taking on a high amount of inflation risk—the risk that his long-term portfolio returns will be too low, increasing the chance of outliving his savings.*

Resetting Kate and Connor's inflation rate to 3.25 percent, we adjust the rates of return earned during their accumulation years to isolate the effect of holding different amounts in bonds (assuming that holding higher percentages in bonds results in lower long-term investment returns).

**Scenario 2: Kate and Connor begin saving 20 percent of gross income at age thirty-five, retire at age sixty, at various investment rates of return**

| | |
|---|---|
| Begin saving at age: | 35 |
| Saving rate (percent of income): | 20% |
| Retire at age: | 60 |
| Inflation rate: | 3.25% |
| Annual rates of return: | 8% / 7% / 6% |
| Balance at retirement: | $7,271,612 / $6,350,625 / $5,563,849 |
| Savings depleted at age: | 93 / 86 / 81 |

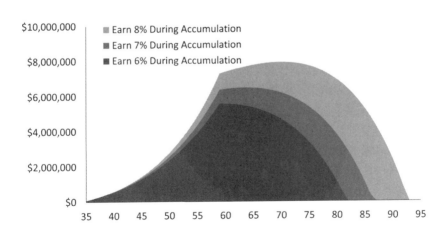

Whereas Kate and Connor's 8 percent rate of return lasts them until ninety-three, earning 7 percent during their accumulation years sees their savings depleted at eighty-six, and the 6 percent portfolio ends at eighty-one. This graph is not meant to suggest an 8 percent rate of return is needed for your investments to last through retirement. It is instead meant to illustrate the potential risk of holding too much in bonds or cash in a portfolio with a long-term time horizon. We again see that misaligning your asset allocation with its time horizon may lead to an unfavorable result, in this case a higher chance of outliving your savings. We could alternatively say that for long-term investment goals, you need to take on enough price volatility risk, in the form of equity mutual funds, to lower inflation risk. Failing to do this increases the probability of exhausting your savings during your life expectancy. Investments with a long-term time horizon can afford to weather stock market volatility and should largely be invested in asset classes that have tended to outpace inflation over long periods, such as equity (stock) mutual funds.

## Portfolio Structure in Retirement

"Okay, okay. Point taken. I will add more equity mutual funds," said Robert. "But what about when we get closer to retirement? I can't imagine holding almost all of my money in stocks when I retire …"

Robert is on the right track here. As he enters retirement, his time horizon changes to reflect both short-term and long-term risks. Retirees withdraw some of their investments each year, so in this respect a portion of their savings has a very short-term time horizon and is therefore susceptible to price volatility risk. They need part of their savings to provide current income in the form of dividends, interest, or withdrawals of capital and cannot afford to have these funds lose significant value. A retiree may hold two or three years of living expenses in cash and a few more years' worth of expenses in a conservative bond allocation to guard against a stock market decline. If we have an economic recession, and we would expect at least a few throughout a twenty-plus year retirement, then Robert can live off this cash and bond balance to allow his equity investments time to recover. With price volatility risk accounted for, retirees will position the rest of their portfolio to have more stock exposure to provide income for later years in retirement, when inflation remains a risk.[1]

## Chapter Summary

"We came here to settle our debate …"

"And we sure did," said Luke. "Looks like we each had half the answer; now we both have the full picture."

Luke summarizes this chapter well. Appropriate asset allocation requires a clear understanding of the risks you face as an investor over both short and long-term time horizons. Investment goals coming up in the next few years are susceptible to price volatility risk, as equity investments may take several years to fully recover from a stock market decline. We can protect against this by avoiding the stock market and holding short-term money in cash and bonds. In contrast, investors with a long-term time horizon do not need to sell their investments for many years and therefore have time to let the stock market rebound. Young physicians with at least twenty years until retirement should have minimal concern for market fluctuations and view market declines as good buying opportunities. Instead, there is a different risk to consider, inflation, which gradually erodes your purchasing power. Allocations with more equity weighting should hold up better against the effects of inflation over many years.

Before we cover asset class diversification in detail, we need to know *where* you will be holding your investments. Which investment accounts do we use? And why does this matter?

---

[1] Interested readers can turn to the appendix for additional insight on portfolio design for retirees.

## Key Takeaways

Your *time horizon* is how long until you need to spend your investments on your goal. This helps us understand which type of risk your investments are most vulnerable to. Your time horizon should therefore be a large driver of your asset allocation.

Two types of investment risk are *price volatility*, which is more evident over short-term time horizons, and *inflation*, which reduces your purchasing power due to the increased cost of living.

We protect against price volatility by holding low-volatility investments, such as cash and high credit quality bonds. We expect these investments to lose minimal, if any, value during stock market declines. Equities exhibit much higher levels of price volatility and may take several years to fully recover from a decline in value, causing stock investments to be an unpredictable choice for near-term goals.

We protect against the risk of inflation in the opposite way. Holding an adequate amount of stock in your portfolio should generate higher long-term returns that outpace inflation. We expect cash and bonds to have low, or even negative, real rates of return after adjusting for inflation. These low-volatility investments are therefore seen as poor long-term inflation hedges.

Retirees face the predicament of both short-term and long-term time horizons. Holding part of their portfolio in cash and bonds with another part mainly in equities allows them to protect against short-term stock market declines and the long-term loss of purchasing power due to inflation.

# CHAPTER 19

# TAX TREATMENT DIVERSIFICATION

DAVID AND MARIA recently finished their residencies and were eager to begin their retirement savings plan. They were hospitalists with base salaries of $200,000 each and were aware they need to dedicate a fair amount of their new income for later in life. They were each making the maximum salary deferral contributions to their 403(b)s of $18,500 per year but were unsure where to save additional amounts for retirement.

"We know we can't contribute to Roth IRAs because of our high income," explained David.

"And we are concerned that investing in a typical brokerage account will add to our already large tax bill with the dividends and capital gains from our investments," added Maria. "We want to save more, but we don't know where to turn next."

David and Maria raise valid concerns that many new doctors face when setting up their retirement plans. When saving for retirement, it is important to consider not only the type of investments you own but also the tax treatment of the accounts in which they are held. If your time horizon answers the "Why?" of investing—to protect against market dips in the short term or to outpace inflation over the long term—then deciding which accounts to use answers the "Where?" Investment accounts determine how your funds are taxed upon contribution, as they grow, and as they are withdrawn. Along with inflation, taxes will be one of your retirement's strongest headwinds, making it essential to consider this in your planning. Continuing the theme of diversification, this chapter will cover the importance of spreading your money among accounts with different tax characteristics. We will begin by reviewing a few key terms before analyzing how accounts differ. We will then apply these rules in a hypothetical savings plan to illustrate how efficient tax management can be beneficial with emphasis on distributions in retirement. Saving enough leading up to retirement is only half the battle. As your career comes to an end, having the ability to reduce your tax bill by adjusting the source of your withdrawals can stretch your savings and increase the probability of a successful retirement.

As we have mentioned, the authors are not tax professionals and recommend you consult with one for tax advice specific to your situation. Many of the numbers that follow, including tax rates and contribution limits, relate to the 2018 tax year, and we expect these to change over time.

**Tax-Deductible Contributions and Tax-Deferred Growth**

The Tax Basics chapter illustrated how our income tax system is progressive and marginal in nature. Income above the upper limit of the previous tax bracket is taxed at a higher rate, resulting in larger tax burdens on higher earners. We also covered capital gain tax, which is assessed when you sell an investment for an amount greater than its basis and has historically been at lower rates than ordinary income tax. Two ideas we have yet to fully cover include tax-deductible contributions and tax-deferred growth.

*Tax-deductible contributions.* Making a tax-deductible contribution allows you to deduct the amount contributed from your gross income for that year. This will lower your adjusted gross income and your taxable income, resulting in a lower tax bill than if you had not made the contribution. Tax-deductible contributions will be taxed in the future, usually upon withdrawal, which is why they are also referred to as "pretax contributions." You are contributing before paying tax on this money, but it will be taxed later at ordinary income tax rates.

*Tax-deferred growth.* When you earn dividends, interest, or realize capital gains on your investments, you do not pay tax on these earnings in accounts that offer tax-deferred growth. Your investment growth may or may not be taxed upon withdrawal depending on the type of account your distribution is taken from.

## Tax Treatment of Investment Accounts

When you take distributions from your investment accounts, your money will generally be taxed in one of three ways—as ordinary income, as a capital gain, or it may be tax exempt. This difference depends on which type of account you withdraw from. Qualified distributions from pretax retirement plans, such as 401(k)s, are treated as ordinary income and will be subject to income tax. Qualified distributions from post-tax retirement accounts, such as Roth IRAs, are tax-free, and therefore no tax is due regardless of the amount withdrawn or amount of growth. Qualified distributions are made after the account owner's age fifty-nine and a half, commonly referred to as the fifty-nine and a half rule. In general, with Roth IRAs, distributions must also be taken at least five years after the initial contribution for the withdrawal to be qualified. If a distribution is not qualified, then earnings are taxed at ordinary income rates, and there may be a 10 percent penalty. Withdrawals from non-retirement accounts are potentially subject to capital gain taxes depending on the cost basis of the underlying investment sold to free up the cash withdrawal. In addition to how withdrawals are taxed, each account type—pretax, post-tax, and non-retirement—has a unique set of characteristics for whether contributions and investment growth are taxed.

## Pretax Retirement Accounts

Contributions:     Tax-deductible
Growth:            Tax-deferred
Distributions:     Taxed at ordinary income rates
Examples:          401(k), 403(b), 457(b), traditional IRA,
                   SEP IRA, SIMPLE IRA

## Post-Tax Retirement Accounts

Contributions:     After-tax (no tax deduction is given for
                   contributions)
Growth:            Tax-free (growth is not taxed in the future)
Distributions:     Qualified distributions are tax-free
Examples:          Roth IRA, Roth 401(k), Roth 403(b)

## Non-Retirement Accounts

Contributions:     After-tax
Growth:            Taxable (taxed on dividends, interest, and realized
                   capital gains each year)
Distributions:     Capital gains are realized and taxed at capital
                   gain rates when sold
Examples:          Non-retirement brokerage account

## Long-Term Savings Plan by Tax Treatment

Now that we have dusted off the cobwebs from the Tax Basics chapter and are familiar with the taxation of different accounts, let's look at the steps David and Maria take to diversify their savings plan from a tax standpoint. With their combined income of $400,000, they are aiming to save $80,000 each year to meet their 20 percent long-term savings goal.

*Employer Retirement Plans*

The first $37,000 they save is going to their employer retirement plans with $18,500 into each of their 403(b)s. This will provide them with an immediate tax deduction at their highest marginal tax rate, 32 percent, to save them $11,840 in taxes at the federal level. As their contributions are invested and grow over time, they will not have to pay taxes on capital gains, dividends, or interest they receive because their 403(b)s provide tax-deferred growth. This is a good start, though every dollar David and Maria withdraw from their 403(b)s in retirement will be taxable at ordinary income rates. This exposes them to potentially paying a high amount of income taxes in the future, depending on tax rates in retirement.

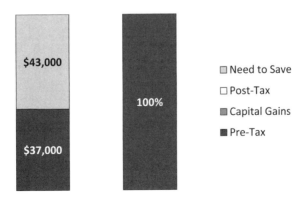

*Roth IRAs (Indirectly)*

"What? I thought we couldn't contribute to Roth IRAs because our income is too high!" exclaimed David.

David is correct, at least partially. However, since 2010, there has been a strategy available to high-income earners that allows them to contribute *indirectly* to Roth IRAs. The two most common types of individual retirement accounts (IRAs), or "individual retirement arrangements" as the IRS titles them, are traditional IRAs and Roth IRAs. Traditional IRAs are pretax retirement accounts that share the same tax characteristics as 401(k)s and 403(b)s. Roth IRAs are post-tax retirement accounts, which do not offer tax-deductible contributions but provide tax-free income when withdrawn. The IRS imposes different restrictions on each of these accounts if your income exceeds certain limits.

You are able to contribute to a traditional IRA independent of your income, but there is an income limit on being able to deduct your contributions from your gross income if you have access to a retirement plan through your employer. In 2018, the ability to deduct contributions to traditional IRAs was phased out between $99,000 and $119,000 of adjusted gross income for couples filing jointly, so David and Maria are well above this. There is also an income limit on being able to directly contribute to a Roth IRA. Couples making above the phase out range of $189,000 to $199,000 of MAGI cannot contribute directly to Roth IRAs. David is correct that he and Maria are unable to *directly* contribute to Roth IRAs.

Prior to 2010, the IRS also had a $100,000 income limit on being able to convert traditional IRAs and other pretax retirement accounts to Roth IRAs. This restriction was lifted in 2010 and is currently not in place. However, Congress may reintroduce this rule in the future. The current tax environment allows for a handy strategy that has been nicknamed the "backdoor Roth IRA." To implement this, David and

Maria will each need a traditional IRA and a Roth IRA. They will first make their contributions to their traditional IRAs and not take the tax deduction because their income is too high and the goal is to get their money into their post-tax Roth IRAs. Holding money in a traditional IRA that has already been taxed is referred to as a nondeductible IRA to indicate the funds did not receive a tax deduction. They will then convert the balance in their nondeductible IRAs to their Roth IRAs. That's it. Once their money is in their Roth IRAs, it is as if they made direct contributions and will not be taxed again.

It is important to be aware of a few items with this approach because the conversion step can be a tax nightmare if not implemented correctly. For example, this can backfire and result in additional taxes owed if you have pretax money in any IRA (traditional IRA, SEP IRA, or SIMPLE IRA) at the end of the year in which you contributed. It is also advantageous to make the entire year's $5,500 IRA contribution and Roth conversion at one time. If there is any growth between these two steps, then this growth is taxed. You will also need to complete Form 8606 when filing your tax return, as this establishes a tax basis for your nondeductible IRA contribution, documenting to the IRS that you did not take a deduction so these funds should not be taxed upon conversion to your Roth IRA.[1]

The current IRA contribution limit is $5,500, so David and Maria each contribute $5,500 to their nondeductible IRAs and convert these to their Roth IRAs, which will result in tax-free income in retirement. Combined with their 403(b) contributions, they are now saving 12 percent of their income and have $32,000 left to save.

---

[1] Be aware that the income limit on Roth conversions may be reinstated, or other tax legislation may arise that restricts the use of this strategy in the future. We recommend consulting with a tax professional before implementing this method of making nondeductible IRA contributions and Roth IRA conversions.

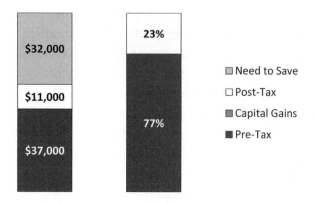

*Non-Retirement Brokerage Account*

With salary deferrals to their employer retirement plans and indirect Roth IRA contributions maximized, David and Maria are now forced to look outside of formal retirement accounts for the remainder of their savings. This will be a common issue for most doctors. The other concern so far is that all of their savings are in accounts they cannot access before age fifty-nine and a half. There are some exceptions, but in general you want to consider the money in your retirement accounts untouchable until fifty-nine and a half or later to avoid the 10 percent penalty on early distributions.

The options for the remaining amount to save are a non-retirement account, cash value life insurance, or a combination of these. We covered how permanent life insurance can be used as a component of a savings plan in the Life Insurance chapter, so we will focus on using a non-retirement account. While these accounts do not provide the same tax advantages as employer-sponsored plans and Roth IRAs, they are liquid and can be accessed without penalty at any time. This makes them a good option for a portion of your savings, especially for an early retirement if you wish to leave medicine or scale back your hours before fifty-nine and a half.

David and Maria round out their savings plan by contributing $32,000 each year to their non-retirement account, resulting in the following tax breakdown: 46 percent to their employer plans made on a pretax basis (withdrawals will be taxed at ordinary income rates in retirement), 14 percent to their Roth IRAs made on a post-tax basis (withdrawals will be tax-free in retirement), and 40 percent to their non-retirement accounts (previously untaxed capital gains will be realized and taxed at capital gain rates when investments are sold for withdrawal).

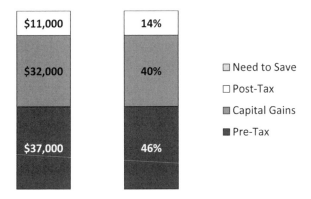

There is not a specific tax percentage breakdown to aim for, though it is generally beneficial to maximize your tax-advantaged pretax and post-tax accounts before contributing to a non-retirement account. The goal is to benefit from tax deductions today while also providing flexibility to vary the source of your withdrawals in retirement depending on income and capital gain tax rates each year.

**Taxation of Retirement Withdrawals**

"That's helpful to see, particularly about the indirect Roth IRA contributions," noted Maria. "How does this look if we fast-forward to retirement?"

"And you've mentioned taxes may change by the time we're retired. Can you show an example of how this could affect us?" David added.

One of the keys to a successful retirement is having the ability to withdraw your savings from different types of accounts, thereby choosing which type of tax and how much you pay. Income and capital gain tax rates change every few years, depending on the fiscal situation our government is facing, who is in the White House, and the reigning party in Congress. Both taxes have been significantly higher in the past, and with our increasing national debt, many people believe current rates may trend up. At the same time, we are unsure which direction tax rates will move in the near term, let alone in thirty years. Spreading your savings among different accounts is the takeaway from Tax Treatment Diversification 101, but what are we specifically diversifying against?

*At a deeper level, we are aiming to reduce the chance that a period of high income tax rates, high capital gain tax rates, or both causes your hard-earned savings to be depleted at an accelerated pace as you take distributions.* We are familiar with graph 1 from the Tax Basics chapter, which shows how $700,000 of taxable income is distributed among the various tax brackets and their rates for a married couple filing jointly.

Graph 1. Taxable income in each tax bracket
($700,000 of taxable income for a couple Married Filing Jointly in 2018 at ordinary income rates, tax liability of $198,379, effective tax rate of 26.5 percent on gross income of $750,000)

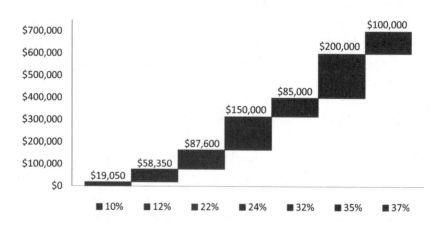

Because only $100,000 of their taxable income is in their highest marginal bracket of 37 percent, their $198,379 tax liability results in an effective tax rate of 26.5 percent on gross income of $750,000. The

$750,000 of gross income serves as a common denominator to compare effective tax rates to other time periods.

Subsequent graphs adhere to this layout of taxable income on the vertical axis, tax rates on the horizontal axis, and amount of income or capital gain taxed at each rate as the steps that make up the tax staircase. All graphs reflect a Married Filing Jointly tax rate schedule. For simplicity, we will ignore deductions and exemptions on retirement withdrawals to focus on how much tax liability each amount of taxable income creates. When reviewing scenarios in which retirement distributions are taxed at income or capital gain rates, or result in tax-free withdrawals from a post-tax account, we will use the following key to differentiate the type of tax being applied with income taxes in dark gray, capital gain taxes in light gray, and tax-free in white.

■ Income Tax Rates   ■ Capital Gain Tax Rates   □ Tax Free

White bars also represent withdrawals that count as a nontaxable return of basis from non-retirement accounts (money that that has already been taxed). We will treat non-retirement account distributions as being one-third tax-free return of basis and two-thirds as long-term capital gain of previously untaxed investment appreciation.

"That make sense from when we went over taxes a while ago," Maria said. "One of the attendings is retiring at the end of the year, and that got me thinking. How would this look for us if we were to retire today on, say, 75 percent of our current income?"

Our first scenario sees Maria and David withdraw all $300,000 of their retirement income from their 403(b)s taxed at ordinary income rates, resulting in a tax liability of $66,479, or 22.2 percent of their distribution owed in taxes. They do not reach the 35 percent or 37 percent income tax brackets, and because they are not taking withdrawals from their Roth IRAs or non-retirement account, the 0 percent tax-free and 15 percent long-term capital gain bars are also empty (assuming Maria and David's income for all 2018 scenarios puts them in the 15 percent capital gain tax rate).

## Graph 2. Retirement withdrawals taxed at each rate, 2018 tax rates, all pretax

($300,000 of taxable income at ordinary income rates (dark gray), tax liability of $66,479, tax as a percent of total withdrawal—22.2 percent)

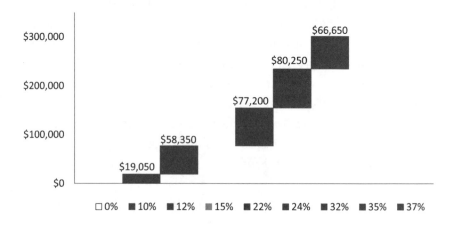

□0%  ■10%  ■12%  ■15%  ■22%  ■24%  ■32%  ■35%  ■37%

The goal with tax diversification is to have the ability to avoid the higher tax rates on the right side of the graph and shift income to lower rates on the left by taking withdrawals from post-tax and non-retirement accounts.

This is what we see in our second scenario when Maria and David withdraw only half of their income from their 403(b)s and a quarter each from their Roth IRAs and non-retirement account. Of their $75,000 non-retirement account withdrawal, $25,000 is tax-free return of basis and makes up $100,000 of tax-free distribution in the white column along with their $75,000 Roth IRA withdrawal. The remaining $50,000 withdrawn from their brokerage account is taxed at 15 percent as a long-term capital gain in the light gray column (with the 3.8 percent net investment income tax not applying due to their income falling below $250,000).

## Graph 3. Retirement withdrawals taxed at each rate, 2018 tax rates, diversified withdrawals

($150,000 of taxable income at ordinary income rates (dark gray), $75,000 tax-free income withdrawn from post-tax accounts (white), $75,000 withdrawn from non-retirement account with $25,000 as tax-free return of basis (white) and $50,000 of realized capital gain taxed at 15 percent (light gray), tax liability of $32,379, tax as a percent of total withdrawal—10.8 percent)

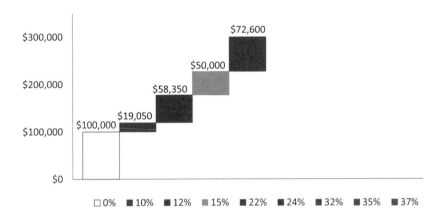

Structuring distributions in this manner allows Maria and David to sidestep the 24 percent and 32 percent income tax brackets and instead pay taxes at 0 percent and 15 percent. This results in a tax liability of $32,379, saving them $34,100 in taxes and causing their taxes as a percent of total withdrawal to fall from 22.2 percent to 10.8 percent.

Maria and David could minimize their tax liability in retirement by taking withdrawals only from their post-tax accounts to eliminate their tax bill entirely. This may not be necessary and could cause them to deplete their Roth IRA balances sooner than ideal. A completely tax-free retirement is difficult, but we can get close with 2018's tax code. Capital gains are taxed at 15 percent for taxpayers in the 22 percent through 35 percent tax brackets but are taxed at 0 percent for taxpayers in the 10 percent and 12 percent brackets. Limiting their pretax distributions to $75,000 to stay in the 12 percent tax bracket allows them to withdraw $225,000 from their non-retirement account with $75,000 as a nontaxable return of basis and $150,000 as a long-term capital gain taxed at 0 percent.[1] In addition to paying no tax on $150,000 of investment appreciation, Maria and David also delay taking withdrawals from their Roth IRAs, saving this precious tax-free money for other years when it may be more valuable with different tax rules.

Graph 4. Retirement withdrawals taxed at each rate,
2018 tax rates, $75,000 pretax withdrawals

($75,000 of taxable income at ordinary income rates (dark gray), $225,000 withdrawn from non-retirement account with $75,000 as tax-free return of basis (white) and $150,000 of realized capital gain taxed at 0 percent due to staying in the 12 percent ordinary income marginal tax bracket (white), tax liability of $8,619, tax as a percent of total withdrawal—2.9 percent)

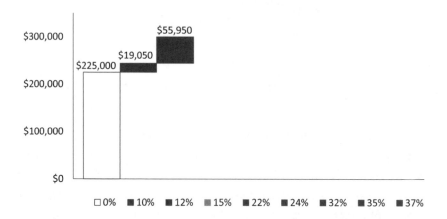

Maria and David have further shifted their retirement income to the left, reducing their tax liability to $8,619 or 2.9 percent of their total withdrawal. It's not 0 percent, but it's not bad either. Qualified dividends

---

[1] Keep in mind that part of Social Security benefits may be taxable as income. David and Maria may also claim income from dividends, interest, and realized capital gains from investments held in non-retirement accounts. If they are aiming to stay in the 12 percent tax bracket, they may want to withdraw well below $77,400 to avoid having their investment income push them into the 22 percent tax bracket, causing capital gains to be taxed at 15 percent instead of 0 percent.

are also taxed at 0 percent if your income is low enough, highlighting another benefit of decreasing a retiree's ordinary income when taking distributions.

The uncertainty around future tax rates is another recurring theme. Overall, we are in a relatively low income tax rate environment compared to most of the past eighty years when looking at the highest marginal income tax rate.

Graph 5. Highest historical income and long-term capital gain tax rates

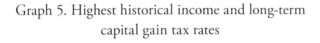

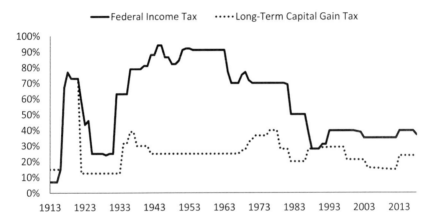

We are not sure what rates will be in thirty to fifty years, but a rise to 50 percent or 60 percent would not be unprecedented compared to what they were between the 1930s and 1970s. Many of the tax brackets below the top rate were higher than the top rate today, causing higher effective tax rates in the past. If this is the case for even a short period of your retirement, it will be important to have the ability to withdraw money from accounts that do not result in income tax. Your retirement savings could be evaporated quickly with a substantial amount going to the government before it reaches your wallet if you do not have this option. How has this looked in the past?

Let's hop in our DeLorean and take it back to 1985.

With dollar amounts adjusted for inflation, 1985's federal income tax brackets are shown in the following table.

### 1985 Federal Income Tax Brackets
### (In 2017 dollars)

| Tax Rate | Married Filing Joint | | |
|---|---|---|---|
| 0% | $0 | to | $8,148 |
| 11% | $8,148 | to | $13,166 |
| 12% | $13,166 | to | $18,207 |
| 14% | $18,207 | to | $28,519 |
| 16% | $28,519 | to | $38,325 |
| 18% | $38,325 | to | $48,384 |
| 22% | $48,384 | to | $58,926 |
| 25% | $58,926 | to | $71,632 |
| 28% | $71,632 | to | $84,315 |
| 33% | $84,315 | to | $109,726 |
| 38% | $109,726 | to | $143,747 |
| 42% | $143,747 | to | $205,067 |
| 45% | $205,067 | to | $262,082 |
| 49% | $262,082 | to | $389,049 |
| 50% | $389,049 | to | No Limit |

This creates the following marginal income tax rate graph on $700,000 of taxable income. Due to the numerous income tax rates in 1985, we have removed the dollar label from each tax bracket's column, but all other formatting is the same as previous graphs, with taxable income on the vertical axis and tax rates on the horizontal axis.

Graph 6. Taxable income in each tax bracket, 1985 tax rates
($500,000 of taxable income at ordinary income rates, tax liability of $205,441,
effective tax rate of 37.5 percent on gross income of $550,000)

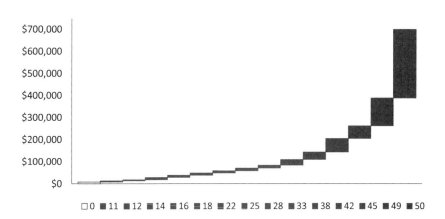

Apart from several more tax brackets, the other key difference we notice is greater weighting toward the higher rates in 1985 than in 2018. For example, $250,000 of taxable income applied to the 2018 rate schedule is still well within the 24 percent marginal rate. Taxable income of $700,000 at 2018 rates results in only $100,000 taxed at the highest rate of 37 percent. A $198,379 tax liability on $700,000 of taxable income equates to a 26.5 percent effective tax rate (assuming $750,000 of gross income). The 1985 tax rates were not as kind to high earners. By $250,000 of taxable income, you will have already had over $140,000 taxed in the 38 percent, 42 percent, and 45 percent brackets. With $700,000 of taxable income in 1985, your tax bill swells to $305,441 with an effective rate of 40.7 percent (again assuming $750,000 of gross income). An adjustment in tax rates to 1985 levels would be unpleasant for today's workers but could be particularly damaging to retirees.

Graph 7. Retirement withdrawals taxed at each rate,
1985 tax rates, all pretax

($300,000 of taxable income at ordinary income rates (dark gray), tax liability
of $106,332, tax as a percent of total withdrawal—35.4 percent)

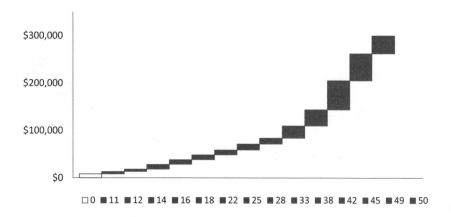

Compared to withdrawals at 2018 rates, 1985 rates cause Maria and David to pay about $39,000 more in taxes, over 13 percent of their total distribution. This is the accelerated depletion of retirement savings in action.

Capital gain taxes were also assessed differently in 1985. Instead of having their own rates, capital gains were taxed at the taxpayer's highest income tax rate with one caveat: taxpayers could exclude 60 percent of their capital gains from their income. For example, if you realized a $1,000 capital gain and were in the 50 percent income tax bracket, you would exclude 60 percent of this gain, leaving only $400 to be included as income. This $400 would then be taxed at the 50 percent income rate, causing a capital gain tax of $200, or a 20 percent effective rate when compared to the gross capital gain of $1,000.

Applying tax diversification to Maria and David's 1985 withdrawals, they take $150,000 from their pretax plans and $75,000 each from their post-tax accounts and non-retirement account. Their highest income tax bracket of 42 percent causes their $50,000 in realized capital gains to be taxed at an effective rate of 16.8 percent. Consistent with the concept, they successfully shift income from the 42 percent, 45 percent, and 49 percent brackets to instead be taxed at 0 percent and 16.8 percent.

Graph 8. Retirement withdrawals taxed at each rate, 1985 tax rates, diversified withdrawals

($150,000 of taxable income at ordinary income rates (dark gray), $75,000 tax-free income withdrawn from post-tax accounts (white), $75,000 withdrawn from non-retirement account with $25,000 as tax-free return of basis (white), $50,000 of realized capital gain taxed at 16.8 percent (light gray), tax liability of $47,367, tax as a percent of total withdrawal—15.8 percent)

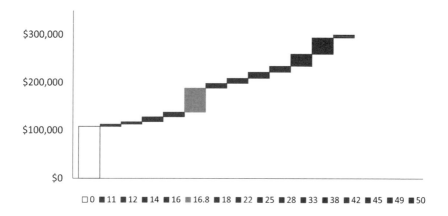

Compared to the pretax scenario, Maria and David have reduced their tax bill from $106,332 to $47,367. However, it was still higher than the $32,379 tax bill seen in the 2018 equivalent scenario.

We round out Maria and David's hypotheticals by analyzing how $75,000 withdrawn from pretax accounts, $75,000 from post-tax accounts, and $150,000 from their non-retirement account is taxed. The tax system in 1985 did not have a 0 percent capital gain tax rate, so their $100,000 of realized capital gain is taxed at 11.2 percent.

Graph 9. Retirement withdrawals taxed at each rate,
2018 tax rates, $75,000 pretax withdrawals

($75,000 of taxable income at ordinary income rates (dark gray), $75,000 tax-free income withdrawn from post-tax accounts (white), $150,000 withdrawn from non-retirement account with $50,000 as tax-free return of basis (white), $100,000 of realized capital gain taxed at 11.2 percent (light gray) due to highest marginal ordinary income tax rate of 28 percent and 60 percent exclusion on capital gains (1985 tax rule), tax liability of $19,886, tax as a percent of total withdrawal—6.6 percent)

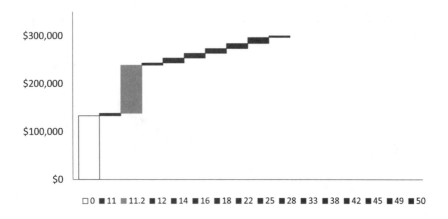

As expected, their $19,886 tax bill is an improvement from the past two 1985 withdrawal strategies, but still higher than under 2018's tax rules for a similar distribution method.

These scenarios confirm the idea that varying the source of your withdrawals can lower your tax bill in retirement across different tax environments. This is particularly evident when income is shifted from the higher income tax brackets to under 20 percent for long-term capital gains and 0 percent with tax-free distributions. The authors are by no means experts in tax, let alone the tax system in 1985, and our calculations have been greatly simplified to focus on the concept. The key is to have the ability to withdraw income from different accounts depending on income and capital gain tax rates in retirement. If you find yourself in an environment in which income taxes are relatively high compared to historical standards, but capital gain rates are low compared to their past rates, then you may want to withdraw only enough income from your pretax accounts to fill the lower brackets and then take the remainder of your distributions from other accounts. If income tax rates are low compared to their historical average, then you could instead favor your pretax accounts and withdraw more income from your 401(k) or 403(b) and pull less from your non-retirement account. If both income and capital gain rates are high in retirement, then you can take greater distributions from your post-tax accounts for tax-free income.

## Other Tax-Related Investment Strategies

In addition to how you take withdrawals, there are other tax-related investment strategies you can implement.

### Asset Location

One of the concerns Maria voiced is that a non-retirement brokerage account does not have any tax advantages. As these accounts do not provide tax-deferred growth, any interest, dividends, and capital gains realized within them will be passed through to the owner and taxed accordingly each year. We want to keep this in mind when designing an investment portfolio with a concept called asset location. Asset location refers to the strategy of considering both the tax characteristics of the account and the investment itself when deciding which securities to hold in each account to lower the amount of taxes and earn a higher after-tax return.

For example, holding investments that are relatively tax efficient within non-retirement accounts can lower your tax bill and possibly increase your after-tax investment return. Municipal bonds (issued by state and local municipalities) are convenient from a tax standpoint because the interest they provide investors is exempt from federal income tax. Interest from bonds issued by corporations and the federal government is taxable, so you may want to hold these investments in accounts that offer tax-deferred growth, such as a Roth IRA.

*Exchange-Traded Funds (ETFs)*

Another strategy to reduce taxes in your non-retirement account is to hold exchange-traded funds, or ETFs, over their mutual fund equivalent. Like mutual funds, ETFs are pooled investments and allow investors to buy into a diversified portfolio. They are structured differently from mutual funds, and this allows them to be more tax efficient, particularly during the process of selling, or redeeming, the ETF. In general, they pass fewer capital gains incurred within the fund through to investors than mutual funds with the same underlying investments. ETFs are also traded throughout the day, and therefore their share price varies by the second, like stock. Mutual fund shares are priced at the end of a trading day at the fund's net asset value.

*Harvest Capital Losses*

A third method to reduce taxes within non-retirement accounts is to use tax loss harvesting to your advantage. To do this, you would sell an investment for a loss and immediately purchase a similar, but not identical, investment (which should have also decreased in value recently). This strategy realizes capital losses in down years, which can then be used to offset current and future capital gains. When implementing this strategy, you will want to avoid the wash sale rule, which causes your loss to be disallowed.

**Chapter Summary**

Taxes will play a large role in your financial plan. As a doctor, you will likely be paying more in taxes than most non-physicians, but there are strategies you can use to limit the overall effect of taxes on your lifestyle. With proper planning in the years leading up to retirement, you can position your investments to be diversified from a tax standpoint by spreading your savings among accounts with different tax characteristics. This will provide flexibility to take your withdrawals from different accounts to lower the overall amount of taxes you pay, leaving more for you and your family to enjoy.

**Key Takeaways**

Pretax retirement accounts provide a current tax deduction for contributions, investments grow tax-deferred, and withdrawals are *taxed at ordinary income rates.*

Post-tax retirement accounts do not receive a current tax deduction, investments grow tax-deferred, and withdrawals are *tax-free.*

Non-retirement accounts do not receive a current tax deduction, do not provide tax-deferred growth, and investments that have appreciated in value will have their capital gains realized and *taxed at capital gain tax rates* when sold to be withdrawn.

It is common to use all three types of accounts when saving for retirement due to the contribution limits on employer pretax retirement plans and IRAs, as well as the goal of diversifying your investments from a tax perspective.

*Tax treatment diversification* aims to reduce the likelihood that a period of high income tax rates, capital gain tax rates, or both causes your retirement savings to be depleted at an accelerated pace as you take distributions. We accomplish this by varying the source of withdrawals to avoid high tax rates and shift distributions into lower tax rates. This concept is consistent across tax environments in the past, and despite the uncertainty around future tax legislation, we expect it to be applicable in the years to come.

*Asset location* is the strategy of considering the tax characteristics of the account and the investment itself when deciding which securities to hold in each account to lower the amount of taxes and earn a higher after-tax return.

# CHAPTER 20

# ASSET CLASS DIVERSIFICATION

"SO, THIS IS when you teach us how to get rich, right?" said Connor.

"Always the joker," Kate said, rolling her eyes. "The last few sessions have been great. We have a good idea of what investing is, why we need to do it, and where to hold our investments, but we're still not confident *how* to invest."

"I assume there's more to it than simply pushing the '8 percent return button' on our Roth IRAs and letting them ride for thirty years," Connor continued. "But that's where our knowledge stops. If you could pull back the curtain and show us how it's done, that would be great."

Connor is right. Until the constant 8 percent return button has been invented, we need to go about investing the traditional way. Inflation's eroding power necessitates that young doctors aim for investment returns well above the rising cost of living to grow their wealth. Failing to do so could put your plans for a successful retirement in doubt. Similar to how the Tax Basics chapter is the prerequisite to the Tax Treatment Diversification chapter, the Introduction to Investing chapter is a prelude to this one. You should have a basic understanding of stocks, bonds, and their general characteristics with regard to return and risk (market volatility and inflation risk). You can flip back to page 179 if a review of stocks, bonds, and mutual funds would be helpful. In this chapter, we are going to expand on that knowledge and introduce new techniques that can be applied to your investment portfolio. This chapter is not "The Stock Picker's Guide to Getting Rich Quickly." Instead, our focus will be on diversifying your money among multiple asset classes to lower your portfolio's volatility and provide rebalancing opportunities. This creates a repeatable process for managing your investments that, over time, should generate a rate of return that puts your financial plan on the path to success.

## Types of Asset Classes

We previously covered stock (units of company ownership, equity) and bonds (debt securities, fixed income). In broad terms, stocks tend to exhibit greater price volatility than bonds and have historically provided investors with higher long-term rates of return than bonds to act a better hedge against inflation. Each can be divided into sub-asset classes that further differ with their levels of risk and potential return, sometimes considerably from their parent asset class. On the equity side, we will analyze company size, style, and geographic location. Fixed income will be broken down by issuer and their respective credit rating, as well as level of interest rate sensitivity. We will briefly cover a third asset class, known generally as alternatives, though will not spend much time here, as the majority of portfolios are usually held in equity and fixed income investments.

### Stock (Equity)

A common way to divide the equity market is by the size of the company, usually split into large, medium, and small categories by market capitalization. A company's market capitalization is the metric of choice for calculating a company's size, arrived at by multiplying the number of shares of stock outstanding by the stock's current price. Large companies typically have a market capitalization above $10 billion, companies falling in the middle capitalization range are usually between $2 billion to $10 billion, and small-caps are under $2 billion, though these ranges may differ depending on the news source or classification service. Large companies have more established business operations and are generally perceived to be less risky than smaller companies. Many large firms are multinationals integrated within the global economy, causing them to be more affected by economic conditions abroad than smaller companies, which derive the majority of their revenue from their country of domicile. In addition to being more dependent on their home economy, small-caps are seen as having more growth potential than large-caps; it is theoretically easier to double in size from a $2 billion company to a $4 billion one than from $20 billion to $40 billion. However, smaller companies are not without their own challenges, such as being crowded out of their industry by larger or more innovative competitors, and are therefore viewed as being riskier than larger, more mature companies. As you would expect, midsized companies share characteristics of their larger and smaller cousins. They may have more of a foothold in their marketplace than small companies but have not yet achieved the level of growth or scale that larger companies have.

Stocks are also classified by their style, usually as either value or growth based on their operations or metrics. Value stocks often pay a regular dividend to their shareholders, passing through the company's excess profits to their owners. They may also exhibit lower price valuations compared to growth stocks. Company valuations are one way to gauge how expensive a stock is relative to their earnings, with the price-to-earnings ratio (PE ratio) being a frequently used measure. The PE ratio is calculated by dividing a company's current stock price by its earnings per share (EPS), which is its profit divided by number of shares outstanding. The higher a company's PE ratio, the more investors are paying to own a portion of the company's profits. Periodic dividend payments and attractive valuations cause many investors to consider quality value stocks to be a bargain. Examples of value stocks include General Mills and Coca Cola. Food and beverage companies may not be the flashiest of stock picks, but you have probably seen their products lining grocery store aisles and perhaps even consumed them today.

Whether a stock is classified as value or growth, the company's mandate is the same: they are required by their board of directors to maximize shareholder value to you, their owners. They just go about this in different ways. Growth stocks aim to provide shareholder value by pursuing more aggressive plans to grow their size and profitability. Instead of distributing their extra profits to shareholders, these companies reinvest their earnings to create new products through research and development, improve their manufacturing capabilities, or expand into a new market. The goal of these efforts is to increase the overall value and profitability of the company, hopefully driving their share price higher. Amazon, Google (also known as its parent company, Alphabet), and Tesla are examples of growth stocks. They don't have extra cash to give out to their owners; they have growing to do! Combining low earnings (Amazon had negative or razor-thin profits for several of its early years as it reinvested heavily in its infrastructure) with high stock prices can cause PE ratios of growth stocks to be higher than value stocks. Apple also exemplified growth traits as it reinvested its profits into the next iProduct and saw their share price appreciate considerably over the past decade. Some stocks exhibit both value and growth characteristics. Mutual funds that hold these types of stocks, or a combination of value and growth stocks, are referred to as a blend.

The equity style box combines company size and style to give us nine sub-asset classes within the broader stock asset class.

Equity Style Box

| Large Value | Large Blend | Large Growth |
|---|---|---|
| Mid Value | Mid Blend | Mid Growth |
| Small Value | Small Blend | Small Growth |

In addition to categorizing stocks by size and style, the last screen we will look at is by geographic location. International stocks are shares of companies based in foreign countries, usually divided between developed nations and developing, or emerging, markets. The differences between these are based on a country's economic stability, size, and advancement, as well as other characteristics. In general, international investments in both developed and developing countries are perceived to be more risky than domestic investments. While the United States is the largest economy, it only accounts for about 25 percent of worldwide economic production, down from 40 percent in 1960. Investors not holding international stocks fail to benefit from the profits and innovation occurring outside of our borders and three-quarters of global economic activity.

Developed international markets broadly include Canada, Western Europe, Japan, and Australia, headquartering companies such as Nestlé (Switzerland), Toyota and Honda (Japan), Volkswagen (Germany), and Royal Dutch Shell (Holland and the United Kingdom). These countries tend to exhibit stable political systems, economies, and currency valuations. Despite additional risks, developing nations should not be ignored. China boasts the second largest economy, and its 1.4 billion people has a middle class projected to reach 550 million consumers within the next decade. India, home to 1.3 billion, is expected to surpass China as the world's most populous by 2024. The two Asian giants account for more than one in three people on the planet. The developing world is home to over 85 percent of global population but only 40 percent of economic production measured by gross domestic product (GDP)—a number that could rise as emerging economies modernize. This was exemplified in the early 2000s as the United Arab Emirates, Qatar, and other Gulf states became more integrated in world economy. Brazil is leading development in South America, though not without the speedbumps of one president being impeached and her predecessor being convicted of corruption. Many emerging markets rely on commodity exports for continued growth, a dependency that can be crippling if global supply and demand forces cause commodity prices to fall.

Prominent companies based in developing countries include Alibaba and Baidu (China), Infosys and Tata (India), Embraer (Brazil), and Etihad Airways and Emirates Airlines (United Arab Emirates). This sub-asset class offers plenty of potential as economies advance, but investors should be aware of the growing pains these countries and the companies based within them may experience.

*Bonds (Fixed Income)*

When you invest in bonds, you care not only about how much interest you will earn but also the probability of receiving each payment as planned. These factors relate to the issuer's credit rating and, along with the bond's term to maturity, define the characteristics of bonds and their sub-asset classes. The interest rate a bond carries is derived from the risk of the issuer, which makes sense if you are lending your money to another entity. If you are deciding between two parties that want to borrow money from you, you will charge the riskier, less creditworthy borrower a higher rate of interest than the safer, more creditworthy borrower to compensate you for the greater probability that the riskier party will not pay you back in full.

Some of the highest quality bonds are issued by the US Treasury and backed by the full faith and credit of the US federal government. These bonds are seen as having virtually no credit risk and are therefore issued at lower interest rates. Corporate bonds add credit risk to the equation. Because companies do not have unlimited taxing power or the ability to print money, there is a chance they may not have the resources to service all of their debt payments, and investors demand higher interest rates in return. Companies in strong financial shape will issue bonds awarded an investment grade rating by the two major bond rating agencies, Moody's Investors Service and Standard & Poor's. However, if a company's creditworthiness deteriorates far enough, they will fall out of investment grade and into the high-yield category, also known as "junk bonds." As their name implies, high-yield bonds are issued to yield higher interest rates to attract investors for taking on greater risk.

Municipal bonds are issued by states, counties, cities, and other municipalities. While their interest rates are also based on issuer creditworthiness, their coupon payments receive preferential tax treatment and are received free of federal income tax. Interest earned on corporate and US government bonds is taxable at your highest federal income tax bracket. Because of this, municipal bonds are an attractive bond option to hold in taxable investment accounts, particularly for high earners. For example, let's say you are in the 32 percent federal income tax bracket and are evaluating two bonds, a municipal bond with an interest rate of 4 percent and a corporate bond. What interest rate would the corporate bond need to provide for you to be indifferent between the two? To answer this, we need to calculate the municipal bond's taxable equivalent yield:

$$\text{Taxable Equivalent Yield} = \text{Municipal Bond Yield} / (1 - \text{Marginal Tax Rate}) = 4\% / (1 - 32\%) = 5.88\%$$

If the corporate bond was yielding an interest rate below 5.88 percent, then you would prefer the municipal bond's tax-free interest. Only an interest rate above 5.88 percent would make the taxable corporate bond more favorable. Note that you can arrive at the same conclusion starting from the corporate bond's interest rate by calculating a taxable bond's yield after tax:

$$\text{Yield After Tax} = \text{Taxable Bond Yield} \times (1 - \text{Marginal Tax Rate}) = 5.88\% \times (1 - 32\%) = 4.00\%$$

In addition to the interest rate and issuer, you will also want to consider how the bond's price may change depending on its level of interest rate sensitivity if you may be selling your bond before maturity. On page 183 we saw how bond prices are susceptible to changes in the interest rate environment. In general, bond prices have an inverse relationship to interest rate changes; bond prices fall as interest rates rise. When we talk about interest rate sensitivity with bonds, we are talking about *how much* a bond's price changes with a corresponding change in interest rates. This is closely linked to the bond's maturity, though more specifically relates to an investing metric known as *duration*. For our purposes, we will think of duration as how much a bond's price will theoretically increase or decrease with a change in interest rates. For example, if a bond's duration is 5, then we would expect a 1 percent increase in interest rates to cause a 5 percent decline in this bond's price. With all else equal between two bonds, the bond with a longer maturity will have a higher duration and therefore its price will adjust more to interest rate changes than the shorter-maturity, lower-duration bond. Keep in mind that if you hold a bond to maturity to receive the principal payment from the issuer, any fluctuations in the bond's price throughout your holding period are irrelevant.

*Alternatives*

In addition to stocks and bonds, investors may choose to hold part of their portfolio in alternatives, which include securities that invest in real estate, commodities, and precious metals. Each category of alternatives carries different levels of risk and return potential that may vary substantially from equities and fixed income. Alternative asset classes typically account for a small portion of a portfolio's allocation, though can play an important diversification role, particularly during stock market declines.

The following graph plots several of these asset classes by their volatility, measured by standard deviation on the horizonal axis, and historical return on the vertical axis. The top left quadrant would be ideal with low volatility and high returns, while the bottom right would be quite frustrating for investors with a high level of volatility and low returns. Instead, we tend to see asset classes populate the lower left and extend diagonally to the upper right. This makes sense and reinforces what we already know. We expect higher credit quality bonds to be among the least volatile of investment categories while providing a lower rate of return. Bonds in the southwest quadrant should hold up well against the risk of price volatility but serve as a poor long-term inflation hedge. Investors are rewarded with higher rates of return as they accept greater levels of price volatility, seen with stocks in the northeast quadrant.

### Graph 1. Asset class risk and return profiles

Risk and return profiles of several asset classes over twenty-five years, from 1993 to 2017. Risk is measured by standard deviation. Return is measured by annualized returns.[1]

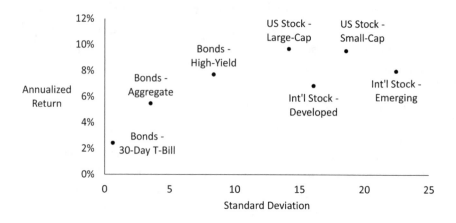

However, this chart should not be interpreted to mean that investors with a long-term time horizon should hold only asset classes in the upper right. Continuing this chapter's theme of diversifying among multiple asset classes, we will take a look at why holding some of your portfolio in categories across the volatility spectrum can be beneficial.

**Why Invest in Multiple Asset Classes?**

Why should you hold multiple asset classes? Well, investment choices may be clear in hindsight, but our crystal ball is foggier looking ahead. The dot-com bubble and 2008 emerging markets stock correction are

---

[1] Measured by the S&P 500 Total Return Index; Russell 2000 Total Return Index; Morgan Stanley Capital International's Europe, Australasia and Far East Index; Morgan Stanley Capital International's Emerging Markets Index; Bloomberg US Barclays Aggregate Bond Index; Bloomberg Barclays US Corporate High Yield Total Return Index; and Ibbotson Associates SBBI US 30 Day TBill TR USD.

two examples of declines in asset classes that have caught investors unaware in the past.

The dot-com bubble of the late 1990s saw prices of technology stocks grossly inflated, only to lose their momentum in dramatic fashion in the early 2000s. The price level of the NASDAQ, an index heavily weighted to technology stocks, rose from 694 in 1994 to a trading day close of 5,048 by March 2000. The next two and half years saw the NASDAQ fall nearly 80 percent before bottoming out at 1,114 in October 2002.[1]

Emerging market stocks saw a similar rise and fall in the mid-2000s. From 2003 through 2007, the MSCI Emerging Markets index posted five consecutive years of impressive returns ranging from 26 percent to 56.3 percent annually. The index then fell 53.2 percent in 2008 during the global financial crisis.[2]

If your portfolio was over-weighted to technology stocks heading into 2000 or emerging market stocks in 2008, then you could have seen a substantial decline in your portfolio's value. It would have been helpful to have other asset classes that did not fall as far as these to offset some of their losses. By spreading risk across multiple asset classes that perform differently in different market environments, you are increasing the chance that some of your investments will perform relatively well and aid your portfolio's return when others perform poorly. It is understandable for investors living in the United States to look through the lens of the American economy and stock market as their frame of reference. While broad exposure to domestic equities is an excellent start, let's take a look at the benefits of holding international stocks and bonds.

---

[1]  Measured by the NASDAQ Composite PR USD.
[2]  Measured by the Morgan Stanley Capital International's Emerging Markets Index.

*Why international stocks?*

In addition to accounting for the majority of global economic production and vast majority of population, countries outside of the US play an important investment diversification role. The thirty-three-year period from 1985 through 2017 saw an epic bout between the two heavyweight equity indices—the S&P 500 in one corner representing the large-cap US stock market and Morgan Stanley Capital International's Europe, Australasia and Far East index (MSCI EAFE) in the other, representing companies based in developed countries outside of the United States and Canada. Round one went to the MSCI EAFE as it bested the S&P 500 in the late 1980s, including a return of 69.9 percent in 1986 compared to the S&P's 18.6 percent. US equities rallied in 1989 and outperformed their international counterparts in ten of the next thirteen years. The tables turned in the 2000s when the MSCI EAFE again gained the upper hand for seven of the next eight years from 2002 through 2009. Aggressive stimulus measures by the US Federal Reserve in the aftermath of the 2008 Great Recession aided the US economy and helped the S&P 500 fare better than the MSCI EAFE in six of the next seven years. At the final bell, the S&P 500 posted an annualized rate of return of 11.3 percent compared to the MSCI EAFE's 9.3 percent.[1] Now, this is not to say international investing is not without its merits. The MSCI EAFE tallied sixteen years of outperformance, barely trailing the S&P 500's seventeen. In years when it outperformed, the MSCI EAFE did so by an average of 13.0 percent a year over the S&P 500, returns American investors would have missed if not invested abroad.

---

[1] Measured by geometric mean. You cannot invest directly in an index.

Graph 2. Outperformance of US stocks
(S&P 500) versus international stocks in developed
countries (MSCI EAFE), 1985–2017
(excess return of the S&P 500 Index over the MSCI EAFE Index)

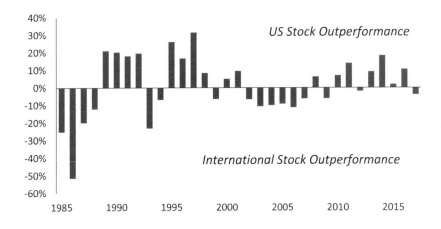

Investors would do well to remember that past performance does not necessarily indicate future results. While the S&P 500 won over the last three decades, are you confident which asset class will perform best over the next thirty-three years?

What's this? A late entrant! Let's not forget developing nations. Tracking the MSCI Emerging Markets index back to 1999 gives us nineteen years of investment returns to compare to the S&P 500 and MSCI EAFE. Over this period, the MSCI EM was the top performing index in twelve of these years, with an annualized return of 10.2 percent compared to the S&P 500's 6.2 percent and MSCI EAFE's 5.0 percent. Investing in emerging markets further diversifies your holdings and provides another geographic area to benefit from.

Graph 3. Outperformance of US stock (S&P 500) versus
international stock in emerging markets (MSCI EM), 1999–2017
(excess return of the S&P 500 Index over the MSCI EM Index)

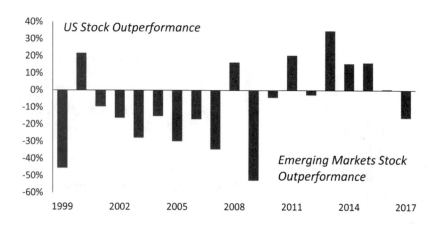

*Why bonds?*

We know that bonds, as a broad investment category, tend to be more of a slow and steady asset class compared to stocks. Because of this, we would not expect bonds to outperform equities when the economy is going well and the stock market posts a decent positive return. However, bonds can more than hold their own when the stock market has a negative return. You can think of bonds as playing defense in your portfolio, to some degree, as seen in two major US stock market corrections.

When the dot-com bubble popped in 2000, the S&P 500 experienced three successive years of negative returns, falling 9.1 percent in 2000, 11.9 percent in 2001, and 22.1 percent in 2002. Bonds, represented by the Bloomberg US Barclays Aggregate Bond Index, returned *positive* 11.6 percent, 8.4 percent, and 10.3 percent over the same period.

The S&P 500 declined 37 percent in 2008 in the midst of the global financial crisis. The Bloomberg US Barclays Aggregate

Bond Index rose 5.2 percent as investors sought safer havens for their money.

Allocating 20 percent to a mutual fund representing the bond index would have helped mitigate losses compared to an all-stock portfolio, raising the returns of an all-stock portfolio from negative 9.1 percent, 11.9 percent, 22.1 percent, and 37 percent to negative 5.0 percent, 7.8 percent, 15.6 percent, and 28.6 percent in an 80 percent stock / 20 percent bond split. Holding bonds to offset downside risk not only gives investors a shallower hole to climb out of following a stock market decline but also positions your portfolio to take advantage of the subsequent rebound in equity markets, as we will soon see.

Graph 4. Outperformance of US stock (S&P 500) versus the Bloomberg Barclays US Aggregate Bond Index, 1980–2017
(excess return of the S&P 500 Index over the Bloomberg Barclays US Aggregate Bond Index)

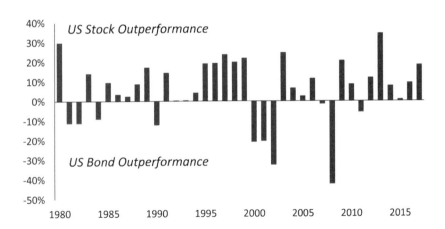

As we expect, stocks (represented by the S&P 500 Index) outperform bonds (represented by the Bloomberg Barclays US Aggregate Bond Index) in most years. Bonds posted their best relative returns during the bear markets of 2000 to 2002 following the dot-com bubble and 2008 following the financial crisis.

**Target Allocation**

"Great, we're starting to understand the benefits of diversification by asset classes. How much should we have in each category?"

This is answered by creating your target allocation, which is the proportion of each asset class held in your portfolio. Each asset class provides a certain level of risk and return potential. The goal of an investor should be to develop an asset allocation that provides them with a targeted rate of return with as little risk as possible. This is the cornerstone behind the investment concept called the efficient frontier; there are many combinations of asset classes projected to earn a certain level of investment return but at varying degrees of risk (volatility measured by standard deviation). The combination of asset classes that minimizes risk for a desired level of return is deemed to be efficient, and all other mixtures of asset classes that project to earn the same return, but at a higher risk level, are considered inefficient.

We previously saw that Kate and Connor may need to earn an annualized return of 8 percent during their accumulation years for a successful retirement. There is a target allocation with an expected 8 percent return with the least amount of volatility, whereas other combinations of asset classes projected to return 8 percent do so with higher risk. We expect these inefficient portfolios to display a greater dispersion of returns from year to year due to their higher level of volatility. Why is this important? Because lowering your portfolio's volatility increases the probability of successfully reaching your goal. For example, an inefficient portfolio has a greater chance of sub-8 percent returns compared to the efficient portfolio because of its higher risk. Several years of low returns would cause Kate and Connor to fall behind in their retirement savings, requiring them to either increase their contributions or accept a greater level of risk in an attempt to catch up. Intentionally choosing a higher amount of risk than necessary is not so much investing as it is gambling. If your bets pay off, then perhaps you are able to retire earlier or with more assets than planned. If they do not work out, however, then lackluster returns may put your retirement in jeopardy.

The target allocation appropriate for you will largely be driven by your investment time horizon and risk tolerance. As we covered in the Time Horizon Diversification chapter, goals further out can accept a higher portion invested in stocks, whereas greater portions in cash and bonds are suitable for near-term goals. Your risk tolerance is how much volatility, specifically downward volatility, you can stomach before feeling the need to deviate from your plan. We will pay more attention to investing tendencies and sticking to your strategy in the next chapter. Younger investors with a long-term time horizon until retirement can afford to weather dips in the stock market and may choose to have 90 percent of their holdings in equities with the remaining 10 percent in bonds, as an example. We call this a 90/10 target allocation. As investors approach retirement, their time horizon shortens, and risk tolerance lowers to the point where having 90 percent invested in stocks is no longer appropriate. Investors may gradually scale their equity exposure down to the 50 percent to 70 percent range, with bonds and other low-volatility asset classes making up the remainder. Keep in mind all asset class ranges discussed are used purely for educational purposes and should not be taken as individual advice. The broad asset class target allocations will then be split into sub-asset classes. For example, the 90 percent held in stock will be divided between US and international stocks, which are further separated by developed and emerging markets, as well as other sub-asset classes.[1]

Your target allocation deserves a lot of attention because it is among the most influential decisions you will make. A commonly cited *Financial Analysts Journal* article by Gary Brinson and colleagues found that over 90 percent of the variation of a portfolio's returns could be

---

[1]  If you are working with a financial advisor for your investments, you will receive a document called an investment policy statement. The IPS outlines your target allocation and specifies how your portfolio will be rebalanced. Rebalancing may be triggered based on a certain time frame, such as annually or quarterly, or whether upper or lower asset class thresholds are breached.

attributed to the long-term asset allocation. Market timing (over- or under-weighting of an asset class relative to its target allocation) and security selection (specific choice of investments within a single asset class) contributed less than 10 percent of the variation of a portfolio's returns. Subsequent studies have confirmed the importance of asset class selection, noting "Asset allocation remains the primary determinant of returns in portfolios made up of index or broadly diversified funds with limited market-timing."[1]

Creating your initial allocation is the beginning. Over time, we expect some asset classes to perform better than others, causing your portfolio to become skewed away from your target allocation. Asset classes that have done well relative to others will become over-weighted compared to their desired weights, while underperforming asset classes will see their weights shrink. This causes your allocation to exhibit a different risk and return profile—one that may no longer be in line with your objective. It is now time to rebalance your portfolio.

## Portfolio Rebalancing

Let's say it is January 1 and your portfolio is diversified among several asset classes in your target allocation. Perfect! Then twelve months go by. Over the year, some asset classes have done well, while others have lagged. Your portfolio is no longer in line with your target allocation, so we need to rebalance your portfolio back into alignment. This can be done by selling some of your holdings in over-weighted asset classes and using these proceeds to purchase investments in under-weighted asset classes. It can also be done by redirecting new contributions into under-weighted asset classes.

Let's work through an example to see this in action. For simplicity, we begin with a target allocation of 50 percent US stock and 50 percent international stock and invest $100 into mutual funds representing each. Over the year, the US economy is booming, and your $100 investment generates a 60 percent return, ending the calendar year at

---

[1] © The Vanguard Group, Inc., used with permission.

$160. Unfortunately, international markets had a 20 percent slump, and your $100 investment is down to $80. What we see is that instead of holding your target 50/50 split, your portfolio is now two-thirds in US stock and only one-third in international stock. This is fine *only as long as the US economy continues to outperform.*

| Asset Class | US Stock | Int'l Stock |
|---|---|---|
| Target Allocation | 50% | 50% |
| Initial Investment | $100 | $100 |
| Return | 60% | -20% |
| End of Year Values | $160 | $80 |
| Rebalance | sell $40 | buy $40 |
| Beg. Year 2 Asset Allocation | $120 | $120 |

However, accurately predicting asset class returns from year to year over an extended period is very difficult, if not impossible. Perhaps next year international markets take off, and the United States has a recession. You would not want to be skewed too far toward an asset class that may be ready to underperform or away from one that may outperform. Portfolio rebalancing fixes this situation by selling forty dollars of US stock (capturing the gain) to buy forty dollars of international stock, resulting in your target 50/50 allocation with $120 in each. Your portfolio is now positioned for whichever asset class performs well or poorly next year.

The thirty-eight years since 1980 have seen the US stock market, defined by the S&P 500 Total Return Index, earn a positive rate of return in thirty-two of them, seeing a down year roughly one out of every six. We would like to remind investors of the uncertainty involved when considering returns from year to year, as famed investor Warren Buffett acknowledges: "Let me be clear on one point: I can't predict the short-term movements of the stock market. I haven't the faintest idea as to whether stocks will be higher or lower a month—or a year—from now."

An example of this is the alternating historical performance of growth and value stocks, initially discussed on page 256. The two styles of investing appear a near mirror image when comparing their returns to the US large-cap stock market as a whole.

Graph 5. Relative outperformance of large growth
and value stocks over the S&P 500

(excess performance of large growth and value stocks over the S&P 500, as measured by the S&P 500 Value and S&P 500 Growth Indices from 1995 through 2017)

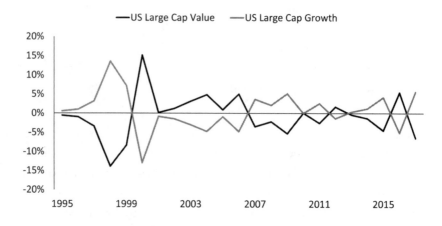

The past decade of returns shows that, in any year, growth or value stocks may outperform the other. If one style has exhibited a sustained period of outperformance, such as growth stocks did during the technology stock run-up of the late 1990s, then rebalancing back to an even equity style box can help lessen the impact a subsequent period of underperformance.

"How often should we rebalance?"

The answer to Kate's well-timed question depends on several variables, such as trading costs and the effect of realizing capital gains and losses when investing in a taxable account. Research from mutual fund giant Vanguard found there is not a single ideal strategy for rebalancing frequency or deviation threshold from the target allocation.[1] Instead,

---

[1] © The Vanguard Group, Inc., used with permission.

rebalancing annually or semiannually can strike a balance between proper account maintenance while not becoming overly time intensive. Another rebalancing strategy is to set threshold criteria for how far an asset class can drift from its target allocation before prompting a rebalance. For example, if your portfolio's desired weight in domestic stocks is 50 percent, you may set lower and upper limits of 45 percent and 55 percent. If the US equity market has a period of good performance, causing its weight in your portfolio to exceed 55 percent, this would prompt a rebalance back to your target allocation.

Periodically rebalancing your portfolio can help avoid becoming overexposed to an asset class, while redirecting gains to another asset class that may be undervalued after a slow year. Failing to rebalance puts you in danger of riding the same investments that have performed well right back down during a period of underperformance. A helpful way to think about this is not that you are buying investments that are out of favor, but you are instead locking in gains from asset classes that have outperformed in the past and giving your portfolio adequate exposure to asset classes that may outperform in the future.

## A School of Fish

"Okay, let us summarize what we've learned so far," Kate began. "We know we should hold investments from different asset classes because we are not sure which ones will perform best or worst each year, let alone over the next thirty years."

"And the proportion of how much we should hold in each asset class is called our target allocation, which is based on our time horizon and risk tolerance," Connor added.

"And from year to year, some asset classes perform better than others, which skews our portfolio toward the outperforming categories and away from the underperforming ones. This causes our portfolio to be more susceptible to a downturn in a particular asset class that has performed well lately and, as a result, has become over-weighted relative to its target allocation."

"Which is why we rebalance our portfolio back to our target

allocation by selling some of our holdings in over-weighted asset classes and using the proceeds to buy shares in funds that represent under-weighted asset classes."

"Is there anything else? The rebalancing example between domestic and international stock was helpful, but I still feel there is a bit more going on."

Kate is on to something. We have mentioned that diversifying your portfolio by different asset classes reduces volatility, which is true, but it does not give us the full picture. You likely endured a statistics class at some point, so let's get a little more use out of it with one more term—correlation. The correlation between two or more variables specifies the degree to which they are related. For our purposes, we will use correlation to mean how investment returns of different asset classes move in tandem.

If two asset classes exhibit a *positive* correlation, their past returns have tended to move in somewhat of a parallel manner.

If two asset classes exhibit a *negative* correlation, their past returns have tended to move in the opposite direction.

If two asset classes exhibit a *neutral* or *no* correlation, their past returns have not shown a significant relationship.

With correlation indicating the direction asset classes move together, the correlation coefficient quantifies this with a range of +1.0 (perfectly positive relationship) to 0 (no relationship) to -1.0 (perfectly negative relationship). The correlation coefficient therefore quantifies the *level of diversification* between asset classes. For example, we would expect US mid-cap stocks and US small-cap stocks to have a highly positive correlation. This makes sense, as companies based in the United States that derive the majority of their revenue from American consumers or businesses should be similarly affected by changes in the domestic economy; a recession should bode poorly for both small-cap and mid-cap companies. How are the main asset classes correlated? We can summarize this with a correlation table showing the correlation coefficients among several equity asset classes along with bonds and gold. The more positive a number is, the more their returns tend to move in tandem together and therefore the less of a diversification effect we get by combining them. Lower correlation coefficients signify a greater level of diversification is achieved by combining the two asset classes. In other words, your portfolio's volatility will be reduced more by adding bonds to US large-cap stock than by adding US small-cap stock.

Table 1. Correlation table

(correlation coefficients between several asset classes over a ten-year period from 12/31/2007 through 12/31/2017 as represented by their respective indices)[1]

| | US Stock - Large-Cap | US Stock - Small-Cap | Int'l Stock - Developed | Int'l Stock - Emerging | Bonds | Gold |
|---|---|---|---|---|---|---|
| US Stock - Large-Cap | | | | | | |
| US Stock - Small-Cap | 0.96 | | | | | |
| Int'l Stock - Developed | 0.94 | 0.88 | | | | |
| Int'l Stock - Emerging | 0.88 | 0.81 | 0.95 | | | |
| Bonds | 0.43 | 0.39 | 0.50 | 0.44 | | |
| Gold | -0.05 | -0.09 | 0.11 | 0.18 | 0.45 | |

We see the correlation coefficient tends to be highly positive for some asset classes, largely among the equity categories, while other asset classes are neutral or negatively correlated. One way to visualize highly positive correlations is by imagining a school of fish swimming together in the ocean. Its coordinated movement has each individual fish swim in the same direction at the same speed at the same time. The neutral or

---

[1] As measured by the S&P 500 Total Return Index; Russell 2000 Total Return Index; Morgan Stanley Capital International's Europe, Australasia and Far East Index; Morgan Stanley Capital International's Emerging Markets Index; Bloomberg US Barclays Aggregate Bond Index; and LBMA Gold Price PM.

negatively correlated fish is the maverick swimming the other way. We saw this in the investment world during the global financial crisis of 2008.

Graph 6. Rates of return for five asset classes, 2005–2010

(annual returns of five asset classes as represented by their indices—S&P 500, Russell 2000, MSCI EAFE, MSCI Emerging Markets, Bloomberg Barclays US Aggregate Bond Index)

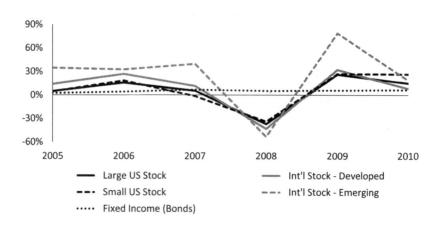

While there is some dispersion of returns in the years leading up to 2008, we clearly notice the highly positive correlation of the four equity asset classes during the market downturn, albeit with negative returns. The school of equity fish is swimming downward together, while the bond fish is bucking the trend with a positive return. Higher credit quality bonds are generally seen as a safe haven for investors during periods of turmoil in the equity market. *Holding investments whose returns are less than perfectly correlated is the essence of asset class diversification. While this does not fully protect against a loss, it decreases the severity and provides rebalancing opportunities.*

In our following 2008 rebalancing scenario, we ignore bonds and split your target allocation equally among four equity asset classes—US large-cap stock, US small-cap stock, developed international stock, and emerging markets international stock. You begin your $1,000 portfolio on January 1, 2008, with $250 in four mutual funds, one representing each asset class, and are blissfully unaware of the economic catastrophe about to unfold. By the end of the year, your returns range from negative 33.8 percent in your US small-cap stock fund to negative 53.2 percent in your emerging markets fund. Your portfolio is now worth $582.43, reflecting a loss of 41.8 percent (ignoring dividends). Each fund did not fall exactly the same amount, so your portfolio is slightly over-weighted to domestic equities (by 2.0 percent in large-cap and 3.4 percent in small-cap) and slightly under-weighted to international equities (by 0.6 percent in developed markets and 4.9 percent in emerging markets). Rebalancing to an even 25 percent in each would require selling $11.89 of US large-cap and $19.92 of US small-cap to purchase $3.26 of developed markets and $28.56 of emerging markets. Selling shares of your US stock funds would realize your losses, and while you can use the capital loss to offset future capital gains, selling shares at a loss is not the goal of successful investing. When all of your portfolio's holdings have positively correlated returns, rebalancing is less effective because the return differential between funds is not very large. Your best performing fund outperformed your worst by less than 20 percent, which does not give you much of a rebalancing lever to pull.

Table 2. A 2008 rebalancing example—all equity

(Hypothetical portfolio rebalance among four equity funds during 2008. Return numbers defined by each asset class's respective index. You cannot invest directly in an index.)

| Asset Class | US Stock - Large-Cap | US Stock - Small-Cap | Int'l Stock - Developed | Int'l Stock - Emerging |
|---|---|---|---|---|
| Target Allocation | 25% | 25% | 25% | 25% |
| Balance - 1/1/2008 | $250 | $250 | $250 | $250 |
| 2008 Return | -37.0% | -33.8% | -43.1% | -53.2% |
| Balance - 12/31/2008 | $157.50 | $165.53 | $142.35 | $117.05 |
| Allocation - 12/31/2008 | 27.0% | 28.4% | 24.4% | 20.1% |
| Over (Under) Weighted | 2.0% | 3.4% | -0.6% | -4.9% |
| Rebalanced to Target | $145.61 | $145.61 | $145.61 | $145.61 |
| Rebalance | Sell $11.89 | Sell $19.92 | Buy $3.26 | Buy $28.56 |

Our second 2008 rebalancing scenario follows the same progression as the first but with one key difference. We now include a mutual fund that represents the broader fixed-income asset class, and your target allocation is split evenly with 20 percent in each of the five funds. The market decline of 2008 is no kinder to your equity funds, but your bond fund holds up well. Its 5.2 percent return is not impressive on an absolute scale, but relative to your stock funds, it has outperformed by 39 percent to 58.4 percent. The bond fund buoys your performance, and while your portfolio has still lost value, it is only down 32.4 percent to $676.42. In addition, the bond fund's large relative outperformance has caused it to swell to 31.1 percent of your portfolio, providing you with a better opportunity to rebalance back to your target allocation. This 11.1 percent over-weighting results in selling $75.20 (capturing the gain in your bond fund) and using these proceeds to buy additional shares in all four of your equity funds after their share prices have decreased—a great time to buy!

Table 3. A 2008 rebalancing example—with bonds

(Hypothetical portfolio rebalance among four equity funds and one fixed-income fund during 2008. Return numbers defined by each asset class's respective index. You cannot invest directly in an index.)

| Asset Class | US Stock - Large-Cap | US Stock - Small-Cap | Int'l Stock - Developed | Int'l Stock - Emerging | Bonds |
|---|---|---|---|---|---|
| Target Allocation | 20% | 20% | 20% | 20% | 20% |
| Balance - 1/1/2008 | $200 | $200 | $200 | $200 | $200 |
| 2008 Return | -37.0% | -33.8% | -43.1% | -53.2% | 5.2% |
| Balance - 12/31/2008 | $126.00 | $132.42 | $113.88 | $93.64 | $210.48 |
| Allocation - 12/31/2008 | 18.6% | 19.6% | 16.8% | 13.8% | 31.1% |
| Over (Under) Weighted | -1.4% | -0.4% | -3.2% | -6.2% | 11.1% |
| Rebalanced to Target | $135.28 | $135.28 | $135.28 | $135.28 | $135.28 |
| Rebalance | Buy $9.28 | Buy $2.86 | Buy $21.40 | Buy $41.64 | Sell $75.20 |

The Great Recession of 2008 was the worst economic recession since the Great Depression of the 1930s, so this example may be extreme, but the concept remains sound. Adding bonds, which had a positive return and negative correlation to stocks, provides an asset class that we can sell for a gain and then deploy the proceeds into under-weighted investment categories. This positions your portfolio to take advantage of bargain prices in the equity market after these asset classes lost value. The 2009 recovery saw emerging markets rebound over 79 percent, rewarding investors for purchasing more shares after rebalancing to your target allocation. The beauty of this process is that it does not require any foresight, and you are not fighting the market's volatility. Instead, holding a diversified portfolio of equity funds along with funds in neutrally or negatively correlated asset classes allows you to take advantage of the natural ebbs and flows we expect to occur in the global economy.

We previously mentioned that sub-asset classes may exhibit risk and return profiles that differ considerably from their parent asset classes. Returns during 2008 provide a good example of this with bonds. With the greater bond asset class posting a 5.2 percent return, long-term US Treasury bonds posted an impressive 24.0 percent return while high-yield junk bonds were down 26.2 percent.[1] What accounts for such a large difference within the same asset class? Investors view these as very distinct investment categories. Treasury bonds are the ultimate safe haven, backed by the full faith and credit of the US government with its taxing and money-printing capabilities. In addition, the Federal Reserve lowered interest rates in 2008 to stimulate the economy. Downward interest rate movements generally cause bond prices to rise, with the prices of longer duration bonds increasing the most from this. Long-term US Treasury bonds with their extended duration therefore benefitted from both the fall in interest rates and increased demand for stable investments. In contrast, high-yield bonds are issued by companies whose assets, debts, and cash flow cause their creditworthiness to fall below investment grade. Companies on shaky financial ground today were not helped by the recession, which further increased investor doubt these entities could pay their obligations as they came due. High-yield

---

[1] As measured by the Bloomberg US Barclays Aggregate Bond Index, Bloomberg Barclays US Long Treasury Total Return Index, and Bloomberg Barclays US Corporate High Yield Total Return Index, respectively.

bonds can sometimes exhibit risk and return characteristics more in line with equities than bonds, as seen in 2008.

We have primarily talked about mutual funds as representing a broad asset class but have not yet given much attention to selecting which funds to invest in.

## The Debate Continues

Chocolate chip or Oreo cookies. Cats or dogs. We develop preferences and feel strongly about them. The mutual fund equivalent of this is the active versus passive debate, introduced on page 187. Passively managed funds are often referred to as index funds and aim to mirror the performance of their benchmark index while keeping their expenses low. Actively managed funds aim to outperform their benchmark on an absolute or risk-adjusted basis and have higher expenses for the additional work involved. With passive funds providing investors with near-benchmark returns at low cost, the point of contention is whether active fund managers can deliver excess performance above their benchmark after accounting for fees.

### The Case for Index Mutual Funds

Investors in the passive management camp assert that the returns of most actively managed funds will underperform their benchmark index net of fees. Sure, some active funds may generate excess returns, but these skilled managers are difficult to identify in advance and may not be able to sustain their outperformance over a long period of time. Because of this, passive investors argue it is better to hold low-cost index funds to earn the benchmark return, less the slim fees they charge.

The SPIVA scorecard, short for S&P Indices Versus Active, is a semiannual report analyzing the performance of actively managed funds against their respective benchmarks. It looks back fifteen years to determine the percentage of active funds that have outperformed or underperformed their index over one-, three-, five-, ten-, and fifteen-year periods. Not all funds that were available to investors fifteen years ago are still around, with many closing due to poor performance. This creates a potential bias in favor of the remaining funds. To control for survivorship bias, the study accounts for funds that were available at the beginning of a time period but have since been liquidated or merged with another fund. SPIVA's 2016 end-of-year findings include:

*Domestic equity underperformance.* The majority of active domestic equity funds underperformed their benchmarks across all market segments and time periods. Sixty-six percent of large-cap funds trailed the S&P 500 over 2016, with the portion of funds underperforming rising to 84.6 percent over ten years and 92.2 percent over fifteen years. Mid-cap and small-cap funds exhibited similar results with 90 percent or higher underperformance for all periods longer than one year.

*International equity underperformance.* The majority of active international equity funds also trailed their indices over all time periods, with 84.9 percent of equity funds focusing on developed countries underperforming their benchmark in 2016. The percentage of underperforming funds fell to 71.1 percent and 67 percent over the three- and five-year reporting periods, respectively, before rising to 94 percent and 89.4 percent over ten and fifteen years. Funds investing in developing countries saw a rate of 63.9 percent underperformance in 2016. This rises to 85.7 percent and 89.9 percent as we look at the ten- and fifteen-year periods.

*Mixed fixed-income performance.* We see our first periods of benchmark outperformance in bonds. Over 80 percent of intermediate-term investment-grade bonds beat their benchmark in 2016 with a 19.8 percent underperformance rate. The majority of funds continued to outperform over three- and five-year periods at 37.6 percent and 34.4 percent underperformance. It is not until we get to the ten- and fifteen-year time horizons when we see underperformance reach 58.6 percent and 72.6

percent. Over 60 percent of general municipal bond funds also outperformed their index in the three- and five-year periods before swinging to majority underperformance at ten and fifteen years.

*The Case for Actively Managed Mutual Funds*

Investors preferring actively managed mutual funds will be quick to point out that, while the majority of active funds have underperformed, there are still ones that have outperformed their benchmark over extended periods. Their task now becomes how to identify these. For insight on the possibility of outperforming actively managed funds, we turn to a paper written by the research division of one of the largest active equity fund firms, Vanguard. Known for pioneering index funds, Vanguard has a long history of its own active funds since its beginning in 1975. Vanguard's "Keys to improving the odds of active management success" study acknowledges the difficulty active managers face when trying to outperform their benchmark, then offers three factors for investors to consider to increase their chance of picking active funds that will beat their index:[1]

> *Low fees.* Mutual fund expense ratios directly reduce their fund's performance. The logical conclusion is that less expensive funds have a lower expense hurdle to clear on their race to top the benchmark. The paper backs this with data showing that three times as many active funds in the least expensive quartile outperformed their benchmark compared to funds in the most expensive quartile over ten-, fifteen-, and twenty-five-year time periods. Building on this, it further asserts that "Low cost has proven to be the most consistent and effective quantitative factor that investors can use to noticeably improve their odds."

> *Talented portfolio managers.* In addition to low expenses, a fund needs a talented portfolio manager. This requires a certain amount of investor due diligence to select a portfolio manager, summarized

---

[1] © The Vanguard Group, Inc., used with permission.

in the "four Ps"—people, process, portfolio, and performance. Does a mutual fund have experienced people managing their portfolio's holdings with a repeatable process to generate positive performance for their investors? A new metric that is gaining recognition for quantifying the portfolio "P" is active share, which measures how much of a portfolio's holdings overlap with the index. An active share of 0 percent indicates identical overlap with the benchmark, which is what we see in index funds. An active share of 100 percent indicates complete differentiation from the index with no overlap in holdings. There is a growing consensus that actively managed funds with low active share, labeled "closet indexers" for their similarity to the index, struggle to beat their benchmark.[1] The active fund's fee applies to all of its assets, but holdings that overlap the benchmark do not contribute to any outperformance. These closet indexers rely on the small portion of their holdings that differ from the index to generate enough outperformance to pay for the fund's entire cost and beat the benchmark, which has been difficult to achieve. Studies have found low active share, particularly below 60 percent, to be predictive of underperformance. Investors can therefore narrow their active fund search by using low measures of active share to weed out closet indexers. What about funds with high active share? These have been dubbed "stock pickers" for their strategy of holding concentrated portfolios of a few dozen stocks compared to the hundreds or thousands that make up an index. The question now becomes "Can this subset of portfolio managers overseeing high active share funds beat their benchmarks over a long period of time?" One paper found that US equity mutual funds in the top active share quintile outperformed their benchmarks by 1.26 percent a year after expenses from 1990 to 2009. When you select an active fund, you are choosing a manager and their team to pick stocks for you. Active share quantifies this and confirms whether they are actually doing their job. As useful as this can be to identify closet indexers, we caution investors against relying too much on any one metric. A thorough evaluation of

---

[1]  © The Vanguard Group, Inc., used with permission.

a fund's four Ps requires consideration of other quantitative and qualitative factors.

*Investor patience.* A low-cost, talented manager will not necessarily lead to superior returns alone. Long-term fund outperformance also requires investors to be patient with stretches of underperformance, often over multiple years. For example, portfolio managers that adhere to the value style of investing (as opposed to growth) aim to identify companies whose stock they believe is undervalued in the market compared to what it truly should be valued at, known as its intrinsic value. Once they make an investment in shares of an undervalued company, it may take a few years for their investment thesis to play out and see the share price rise to what they expect it to be. Other funds and the benchmark may outperform in the meantime, causing investors to doubt their fund. Vanguard's study found that two-thirds of the active funds that outperformed their index over the fifteen-year period from 2000 through 2014 had, at some point, trailed their benchmark for three consecutive years.

The debate between passive and active management will continue with staunch supporters on both sides. The data we reviewed found the majority of actively managed funds failed to beat their benchmarks, though some did exhibit outperformance over an extended period of time. Investors who wish to try for returns above the benchmark with active funds may be able to increase their odds by choosing low-cost funds with talented managers, while also being patient with bouts of underperformance along the way.

## Chapter Summary

"And that's the behind-the-curtain view of asset class diversification and portfolio management!" Connor concluded.

That's it for a mutual fund portfolio invested across multiple asset classes. Like many parts of your financial plan, your investment portfolio is not something that can be set on the shelf and ignored. As certain asset classes outperform others, your portfolio becomes skewed away from your target allocation, prompting a rebalance back to your desired allocation. Holding bonds and other asset classes that tend to have dissimilar returns from the equities can reduce your portfolio's volatility and provide rebalancing opportunities, particularly during stock market declines. Mutual funds, as opposed to individual stocks and bonds, are commonly purchased to provide diversified exposure to an asset class and are split into passive and active funds.

We have covered quite a bit of investment education so far, though it is incomplete without one more topic.

---

### Key Takeaways

*Stocks (equities)* are units of ownership in a company. As an asset class, stocks tend to exhibit considerable market volatility in the short term, while historically outpacing inflation over the long term. Equities can be divided into sub-asset classes based on company size, style (value and growth), and geographic location.

*Bonds (fixed income)* are debt securities issued by companies and government entities. In general, bonds exhibit low levels of market volatility in the short term but may not outpace inflation by much over the long term. Fixed income is separated by the issuer's credit rating, interest rate sensitivity (measured by duration), and tax status (municipal bonds providing tax-advantaged interest payments).

*Alternatives* include commodities and precious metals, like gold, whose returns tend to have low to negative correlations with the greater equity market. Their risk and return characteristics differ from stocks and bonds, providing an additional level of diversification.

We hold investments in different asset classes due to the uncertainty of returns in each category from year to year. In some years, large-cap stocks may perform better than small-caps while US equities outperform international stocks. In other years, the opposite may occur. *By diversifying your investments across multiple asset classes that perform differently in different market conditions, some of your holdings will perform relatively well and aid your portfolio's return when others perform poorly.*

The proportion of how much you should hold in each asset class is called your *target allocation*, which is based on your time horizon and risk tolerance.

Over time, your portfolio will become skewed away from your target allocation as some asset classes perform better than others. This causes your portfolio to exhibit a different risk and return profile that may no longer be aligned with your goals, necessitating a *rebalance back to your target allocation.*

Diversification among asset classes is indicated by their *correlation*, which specifies how returns of two asset classes fluctuate together. Asset classes that are neutrally or negatively correlated provide a greater diversification effect, whereas returns of positively correlated asset classes tend to move in the same direction (the school of fish analogy). The *correlation coefficient* quantifies the level of diversification between asset classes ranging from +1.0 (perfectly positive relationship) to 0 (no relationship) to -1.0 (perfectly negative relationship).

*Passively managed mutual funds*, or *index funds*, provide broad, low-cost exposure to an asset class and aim to mirror their benchmark index's returns. *Actively managed mutual funds* aim to beat their benchmark on an absolute or risk-adjusted basis and have higher expenses than index funds. Studies have found that the majority of active mutual funds do not beat their benchmark after fees. Suggestions for identifying active mutual funds that stand a better chance of benchmark outperformance include funds that have low fees, talented management teams (with active share being one metric of quantifying this), and patience from the investor through periods of underperformance.

# CHAPTER 21

# THE INVESTOR IN THE MIRROR

MEGAN AND CHRIS, both practicing psychiatrists, were a few years out of training and arrived for a review meeting to discuss their savings plan. It was developing well, though they were concerned about a recent stretch of volatility in the stock market.

"We're pleased with our investments so far," began Megan, "but worried about the market's recent drop."

"And it's not just what has already happened," continued Chris. "We're not sure about the current administration's policies and how they might affect the economy. The global geopolitical scene seems to be getting more uncertain by the week too. We're wondering if now is a good time to take our money out of the market and sit on the investment sidelines for a while until things get resolved."

Megan and Chris raise understandable concerns. You work hard for your money, and it can be discouraging to see your investments lose value with no control over how the market performs. Do not be alarmed if doubts arise, as this is normal. What you need to be keenly aware of is how you interpret these doubts and what action, if any, is needed with your portfolio.

Had this book been written before 1979, it would have ended after our review of asset class diversification. Since then, developments in the field of economics and psychology have changed the way we view investing. Today, writing about investment management would be incomplete without discussing the most important factor—you. If the three forms of diversification is the road map to investing for retirement, then you are the driver who must navigate the way. Even the best map will not get you there if you deviate from the course. This chapter will review published findings on investor behavior so you can be aware of the pitfalls of investors who have come before you.

## Behavioral Finance

The star of traditional economic theory is the rational agent, or rational investor as we will refer to him or her. Our rational investor is calculating and logical, always selecting the course of action that will maximize his or her wealth with a carefully diversified portfolio at the appropriate level of risk. In *Star Trek* terms, the rational investor is Spock. In reality, investors act more like Captain Kirk—emotional and impulsive, sometimes to their detriment. Investor behavior is not simply a conglomeration of random, personal deviations from the rational model, unrelated from one person to the next. Instead, studies have found that the decisions of individual investors, as a group, are made in a predictable, systematic manner. Enter the emerging field of behavioral economics and subfield of behavioral finance. In their 1979 landmark paper "Prospect Theory: An Analysis for Decision Under Risk," cognitive psychologists Daniel Kahneman and Amos Tversky examined decision-making and introduced ideas that would have far-reaching implications, including:

> *Prospect theory.* A theory for decision-making that incorporates human tendencies and challenged the traditional economic decision model based on a rational agent (expected utility theory).

> *Change in value matters more than final states.* Whereas expected utility theory asserts decisions are made to maximize the subject's final state of wealth, prospect theory proposes that subjects

instead view outcomes as gains or losses from an initial reference point. Changing the subject's reference point, such as by framing the proposition in a different manner, affected their decisions.

*Loss aversion.* Decision makers are loss averse to the point of feeling more displeasure from a loss than happiness from an equivalent gain. Their decisions will therefore favor minimizing losses unless there is a suitable chance of a larger gain. Kahneman and Tversky found that decision makers experience losses over twice as severe as gains. Put another way, subjects required the chance of a gain be at least twice as large as the loss they might incur before they would accept the offer.

A simple way to understand loss aversion is the proverbial coin-flip example. Let's say we propose a wager to you: we flip a coin, and if it lands on heads, then we give you $100, but if it lands on tails, then you give us $100. Do you want to take this bet? Probably not, but why? It's a fair bet, and you have equal chance of gain or loss. Spock would be indifferent. Loss aversion suggests you would be unhappier to lose $100 than satisfaction you would feel by winning $100. What if we tip the odds in your favor by giving you a payout of $105. Would you take the bet now? Spock would. Most humans would probably still not. The extra five dollars of possible gain is not enough to offset the displeasure of losing $100. Kahneman and Tversky suggest we would likely need to offer you the chance to win $200 or more before you find the coin flip acceptable.

Behavioral finance studies why people make certain decisions regarding their finances, particularly with their investments. Kahneman and Tversky are considered two of the founding fathers of behavioral finance and, along with economist Richard Thaler, laid the groundwork for other minds to develop this field into what it is today. Further additions include investor overconfidence, herding (copying other investors), lack of portfolio diversification, and the disposition effect. We would not pay much attention to them if these findings were limited to a small subset of investors. However, the prevailing view is that individual investors, as a whole, exhibit similar tendencies. We do not mean to presume that you or all investors act in these ways. Rather, we feel it is important to share what has been observed so you can be aware of these concepts and mindful of your investment decisions.

## Investor Behavior

Among the growing body of research on investor behavior, two of the most prevalent findings are the disposition effect and trading tendencies based on investor confidence. These provide insight into how investors manage their portfolios specifically relating to trading patterns. They do not represent the entire scope of investor behavior but do demonstrate some of the choices investors make.

### The Disposition Effect

The disposition effect is a phenomenon in which investors prefer to sell stocks whose value has appreciated since they were purchased (winners) and continue holding stocks that have decreased in value (losers). Upon first glance, this may appear to be a rational decision. Investors are locking in their gains from an appreciated stock while giving their losers time to potentially rebound. The reason this is deemed to be a blunder is due to its tax inefficiency of maximizing realized capital gains while not harvesting capital losses to offset them. Investors are incurring a higher tax liability than necessary. The ideal tax strategy would instead postpone realizing capital gains as long as possible and realize capital losses when the losing stock is no longer considered a suitable holding. There are different theories on why investors behave this way, including their aversion to losses. Selling for a loss causes regret while capturing a gain elicits a sense of pride from a successful pick. Take note that this is different from rebalancing a mutual fund portfolio back to its target allocation. Observations of the disposition effect have primarily been through data sets of individual stock holdings.

While on the subject of individual stocks, we would like to take this opportunity to remind you about the difficulty of trading them. Nonprofessional investors are at a large disadvantage compared to professional analysts and traders. These specialists earn a living by valuing companies and trading based on perceived under or overvaluations in their stock price. When you buy or sell a stock online, you may be trading with your neighbor across the street who has no more insight into the company than you do, but you could also be trading against a Wall Street professional whose firm has considerable resources devoted to knowing where the stock's price may be heading. This is backed by research that found stocks individual investors sold subsequently outperformed the ones they purchased by 3.3 percent over the following year. Due to this informational asymmetry, we would encourage you to consider trading individual stocks to be more speculative in nature compared to holding a diversified mutual fund portfolio. The stock-picking game is fine if you are doing it for fun, but be wary of betting your retirement on it.

*Think Twice before You Trade*

We previously used the example of rebalancing a diversified portfolio to show how trading can be beneficial; periodic adjustments keep your holdings from straying too far from your target allocation. With that said, investors trade for reasons other than rebalancing and studying the effects of trading has become a popular topic. One review compared the performance of investors who switched investments at least once during the five years from 2008 through 2012 to those who did not. It found that investors who traded trailed their benchmark by 1.50 percent annually, while investors who refrained from trading trailed by only 0.19 percent. This included the 2008 recession and market volatility that accompanied it, suggesting that when investors traded, they did so to their detriment as opposed to opportunistically taking advantage of the market dip.

A separate study looked at the difference in investor returns compared to returns of the underlying funds they invested in to highlight investor fund flows (when investors make contributions into mutual funds and withdrawals from them). A negative difference for investors' returns can indicate performance chasing; more investor contributions flowed into a fund *after* it achieved a stretch of impressive returns, causing lower returns for investors who missed out on the fund's above-average performance. Results were categorized based on which quadrant of the equity style box each fund was associated with.

Figure 1. Investor returns versus fund returns, ten years ended December 31, 2015

| | Value | Blend | Growth | Conservative allocation | Moderate allocation |
|---|---|---|---|---|---|
| Large-cap | 5.59% | 6.44% | 7.33% | 4.15% | 5.23% |
| | 3.70 | 5.06 | 5.69 | 3.29 | 4.08 |
| | -1.88 | -1.38 | -1.64 | -0.86 | -1.15 |
| Mid-cap | 6.59 | 6.50 | 7.16 | | |
| | 4.30 | 4.68 | 5.53 | | |
| | -2.28 | -1.82 | -1.63 | | |
| Small-cap | 6.01 | 6.27 | 7.14 | | |
| | 4.45 | 4.63 | 5.20 | | |
| | -1.57 | -1.64 | -1.94 | | |

▨ Time-weighted return
■ Investor return
☐ Differential

Notes: Morningstar Investor Return™ assumes that the growth of a fund's total net assets for a given period is driven by market returns and investor cash flow. To calculate investor return, a fund's change in assets for the period is discounted by the return of the fund to isolate how much of the asset growth was driven by cash flow. A proprietary model, similar to an internal rate-of-return calculation, is then used to calculate a constant growth rate that links the beginning total net assets and periodic cash flows to the ending total net assets. Discrepancies in the return "difference" are due to rounding.

Source: Morningstar, Inc.

While there is some variation throughout the style box, the returns for investors compared to their funds are consistently negative across the board. This suggests the average investor has shifted money among funds in a manner that misses a fair amount of the fund's above-average performance and instead captures more of the fund's below-average returns.[1]

This is insightful, but there is only so much we can take from the average investor. "Average" is not very flattering, and we doubt many readers would select it as their descriptor of choice. Most people with a positive self-image view themselves as above average in many areas of life.

---

[1] © The Vanguard Group, Inc., used with permission.

For example, when you think of your driving ability, do you consider yourself to be an above-average driver or worse than the average driver? If you chose "above-average," you are in good company. One survey found 93 percent of American drivers polled consider their driving skills to be above average. This cannot be higher than 50 percent by definition, so some drivers clearly have an undeserved appreciation of their ability behind the wheel. The study concluded by stating "there was a strong tendency to believe oneself as safer and more skillful than the average driver." What does this have to do with investing behavior? Well, the paper also noted that "believing oneself as more skilled than others may lead to greater risk taking which is positively reinforced for those who 'win the game' and are successful."

Further research into investor behavior focuses on how confidence affects trading patterns and results. Several studies have linked increased investor overconfidence to higher levels of trading. While there is nothing wrong with being confident in your abilities, there also needs to be an understanding of your limits and knowing when you may be approaching them. One paper found investors with an average level of trading trailed the market by 1.50 percent a year, whereas investors who traded the most underperformed by 6.50 percent annually, citing overconfidence and transaction costs as contributors. Dividing investors by gender found that men, on average, were more overconfident in their investing abilities than women. Overconfidence was noted as the primary reason for men trading 45 percent more than women and subsequently earning lower returns. Empirical research indicates that excessive trading, at least partly based on overconfidence, does not help investor performance. The next time you are considering a change to your portfolio, take a moment to pause and think about what you are aiming to accomplish.

**Chapter Summary**

"Whoa, that's interesting," Chris said. "If anyone appreciates the intricacies of the human mind, it's a couple of psychiatrists!"

As the past few chapters have demonstrated, there is a lot that goes into building and managing your financial plan. Studies have shown that one of the biggest roadblocks for the investing component of this can be our own human tendencies. Even if investors understand the concepts, they are conditioned to make mistakes that erode their returns. These range from the disposition effect to excessive trading to chasing performance. Picking individual stocks—specifically knowing at which prices to buy and then sell—has also been viewed as a losing proposition for the average investor. We continue to be proponents of holding a low-cost mutual fund portfolio diversified across several asset classes that is properly aligned with your time horizon and periodically rebalanced to your target allocation.

That's it. The financial planning topics we feel are most relevant to residents, fellows, and early-career doctors have been laid before you. From here, the decision turns to how you choose to implement your financial plan. Our last chapter will explain what financial advisors do so you can make an informed decision on how to enlist the help of an advisor for your planning.

---

### Key Takeaways

Understanding investment concepts is one thing, while properly implementing them in a thoughtful and objective manner is another. Investors are (understandably) emotionally tied to their investments, and this connection can cause suboptimal behavior. *Behavioral finance* is the study of why people make financial decisions that differ from the rational agent found in traditional economic theory.

The *disposition effect* is exhibited when investors sell stocks whose value has appreciated since they were purchased (winners) and continue holding stocks that have decreased in value (losers). This is an inefficient investment strategy because it maximizes capital gain taxes while not realizing capital losses to offset them.

Studies have found the average investor trails the benchmark by more than their mutual funds' expenses, indicating that investor behavior accounts for some amount of underperformance. Further research focused on investor trading tendencies suggests investors erode their returns by trading at inopportune times. This may be done by purchasing more investments after a period of above-average performance (buying technology stocks in the late 1990s after their prices already appreciated considerably) or by selling after a period of decline (selling equity shares for a loss after the 2008 bear market).

Investors should therefore *be aware of chasing performance*—buying after a period of above-average returns, whether that is of a single stock, a particular asset class, or timing when to invest at all. This practice of buying a stock or mutual fund after a stretch of above-average performance and holding it through a period of below-average performance is one reason why investor returns may be lower than those of their mutual funds.

This is exacerbated by excessive trading, partly attributed to *investor overconfidence* in their ability to pick stocks or mutual funds.

Our framework for investment management involves creating a portfolio of low-cost mutual funds diversified across several asset classes in an allocation that is aligned with your time horizon, while staying disciplined with your contributions and occasionally rebalancing through periods of market volatility. In light of the findings in this chapter, we would encourage you to think about what you are aiming to achieve if you are considering deviating from this approach.

# CHAPTER 22

# IMPLEMENTING YOUR PLAN

AS WE HAVE seen, there is a lot that goes into developing and maintaining your financial plan. It is broad in its scope, and taking a comprehensive approach requires an understanding of the various topics we have covered. Like getting into good physical health, improving your financial health does not happen by accident. It involves a mindset of intentionally living within your means, appropriately managing your debts, properly addressing certain risks, and putting together a savings plan for later in life. Once your plan is established, ongoing effort is needed to revise it as your current situation and future goals change. The good news for young doctors and their families is that you have plenty of time to make up for your training years. If there is one idea you take away from these pages (and we hope there are many), then let it be this:

Start planning now.

Make a commitment to think about your finances on a regular basis.

Even the small steps of creating your net worth statement and monthly cash flow will give you a starting point to build from.

You can then make a list of your short-, medium-,
and long-term goals you would like to accomplish
in training, soon afterward, and in the years that follow.

As we turn to implementing your financial plan, a central idea will be how much responsibility for its outcome you would like to keep or pass along to a financial advisor. This is not an all-or-nothing decision, and successful plans commonly share responsibility between parties. We certainly acknowledge that doctors are responsible people; otherwise, you would not be in medicine. This is different. We are now addressing the degree of research, development, and implementation that you would like to assume for the well-being of your finances over the next several decades. We understand that some readers may have more of a knack for the topics we have covered than others. Combining this with the amount of time you can devote to your plan, your level of interest, and overall personal preference will land you somewhere along the responsibility spectrum.

At this junction, we want to take a moment to admit our bias as financial advisors. Our aim so far has been to objectively present topics while highlighting areas we feel deserve extra attention. We are now getting at the core of how the authors practice, and it is difficult to present this in a detached manner. If you ask a dentist whether you should have regular checkups to evaluate your oral health, you can imagine she will answer in the affirmative. We will similarly acknowledge our bias here. We feel working with a trusted advisor can have a significantly positive impact on the long-term success of a family's financial life, even for multiple generations, as they help to form and maintain strategies that address your goals. What follows is our take on planning, shaped by our experiences and how we feel our clients are best served.

For those of you who wish to do as much planning on your own as possible, we would encourage you to occasionally meet with an advisor rather than proceeding alone without any professional guidance. Financial advisors provide an outside perspective and can point out blind spots in your analysis. Knowing that you have an upcoming meeting can also hold you accountable for completing what needs to be done. At a minimum, working with an advisor includes a review of your plan once a year, which you can think of as your annual financial checkup. You will provide your advisor with updated financial and nonfinancial information ahead of the meeting, such as current investment statements and new goals or concerns. In return, they will review your finances, meet with you for an assessment of your plan, and send you on your way to perform the recommended changes you agree on. This sort of arrangement, at the very least, requires you to be diligently involved with the upkeep of your plan.

Fully maintaining your plan is time-consuming due to the breadth of work involved, in addition to dealing with complicated and emotional financial decisions. Because of this, many doctors will work with an advisor on a more proactive basis. Approaching the middle range sees more frequent meetings and increased email correspondence between sessions. Rather than meeting sporadically, you are committed to meeting on a regular basis of usually twice a year. You still retain some of the actual execution of the plan yourself, but not all of it. This sees you pass off the implementation of certain parts to your advisor, particularly those you do not enjoy or do not want to be responsible for.

On the other end of the spectrum, many doctors prefer to follow holistic financial advice and want an advisor's help with their entire plan, rather than one or two specific areas. Doctors are acutely aware of how limited their free time can be, and you may prefer to spend this with family or engaging in a personal hobby. If you would like to have a planning specialist involved with implementing and monitoring your financial plan, then working with an advisor who will do this for you may be a better fit. Review sessions are conducted at least twice a year, and your advisor will be available to meet for anything that arises between scheduled reviews. They are as committed to your plan's success as you are and will do all they can to relieve you of the time it takes to maintain its course, as well as the stress that comes along with it.

Keep in mind that your position along the responsibility range is not static. You may feel yourself gravitating toward a different part of the spectrum as your interests and available time change. Independent of where you currently fall, it can be beneficial to find an advisor so you have a reliable team in place as your preferences shift.

We feel it is important to inform readers what financial advisors do so you can decide how you may want to work with one. The remainder of this chapter will first look at how advisors operate. It will then aim to clarify what to expect, as the partnership will only be productive if the advisor and client have a shared understanding of the meeting process and possible results. The final section will review considerations when selecting an advisor, ranging from the topic of fiduciary duty to different credentials an advisor may have.

**What do financial advisors do?**

Apart from writing mildly entertaining books, financial advisors work with individuals and families to address their financial concerns and achieve their goals. You likely want to head into your later years in good physical health and without worrying about outliving your money. We can therefore think of financial planning as preventive care for your financial health. In medicine and dentistry, preventive measures reduce the frequency and severity of physical health issues arising. Along the same lines, proactively planning your finances will improve your odds for a successful financial plan throughout your career and retirement. Advisors may recommend beginning a new strategy (enroll in an income-driven repayment plan to have your student loan payments count toward public service loan forgiveness) or may recommend adding a financial product (secure disability insurance to protect your income). As they do, they should explain their reasoning so you are aware of their rationale.

With the care of your physical health, there are actions you can take to lead a healthy lifestyle while seeing your primary care provider and dentist for areas you are unable or not qualified to perform yourself. You can eat a balanced diet, exercise regularly, and brush and floss your teeth without direct oversight from your physician and dentist. Despite this, medical professionals recommend periodic checkups even for healthy people. Your primary care provider analyzes and coordinates the care of your physical health, commenting on lifestyle choices and adding their recommendations when needed. Beyond this, they perform procedures most people are unable to do themselves, such as checking your cholesterol levels with a blood draw. If your results are outside of the normal range, your physician may recommend a medication or refer you to a specialist for additional care. Visits to your dentist include a round of cleaning, which itself is a professional version of what you hopefully do twice a day already. They may also take an x-ray to scan for cavities and remedy the situation if one is found, something most patients are not equipped to do on their own.

Turning to your financial health, you can live within your means and adhere to other planning guidelines without seeing an advisor. Even so, many doctors and families work with financial advisors to analyze and coordinate the care of their finances. Some of the basic questions advisors address may be: Am I managing my debts well? Am I properly insured? Am I saving enough? Are my investments allocated appropriately? In addition to these, financial advisors bring up planning areas and strategies you may not have previously considered. They also use tools that many non-advisors do not have access to, such as software that allows a deep dive into an investment portfolio to look at each holding in fine detail. Most importantly, your advisor will reaffirm your financial goals, whether these have changed, and, if necessary, make recommendations to realign your plan with them.

When planning arrives at a topic beyond the scope of what financial advisors are qualified to handle, they will refer you to a specialist who is. This may be an accountant for tax issues or an attorney for drafting estate planning documents. However, this is not simply passing the planning baton off to the next professional while your advisor recedes into the distance. Your advisor should explain why consulting a specialist is needed and where this fits into the planning process. They will give you direction for your appointment, such as, "Ask your accountant to calculate how much more in taxes you would pay by filing separately instead of jointly," or, "See whether the attorney recommends setting up a trust to serve as the contingent beneficiary on your life insurance for your children." It is common for advisors, accountants, attorneys, and other specialists to connect behind the scenes to organize your plan or to have meetings with all parties present to make sure everyone is on the same page.

With regard to their scope of services, financial advisors do much more than offer insurance products and manage investments. Advisors taking a comprehensive approach must be knowledgeable on a range of topics and work with their clients on them as situations arise. They are trained to increase your net worth as efficiently as possible, which can include advice that is not necessarily groundbreaking, like shifting cash to an online high-interest savings account to earn more interest. Advisors must also be aware of new developments that may impact your plan, whether this is through formal continuing education or keeping up to date with recent stock market trends and proposed legislation. If an opportunity to improve your financial plan presents itself, they will let you know and work with you to achieve this. Serving as your behavioral coach, saving you time for more enjoyable activities, and performing due diligence on investment options are three of the many reasons why doctors choose to work with an advisor.

### Behavioral Coaching

Money, especially in large balances, can elicit certain moods. Some doctors may feel queasy at the thought of how much they owe in student loans. On the investment front, plenty of research has been conducted on how individuals manage their money in a field collectively known as behavioral finance. As an investor, you may find it difficult to keep your feelings separate from your investment decisions, particularly during times of heightened market volatility. One of the more common blunders investors make is succumbing to their emotions (sometimes influenced by the media or colleagues) and selling at an inopportune time during a market dip, precisely when they should remember their long-term time horizon and not make short-term decisions that could have lasting effects. A single big investment mistake could be one too many, which is why serving as a behavioral coach is one of the most important roles financial advisors perform. They may not provide sage advice each and every day, but a key intervention during a time of crisis can more than make up for several years of their cost.

If you are thinking of deviating from your investment strategy because of recent market events, your financial advisor will remind you why they recommended this approach initially and why they stand by it now. They will remind you how common it is for the stock market to rise and fall within a year, perhaps citing recent examples. In the thirty-eight years from 1980 through 2017, the S&P 500 Index has had an average intra-year decline of nearly 14 percent and has gone on to post positive calendar year returns in thirty-two of them, roughly 84 percent of the time.[1] It has dropped by 28 percent or more in five of these years and in two of them had fully recovered by the year's end.[2] We acknowledge it may be against your impulse to purchase more mutual fund shares when the ones you own have lost value, yet this is exactly when an advisor's counseling can be most beneficial.

Financial advisors proactively contact their clients and give the "stay the course" talk, reminding you that you have time to let your investments recover, as you do not need to tap into your portfolio for many years. Realizing that you will be a *net buyer* of stocks over the next couple of decades can help shift your mindset from perceiving a market downturn as a negative event into a positive one. When the market has dropped lately, think of stocks and equity mutual funds as "being on sale" compared to their previous prices. They will remind you to continue your ongoing contributions and investment purchases independent of how volatile the market has been or is believed to be going forward. This concept, called dollar cost averaging, takes advantage of price swings in investments by buying more shares when they have decreased in value.[3] Market dips provide good buying opportunities for long-term investors, something that may not be apparent when they are happening.

Depending on the nature of the stock market decline, advisors may

[1] As measured by the S&P 500 Total Return Index.
[2] Source: J.P. Morgan Asset Management.
[3] See the disclosure at the end of the book regarding dollar cost averaging.

recommend rebalancing your portfolio if recent performance has caused your asset allocation to stray far enough away from its target breakdown. Bonds, precious metals, and other defensively oriented asset classes usually hold up well during stock market dips and may now be over-weighted compared to their desired allocations. If so, then shares in these asset classes may be ripe to sell, locking in a gain after a period of relative outperformance compared to the equity side of your portfolio. You can then use the cash proceeds from the shares sold to purchase shares in under-weighted equity asset classes (see the rebalancing example on page 278 for additional mechanics).

It also is important to understand that the media's job is to report current events, and from time to time, they may do this overzealously. Particularly significant stock market declines can be the result of wider economic recessions, characterized by rising unemployment and declining productivity—news that reporters will not shy away from and will be making the daily headlines. If you feel yourself being influenced to deviate from your investment plan, take a moment to remember that disciplined investors can be rewarded for persevering through difficult conditions. Occasional market corrections are a natural and healthy part of any economy, one that long-term investors should embrace and not fear. It is your advisor's job to remind you of all this and coach you through the emotional roller coaster the stock market can take you on.

*Time Savings*

Imagine you have just had an especially difficult week. A few patients went long, and the electronic medical records system did not do you any favors. You survived to Friday evening and can finally catch your breath. As you begin to unwind, you notice the to-do list pegged to your fridge. It's the last thing you want to pay attention to, but you skipped mowing the lawn last weekend and have already delayed that oil change for too long. Further down, a note in familiar handwriting reminds you that your Roth IRA contribution is not going to invest itself. It has been in cash since your deposit a few weeks ago, and you are well aware that the rate of return on cash will not do the trick for retirement. Your carefree weekend may not be quite as relaxing as you had hoped.

Though you are given 168 hours each week, many of these are accounted for in advance. Budget thirty to fifty for sleep, five to ten for your commute, another handful for cooking and errands, forty to "who knows how many" for work, and over half of your week has already been spent, not to mention the time you would like to be with friends and family. For doctors who enjoy planning their finances, a Saturday of researching mutual funds, placing trades, updating your spending analysis, and looking into mortgage rates is exactly how you would like it to go. If so, the authors have found a kindred spirit. If you prefer to do anything but this, then know that help is available.

Our modern economy is built on specialization. We focus our efforts on becoming very good at our occupation rather than each person developing a rounded set of skills as a Jack or Jill of all trades. Of the newborns populating the hospital nursery, some will grow up to become chefs, some engineers, and a few hard-working souls will choose the medical path themselves. Others will find their calling as financial advisors, intrigued by the financial markets and passionate about serving their clients. They have spent their time becoming an expert in financial matters so you do not have to.

The logical next question is, How much is your time worth? Your employer has an answer to this. Do you? How much time do you have and how much are you willing to commit to your financial endeavors? Financial planning is comprised of many decisions—evaluating options, prioritizing the use of your resources, implementing the strategy, monitoring the plan, and repeating this cycle over your lifetime as circumstances change. Perhaps even more so than money, time is a limited resource, and unlike money, more cannot be created.

In addition to the economic benefit of receiving advice, there is another benefit of working with an advisor that, while difficult to quantify, is quite real. This is the emotional relief that comes with passing the responsibility of managing your financial plan to someone else. Changing your car's oil is less complicated than planning your finances, with a fraction of the cost if you get it wrong, yet many doctors take their car to a mechanic rather than roll up their sleeves. In this respect, having the mechanic change your oil and working with an advisor can be considered services you expect to recover part of the cost as the nonfinancial benefit of not having to perform these yourself. If you are not inclined to manage your investment portfolio or other areas of your plan, then working with an advisor can be well worth the cost through time saved, proper coaching and decision-making during difficult economic times, and the peace of mind your financial plan is receiving professional oversight.

*Investment Due Diligence*

Turning to investment analysis, financial advisors select mutual funds to use, construct asset allocations in line with your time horizon and risk tolerance, place trades, and monitor accounts for recommended adjustments. They also write the investment policy statement that dictates an appropriate asset allocation and outlines how they will manage your portfolio. This is commonly done with their firm's investment research division, which performs rigorous due diligence to screen out funds that do not meet their criteria and provide justification for ones that do. Fund characteristics they analyze include, but are not limited to, investment strategy, fees, management tenure, modern portfolio theory statistics, and other risk and return metrics.

Advisors also meet with mutual fund management teams to receive direct commentary on the fund's performance and any changes the fund has enacted or is considering. This serves as an opportunity to put a mutual fund's team on the stand and cross-examine them on individual holdings within the fund or current macroeconomic themes. If a financial advisor is going to be a responsible steward of their clients' money, then they need to be sure the fund managers they select will be too. This is more evident when selecting actively managed funds due to their higher expenses and greater dispersion of performance than index funds. Advisors recommending an active mutual fund should have a strong understanding of the fund's strategy to support their rationale for why they feel paying up for active management is worth the cost.

A large amount of your retirement savings will likely be as contributions into your employer's 401(k) or 403(b) retirement plan. Financial advisors usually do not manage these directly, though can still provide advice for you to carry out within them. Most employer retirement plans will have around twenty to thirty mutual fund options, which may include a series of target date funds that align with the investor's desired retirement year. Target date funds are managed to be more aggressive (more stock market exposure) when the investor is young with a long-term time horizon before gradually becoming more conservative (less of the fund invested in equities and more in bonds) as it approaches its target retirement date. While these can be appropriate choices, some target date funds contain unimpressive underlying mutual funds or have higher fees than other mutual funds available on the menu of investment options. Advisors review employer retirement plan options and comment on whether your current allocation is appropriate or whether they recommend adjusting your fund selection. As an employee, you may be defaulted into an investment option that is too aggressive or too conservative. If so, your advisor should point this out and propose reallocating your account to a more suitable breakdown.

## Setting Expectations

As skilled as an advisor may be, your work with them will not be fruitful if there is a disconnect between your expectations and theirs. The paragraphs that follow are our take on the planning process, investment performance, and the client-advisor partnership. We expect other advisors to have different perspectives, just as two doctors may have different opinions on how to best treat a patient.

### The Planning Process

If you have not worked with a financial advisor before, it is understandable if you are unfamiliar with the planning process. This can cause hesitation to seek guidance with your finances, which is why it is important to clarify what to expect during sessions with an advisor. Planning generally starts with an initial "get to know each other" meeting, during which the advisor will answer any questions you have and provide an overview of them, their firm, scope of services offered, how they are paid, what it will cost to work with them, and what you will work toward in subsequent appointments. The rest of the meeting then becomes a question-and-answer session. The goal of their prompting questions is to gain an understanding of your current financial and nonfinancial situation, as well as your goals, concerns, and how you prioritize these. If you are not comfortable answering a question, just let them know. The more information you can give, the better the advisor will understand where your financial plan is starting at and where you would like it to go. Following the first meeting, the advisor will review their notes, analyze your information, and begin forming their recommendations (think about how doctors review a new patient's file after you meet them for the first time and before you propose a course of treatment).

At this stage, some advisors review their recommendations in the next meeting. While there is nothing wrong with this approach, we imagine this could be confusing for doctors who do not have much, if any, background in financial planning. You would be quite justified in asking clarifying questions throughout the meeting if this were the first time you heard the phrase "rebalance your mutual fund portfolio back to your target allocation that is aligned with your long-term time horizon." Because many doctors do not receive a formal course in planning their finances, we feel it is important to take the next two or three meetings to educate doctors on the key topics reviewed in this book as a crash-course in financial planning customized for you. Our goal is for doctors to gain an understanding of the strategies that may be suggested and the reasons behind these.

During the recommendations meeting, financial advisors provide their thoughts on how to better position your financial plan going forward based on the priorities you have shared. This can range from "just survive" while in training to rolling out an entire agenda, depending on your goals and career stage. Keep in mind these are the advisor's recommendations and, though they are formed with your input, may not be exactly what you expect to hear. It is normal to adjust the initial recommendations to ones you feel are a better fit. While advisors should respect your feedback and not rigidly cling to their suggestions, they should also be grounded and let you know if they feel certain deviations could cause harm to your plan or expose it to substantial risk. If some of the recommendations agreed on involve additional work with your advisor, then the initial meeting process will extend to include the implementation of these.

Once these are completed, then planning may take a break until your first review meeting. The optimal review meeting frequency is up to you, though connecting every six months or so is common. Extra meetings and brief phone calls often happen around your transition year or other significant events, such as getting married, having children, a home purchase, or a job change.

*Investment Performance*

Another area we want to provide our take on relates to expected investment performance. To us, responsible investment management involves building a portfolio of low-cost mutual funds diversified across multiple asset classes. It will be structured to take a commensurate amount of market risk to hopefully earn a long-term rate of return that will achieve your objective. As we reviewed in the Asset Class Diversification chapter, adequate diversification means spreading your investments among stocks, bonds, and, to a lesser degree, alternatives in a breakdown aligned with your time horizon. These are further divided between sub-asset classes by company size, companies based in developed and developing countries abroad, and different categories of bonds. Understand that when the stock market declines, as it does from time to time, it is likely that your equity investments will too. We are financial advisors, not magicians, and it is difficult for even a diversified portfolio to not lose value when the market experiences a decent drop. When this happens, your advisor will remind you of your long-term time horizon and bring up rebalancing opportunities, as we covered in the preceding section on behavioral coaching. They should navigate you through choppy market periods so your portfolio remains on track for your goals.

We also need to address the idea that an advisor's job as an investment manager is to beat the market. To begin, which market are we referring to? American investors may define the market as the S&P 500 Index, which represents domestic large company stocks. Comparing your portfolio's return to the S&P 500 alone presents a few problems. First, what if large US companies are the underperforming asset class over the next thirty years just as developed international markets lagged over the past thirty? Even if your portfolio outperforms the S&P 500, it could still trail international stocks, small-cap stocks, or worse—inflation! Benchmark outperformance may not be reason to celebrate if your returns do not put you on track to achieve your goals.

Second, there are issues with a few strategies aimed at beating the S&P 500—selecting actively managed mutual funds in the domestic large-cap equity space, investing in other asset classes, and trying to time the market's fluctuations, to name a few. Focusing on only trying to "beat" the market may inject unnecessary risk into your plan relative to your long-term goals.

Third, what time frame do you use to evaluate performance? Since 1926, the average bull market (rising stock market) has been about four and a half years, while the average bear market (declining stock market) has been about two years.[1] Anything less than roughly a seven-year time frame gives you only a partial snapshot of your portfolio's performance over a full market cycle. Seven years is not necessarily the magic number over which to evaluate your returns, though we suggest looking at a single year's return is too short to provide a fair representation of your portfolio's performance. For example, holding bonds during an equity bull market year could cause your return to lag the S&P 500. Despite this, your return may be in line or above what you require to achieve your goals.

---

[1]  Source: J.P. Morgan Asset Management.

The question that should be asked is, What are you measuring your performance relative to? An index's rate of return will differ from the return needed for you to retire comfortably. For this reason, comparing your return to an arbitrary benchmark may be a flawed approach. After all, if your investments achieve a rate of return that allows you to stop working when you want, have exactly the retirement you dream of, and leave an inheritance for younger generations, does it matter if your return happened to be lower than an index's along the way? We suggest a shift in mindset from index outperformance to achieving the rate of return needed to fulfill your objectives.

*The Client-Advisor Partnership*

There are a few expectations of both parties for the client-advisor partnership to be most productive. When you engage an advisor for their services, they will come to each meeting prepared to talk about your situation and will have reviewed any documents you have provided in advance. In return, clients should come to meetings with an open mind and be receptive to what your advisor has to share. Prepare to be actively involved in sessions and ask questions when a concept is not clear. Similar to a business partnership, your financial plan has the best chance for success when both parties are fully committed to achieving agreed-upon goals, rather than one party being disproportionately more invested than the other. Trust is also integral to the partnership and is earned after going through meetings, emails, and life events.

While hiring a financial advisor does not come for free, we believe that working with a caring, intelligent, and trusted advisor will generate far more wealth during your lifetime than their cost. You will need to be comfortable with this cost-benefit analysis for the client-advisor partnership to work. In evaluating whether you are willing to pay for advice, we need to understand the cost and risks of *not* paying for advice. These include, but are not limited to, your time spent researching and coordinating the many areas of your plan we have covered, as well as the monetary cost of a mistake incurred due to inexperience or personal bias. Financial advisors will explain their cost structure in your first meeting, which may consist of a cost per meeting, monthly subscription or retainer, or asset-based fee if they are managing investments for you.

**Okay, I'm considering a financial advisor. What do I look for in one?**

Whether you have worked with an advisor in the past, currently do, or plan to in the future, consider applying the following criteria when screening one. Remember, they are auditioning to be your primary financial-care provider, so you owe it to yourself to properly vet them to see if they are what you are looking for in a partner.

*Fiduciary Standard of Duty*

Loosely defined, being a fiduciary means you are acting in the interest of someone other than yourself. When you engage a financial advisor for planning services, you have every right to expect they will perform these services in your best interest under a fiduciary standard of duty. This contrasts with the lower standard of care that brokers are held to when providing advice or recommending products, which requires their advice or product only be "suitable" for the client at the time of recommendation. Financial advisors that hold a Series 65 or 66 license and are registered with an SEC-regulated registered investment advisor (RIA) are mandated to act in your—the client's—best interest ahead of their own and disclose conflicts of interest by the Investment Advisor Act of 1940. You can verify whether an advisor holds a Series 65 or 66 license on the SEC's Investment Adviser Public Disclosure website.[1]

*Independent*

An advisor is independent when neither they nor their registered investment advisor (the entity that directly oversees their investment activity and transactions) are directly or indirectly affiliated with an

---

[1] The Securities and Exchange Commission (SEC) is a federal government agency that regulates securities markets and enforces rules designed to protect investors, among other responsibilities. The SEC's IAPD website can be accessed at www.adviserinfo.sec.gov.

insurance carrier or investment company that manufactures financial products, underwrites securities, creates research, or engages in investment banking. In addition, an independent advisor is not an employee of an investment or insurance firm that creates their own financial products for distribution. Working with an independent advisor can reduce conflicts of interest when insurance or investment products are used by allowing the advisor to go through a variety of companies to better meet the client's needs.

An advisor is *not* independent when the channels that allow him or her to provide financial products are affiliated with an insurance or investment company. If this is the case, then the nonindependent advisor may have a difficult time providing unbiased advice because they may be required by the terms of their employment or financially encouraged to use one company's products ahead of another's, even if this is not in the client's best interest. For example, if a disclosure on an advisor's website states, "Securities and investment advisory services offered exclusively through ABC Broker-Dealer or ABC Registered Investment Advisor," and further in the disclosure it states, "ABC Broker-Dealer or ABC Registered Investment Advisor is a wholly owned subsidiary of XYZ Insurance Company," then the advisor is likely faced with a conflict of interest. They may only have access to XYZ's products or may be paid more to recommend XYZ's products than the products of other insurance or investment companies.

Continuing this example, let's say the client and advisor have agreed that securing disability insurance is an important part of the client's plan. The advisor now needs to determine which disability insurance carrier they will recommend and has narrowed the selection to disability insurance companies A and B. Company A has stronger features and is better priced for this client, but the advisor is employed by Company B and receives more compensation by selling Company B's policies. Which company does the advisor recommend? We hope the superior policy of Company A; however, we clearly see the conflict of interest here. The advisor is financially incentivized to recommend Company B's products, even if they are not the best fit for the client.

Similar to how the SEC's IAPD website can confirm whether an advisor is held to a fiduciary standard of duty, FINRA's Broker Check website can inform you whether an advisor is employed by or affiliated with an insurance carrier or investment firm that manufactures their own products.[1] Another resource you can research is the advisor's ADV Brochure, which provides an updated disclosure of conflicts of interest. The advisor's ADV Brochure is required to be made available upon request.

*Specializes in Working with Doctors*

Doctors have unique financial situations that make planning your finances different from non-doctors. These include much larger student loan balances, delayed starts to saving for retirement, higher incomes, higher tax burdens, special mortgage programs, and greater asset protection needs. What is the chance that the average financial advisor is acutely aware of the challenges you face? Probably not very high. We doubt you want to be your advisor's first doctor client, with them frantically looking up what "PSLF" means and the many rules associated with it during the minutes before your meeting. Similar to how doctors specialize in certain areas of medicine, advisors commonly focus their practice on a particular demographic, such as pre-retirees at the tail end of their careers or public state employees. We suggest narrowing your search to advisors whose practices are largely or entirely devoted to serving doctors and their families to ensure your advisor stays familiar with trends and issues affecting the medical community.

*Scope of Services*

Another area of advisor differentiation relates to the scope of services they encompass. Financial advisors who work at traditional wealth management shops typically focus on investment management services and may not provide advice on other areas of planning. Some advisors have more of an insurance or student loan tilt to their style. While there is

---

[1] The Financial Industry Regulatory Authority (FINRA) is a self-regulatory organization that regulates securities trading and is responsible for protecting investors. FINRA's Broker Check website can be accessed at brokercheck.finra.org.

nothing wrong with these approaches, you will need to seek advice from a second advisor or outside specialist to fill the gaps in your plan if your advisor does not practice in a comprehensive manner. Understanding which planning topics you desire advice on and which ones an advisor covers can help you decide whether they may be a good fit.

## Advanced Designations

One way to determine if an advisor has an advanced skill set is whether they have an abbreviation of letters after their name, though not all credentials are held in the same regard. There are dozens of designations a financial advisor can obtain, and many of these lack meaningful industry recognition or credibility. Here is a short list of the more respected designations in the financial services industry.

### CERTIFIED FINANCIAL PLANNER™

One of the most widely respected certifications in the financial planning industry. To become certified, a CFP® professional must complete a series of seven college-level courses covering broad aspects of financial planning, have at least a bachelor's level degree from an accredited university, have at least three years of financial planning industry experience, have no ethical violations, abide by the CFP Board code of conduct and practice standards, and pass an exam administered by the CFP Board with a historical pass rate slightly above 50 percent. Furthermore, the CFP® professional must satisfy thirty hours of continuing education approved by the CFP Board every two years.[1]

---

[1] Certified Financial Planner Board of Standards Inc. (CFP Board) owns the certification marks CFP®, CERTIFIED FINANCIAL PLANNER™, CFP® (with plaque design), and CFP® (with flame design) in the US, which it awards to individuals who successfully complete CFP Board's initial and ongoing certification requirements.

### Chartered Financial Analyst® (CFA®) designation[1]

The CFA credential focuses on portfolio management and financial analysis. Someone who has this designation is usually a financial analyst or institutional investment portfolio manager. However, some financial advisors who focus on investment management will obtain the CFA designation. Requirements to earn this designation include passing three rigorous exams, agreeing to uphold the CFA Institute Code of Ethics and Standards of Professional Conduct, having at least four years of qualified experience in investment decision-making, and becoming a member of the CFA Institute.

### Chartered Financial Consultant® (ChFC®)

An all-encompassing financial planning credential awarded by The American College of Financial Services. Advisors must complete eight college-level courses on several aspects of financial planning, including retirement planning, taxes, insurance, and estate planning. Furthermore, recipients of the ChFC® must have at least three years of financial planning industry experience, meet ethics standards, and agree to comply with The American College Code of Ethics and Procedures. Each ChFC® professional must also complete a minimum of thirty hours of continuing education every two years.

### Chartered Life Underwriter® (CLU®)

The premier credential in the insurance profession since 1927. Accredited by The American College of Financial Services, advisors who hold this designation possess an advanced understanding of risk management strategies for individuals and business owners. The average study time for the program is over four hundred hours. Each CLU® professional must also complete a minimum of thirty hours of continuing education

---

[1] CFA® and Chartered Financial Analyst® are registered trademarks owned by CFA Institute.

every two years, adhere to strict ethical standards, and meet extensive experience requirements, ensuring their knowledge is comprehensive and current.

A financial advisor can have a positive impact on your finances over decades. We encourage you to be selective when screening for this role and use the criteria outlined in the previous pages to filter out advisors who do not match what you are looking for. We also suggest keeping an open mind as you interview advisors, giving them a fair chance while holding them accountable for their answers and advice. If you are not sure where to begin your advisor search, asking your colleagues whether they have a recommended advisor can be a good place to start.

## In Summary

We have covered quite a distance since page 1. It may take a while to digest everything, so we boiled down the key takeaways to the checklist laid out over the next few pages.

☐ Net Worth Statement   Have you created your net worth statement
*See page 2.*                to get an idea of your assets and debts?

If not, then a blank template of this spreadsheet can be downloaded at: www.TheFinityGroup.com/Net-Worth-Statement.

☐ Monthly Spending Analysis *See page 5.*

Have you created your spending analysis to get an idea of your monthly cash flow?

If not, then a blank template of this spreadsheet can be downloaded at: www.TheFinityGroup.com/Monthly-Spending-Analysis.

☐ Emergency Reserve *See page 10.*

Do you have three to six months of fixed expenses set aside in a savings account that is safe, liquid, and free?

☐ Credit Card Use *See page 12.*

Do you have two or three credit cards that you use regularly and pay off entirely each month?

☐ Student Loans *See page 42.*

Do you have a plan for your student loans?

If your post-training employment may qualify for public service loan forgiveness, consider enrolling in one of the income-driven repayment plans so your payments count toward the 120 needed for forgiveness.

☐ Home Buying
*See page 69.*

Do you have plans to buy a home in the near future?

If so, then revisiting the Home Buying chapter and working through a detailed spending analysis can be appropriate next steps. Your ability to qualify for a physician loan means you can get a mortgage with far less than a 20 percent down payment.

☐ Insurance–Health
*See page 90.*

Is your health insurance set through your employer?

If you will be taking time off between the completion of your training and start of your next position, then you may need a short-term health insurance policy for you and any dependents to bridge the gap in employment.

☐ Insurance—
Malpractice
*See page 94.*

Is your malpractice insurance set through your employer?

If you are considering a job change, keep an eye out for how your next employer's malpractice insurance is structured. If claims-made, then are you or your employer responsible for obtaining tail insurance if your employment terminates?

☐ Insurance—Umbrella Liability
*See page 101.*

Have you secured an umbrella liability insurance policy?

If not, then it is generally advisable to secure at least $1 million to $3 million of umbrella liability insurance to protect your assets and income against large personal liability claims.

☐ Insurance—Disability
*See page 104.*

Have you secured an individual, own-occupation disability insurance policy?

If not, then consider looking into a policy that you can increase as your income rises in the years out of training. Keep in mind the downsides of employer group disability insurance include a limited benefit and less specific definition of disability (commonly reverting to "any occupation").

☐ Insurance—Life
*See page 118.*

Do you have any dependents who could experience a financial hardship if you were to pass away?

If so, then consider looking into term life insurance.

☐ Estate Planning
*See page 140.*

Have you had a will and other basic estate planning documents drafted?

If not, then consider meeting with an attorney to add these to your plan, especially if you are a parent.

☐ College Planning
*See page 161.*

Would you like to save for a child's college education?

If so, consider opening a 529 plan, while balancing your contributions with the rest of your plan.

☐ Employer Retirement Plan
*See page 235.*

Does your employer's retirement plan offer a matching contribution?

If so, are you contributing at least the minimum to receive the full amount of your employer's match? Is this invested in an allocation appropriate for your long-term time horizon?

☐ Roth IRA                    Are you in a position to fund a Roth IRA?
  *See page 236.*

                              If so, are you able to contribute directly
                              into your Roth IRA or does your income
                              require you to use the indirect "backdoor"
                              method of contributing to a nondeductible
                              IRA and making a Roth IRA conversion? If
                              the indirect method is required, remember
                              that there are special rules you must follow
                              to adhere to IRS guidelines for this strategy.

☐ Non-Retirement             If you are out of training and aiming
  Account                     to save at least 20 percent of your gross
  *See page 238.*             income toward retirement, do you need
                              to use a non-retirement account now that
                              contributions to your employer retirement
                              plan and Roth IRA are maximized?

☐ Asset Allocation           Are your investments appropriately
  *See page 268.*             allocated for their respective time horizons?

You can download a copy of this checklist at
www.TheFinityGroup.com/Planning-Checklist.

## Signing Off

We hope this book has given you a greater understanding of the topics
involved when building a financial plan, serving as a guide on the path
to financial independence. Your extensive training gives you a natural
late start to planning, so even the small steps of outlining your net worth,
cash flow, and goals will be a productive beginning. Some of the topics
we covered will be reserved for after residency or fellowship when your

budget is not as limited. Others can, and should, be prioritized during your training years.

While some of these checklist items can be completed on your own, the decision to manage your entire financial plan without professional guidance should not be made lightly, given its significance. Working with a financial advisor can range from occasional checkups to more frequent meetings and actual implementation, depending on how much responsibility you would like to keep or pass along. Either way, it can be beneficial to get a plan and trusted team in place for when you are able to save for later in life, rather than being ready to save and then having to find your financial partner. Your plan should be designed with an exceptional level of care, competence, and effort. Beyond saving you a vast amount of time, working with an advisor means you have a partner to help remove emotions from your financial decisions while keeping you focused on achieving your goals.

As we sign off, we would like to do so with how we began—with an invitation to share your thoughts. Our aim is to harness the collective feedback of the medical community to refine later editions into an improved educational resource. We welcome any suggestions by emailing info@thefinitygroup.com.

We wish you the best with your financial, personal, and professional endeavors.

---

**Key Takeaways**

The limited budget during your training years will require you to prioritize which planning areas you would like to focus on first, while others may take a back seat until your income increases. *Even if you cannot achieve all of your goals right away, beginning to work on the ones you can and outlining a plan for the rest should instill a sense of confidence.*

Doctors may seek the counsel of a financial advisor for a variety of reasons, including their expertise in *serving as your behavioral coach, saving you time when constructing your plan, and performing investment due diligence.*

The *financial planning process* includes an introductory "get to know each other" meeting, recommendations, and review meetings, as well as educational sessions as needed or desired.

If you are working with an advisor for direct management of your investments or for advice to carry out yourself, *it is important that the return your portfolio earns over a full market cycle puts you on track to achieve your objective*, not necessarily that your returns are higher than one index or another. Depending on your career stage and risk tolerance, certain indices may exhibit more or less volatility and expected returns than required to meet your goals.

Several criteria you can use to select a financial advisor include a fiduciary standard of duty, being independent, specialization in planning for doctors, their scope of services, and having an advanced designation.

*Fiduciary standard of duty.* A fiduciary standard of duty requires an advisor to work in your best interest and place your interests ahead of their own. You can verify an advisor is held to a fiduciary standard at the SEC's Investment Adviser Public Disclosure website.

*Independent.* An advisor is independent when they are not employed by or affiliated with a firm that manufactures their own insurance, investment, or other financial products for distribution. Independence removes bias from an advisor's recommendations with regard to which company's financial products to implement within your plan. You can verify whether an advisor is independent at FINRA's Broker Check website.

*Specializes in working with doctors.* Advisors who cater to doctors should be well versed in the many aspects of what makes a doctor's financial plan different from non-doctors. These include moonlighting income, the public service loan forgiveness program, and which disability insurance carriers provide an own occupation definition of disability and why this is important. They should be familiar with the transition from the meager finances of most residents and fellows to the comfortable lifestyle out of training. The reassurance that you can follow in your predecessors' footsteps and achieve a similar transformation should grow your confidence in an advisor and how your financial plan is progressing.

*Scope of services.* Some advisors take a comprehensive approach to planning and work with their clients on the many topics we have addressed. Other advisors limit the scope of their practice to only a few of these, which will require seeking guidance from another advisor on the areas not initially covered.

*Advanced designations.* Just as you have made a commitment to medicine, advisors show dedication to their profession by earning at least one advanced designation.

The summary *planning checklist* identifies several basic topics and can be used to begin building your financial plan.

# APPENDIX

# PORTFOLIO DESIGN IN RETIREMENT

Robert and Luke's dialogue in the Time Horizon Diversification chapter detailed the two main risks investors face, market volatility and inflation. Market volatility tends to be a greater concern over short-term time horizons and is protected against by holding asset classes that should exhibit low downward volatility in a stock market dip, such as cash and high credit quality bonds. Inflation is a larger concern with long-term time horizons, as small increases in the price level compound over decades. We protect against the rising cost of living by investing in asset classes that have historically well outpaced inflation over long periods, such as stocks. New doctors generally have at least twenty years until they will be taking distributions from their accounts and therefore have time to weather stock market declines, as we covered previously. This changes as doctors approach and enter retirement. Their portfolios are now pressured by short-term and long-term risks due to the immediacy of beginning withdrawals over a decades-long retirement. As with the management of your investments during your working years, your investment policy statement should clearly articulate how your retirement portfolio is to be managed. This appendix will walk through the concepts of portfolio design and management for a doctor near the end of his or her career.

## Sleeves and Buckets

We learned that a young doctor should skew her portfolio to equity holdings and have around 10 percent to 20 percent in bonds for diversification and rebalancing purposes, depending on her time horizon and risk tolerance. How does this change as she enters retirement? Should she have 30 percent in bonds? Fifty percent? Seventy percent? This depends on her situation, but one point we will make is that evaluating a retiree's aggregate portfolio can be misleading due to having both short-term and long-term investment time horizons. To better understand the concept of portfolio design in retirement, we suggest categorizing portions of the overall portfolio into sleeves (by asset allocation) and buckets (by groups of three retirement years). We will limit the detail on asset allocation to three broad investment categories—cash (white), bonds (light gray), and stock (dark gray).

□ Cash         ■ Bonds         ■ Stock

We will consider cash to have no downside volatility and a minimal investment return, such as the low rate of interest earned in your savings account. Bonds should provide a higher rate of return than cash with fairly stable value. We expect our stock holdings to exhibit the highest long-term rate of return and the greatest level of volatility. In our following scenario, we will examine a hypothetical thirty-year retirement of a $1.0 million portfolio. Bond interest and stock dividends will pay for some of our retiree's expenses, with the remainder of living costs covered by withdrawals of the portfolio's $1.0 million principal, which is expected to be fully depleted after thirty years.

*Sleeves*

**100%**

Our retiree's aggregate portfolio will be made of different asset allocation *sleeves*, which align with the risks she faces during different phases of retirement. The most threatening near-term risk is market volatility, prompting us to hold the first sleeve entirely in cash. While cash has the lowest rate of return of the three asset classes, it offers complete protection against an economic decline that could lower the value of her stock holdings, and perhaps bonds too. The average bear market has taken about 3.3 years to recover from, so holding three years of living expenses in cash will serve as a buffer against the less-severe market downturns.

BOND SLEEVE
RETIREMENT YEARS 4 - 6

**100%**

With three years of an economic recession protected against, we can now turn to the next notch up on the risk spectrum. Bonds can lose value, but price declines should be limited, particularly with higher credit quality bonds. Our bond sleeve offers fairly stable principal and regular interest payments that can help fund living expenses. Three additional years' worth of retirement withdrawals held in bonds further reassures against having to sell equity holdings at a loss in the event of a prolonged stock market decline.

## 40 / 60 SLEEVE
## RETIREMENT YEARS 7 - 12

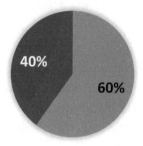

With the first six years of retirement living expenses held in cash and bonds, we now invest a portion of our next sleeve in stocks. Our 40 percent stock / 60 percent bond sleeve is still quite conservative with over half invested in bonds, but we now have exposure to the equity market and higher returns it can provide. Having the next six years of living expenses in this asset allocation offers a combination of principal stability and higher return potential.

## 80 / 20 SLEEVE
## RETIREMENT YEARS 13 - 30

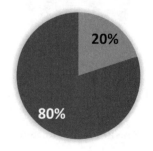

With the first twelve years accounted for, we can now turn our attention to protecting against the loss of purchasing power over the next eighteen. The cost of living could double by your later retirement years, which would cause rapid depletion of your assets if their real return (net of inflation) has not been high enough. For this reason, investing the rest of your assets in an 80 percent stock / 20 percent bond allocation could be appropriate. The risk of a stock market decline has been addressed, and we are now more concerned about inflation in the second half of retirement.

*Buckets*

With sleeves outlining broad asset allocations, *buckets* detail how these sleeves represent withdrawals throughout retirement. We will split our thirty-year planned retirement into ten buckets, each representing three years of principal distributions, as shown in the following graph.

Graph 1. Breakdown of retirement distributions
by buckets (by percent of total portfolio)

(Each bucket represents three years of principal withdrawals. Earlier retirement years face the risk of market volatility, which is why we hold more cash and bonds in buckets 1 and 2 (representing retirement years 1–3 and 4–6, respectively). Heavier weighting to stock in later retirement years acknowledges the risk that inflation poses.)

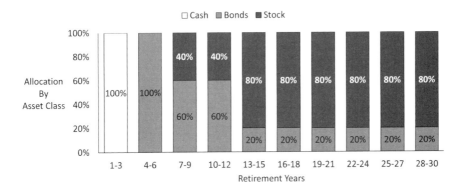

We can visualize the risk spectrum from another point of view if we look at each bucket's expected real, or inflation-adjusted, rate of return. Your portfolio's gross rate of return is the rate at which you see its value increase or decrease on your account statements. While this is insightful, we care more about how this translates into your ability to take distributions to fund your retirement as inflation increases the cost of living over the years, or as market volatility causes the value of your investments to fluctuate in the near term. The following graph illustrates our willingness to accept low, even negative, real rates of return in the short term in an effort to be well positioned against a stock market decline. Inflation risk grows with your time horizon, so buckets further out have a greater portion invested in equities to earn higher expected real rates of return. With our cash sleeve earning a 0 percent return before inflation and subtracting a 3 percent annual inflation estimate, we arrive at an inflation-adjusted return of negative 3 percent.[1] We will estimate the bond portion of your portfolio to earn a 5 percent gross annual return and the stock portion to earn 8 percent. Netting the rest of the buckets' gross returns against inflation, we see their real expected returns range from 2 percent to 4.4 percent. The aggregate portfolio's real rate of return is 3.3 percent, which can be thought of as the rate at which your investments are making you wealthier above the price level in the economy. This equates to roughly a 6.3 percent gross rate of return, similar to the 6 percent annual return we used in the distribution phase of Kate and Connor's projections in the Playing Catch-Up chapter.

---

[1] Subtracting the rate of inflation from an investment's gross rate of return is a simple way to estimate the real rate of return and will suffice for our purposes. More accurately, inflation-adjusted rates of return are calculated by this formula:

$$\text{Inflation-adjusted rate of return} = \frac{(1 + \text{gross rate of return})}{(1 + \text{inflation rate})} - 1$$

## Graph 2. Breakdown of retirement buckets
## by estimated real rates of return

(estimated inflation-adjusted rates of return for each bucket of retirement income with inflation at a constant 3 percent per year, cash earning a 0 percent gross annual return, bonds earning a 5 percent gross return, and stocks earning an 8 percent gross return)

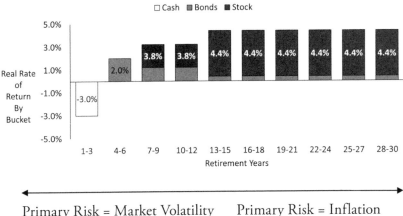

Primary Risk = Market Volatility    Primary Risk = Inflation

Translating our buckets into dollar amounts gives us a third graph, with each bucket now representing $100,000, or three years of retirement distributions.

## Graph 3. Breakdown of retirement distributions
## by buckets (by dollar amount)

(In thousands of dollars. Our $1.0 million portfolio is split into ten $100,000 buckets.)

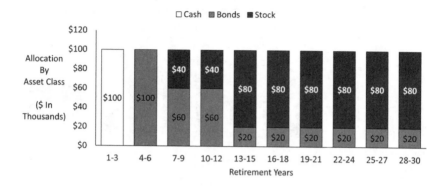

If we combine these buckets, we see that our aggregate portfolio holds 10 percent of its balance in cash, 34 percent in bonds, and 56 percent in stock. A positive year in the stock market will prompt us to sell some of our equity shares, harvesting the gains in the stock portion of our 40 / 60 and 80 / 20 sleeves to replenish the cash bucket that was partially depleted from the year's withdrawals.

## AGGREGATE PORTFOLIO

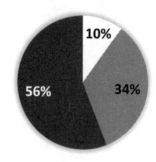

What happens if the stock market declines?

## A Market Dip

If history has given us any precedent, we would expect the stock market to have more positive years than negative ones. Equities would hardly be an enticing investment if they lost value more often than they gained. With that noted, it is common to experience an economic recession roughly once or twice a decade, which is often accompanied by a sizable decline in the stock market. We have so far viewed market dips as good buying opportunities and minor speedbumps that young investors can patiently wait out; however, this optimism does not extend into retirement. Preservation of capital is now our top priority, and we no longer have new earnings coming into the household. The following analysis examines what a significant stock market drop could look like on a retiree's portfolio and why properly laddered buckets should help protect against this event impairing your portfolio's ability to last through retirement.

In this example, we continue our previous allocation and start day one of retirement with a $1.0 million portfolio split into ten $100,000 buckets, as seen in graph 4. Economic conditions sour over the next few months, causing your stock holdings to lose 30 percent of their value. Your cash has neither gained nor lost value, and the value of your bonds has risen 5 percent as investors sought safer havens for their money, similar to what we saw in the bear market of 2008. These factors result in your portfolio falling to $849,000. A 15.1 percent loss early in retirement is not the start we are hoping for, but as we stressed before, focusing on your aggregate portfolio may be misleading. Viewing your portfolio as four sleeves and ten buckets tells a different story.

## Graph 4. Breakdown of retirement distributions
## by buckets after a stock market decline

(In thousands of dollars. No change to the value of cash, 5 percent increase in the value of bonds, and a 30 percent decrease in the value of stocks from graph 3.)

Cash Sleeve (Years 1–3 of Retirement Withdrawals). Your first three-year retirement income bucket represented by the Cash Sleeve has stayed even, giving you three years to allow the equity portion of your portfolio to recover.

Bond Sleeve (Years 4–6 of Retirement Withdrawals). Your Bond Sleeve is up 5 percent. Despite a drop in the stock market, *you have no loss of principal through the first six years of your planned withdrawals* (almost twice the length of the average stock market recovery).

40 / 60 Sleeve (Years 7–12 of Retirement Withdrawals). We do not see your first loss until we get to retirement year seven. Your 40 / 60 Sleeve has declined 9 percent from $200,000 to $182,000, yet this means only a decline of 3.25 percent through the first twelve years of retirement when combined with the previous two sleeves ($400,000 to $387,000).

80 / 20 Sleeve (Years 13–30 of Retirement Withdrawals). As we expect, we see the majority of your portfolio's loss occurring in the 80 / 20 Sleeve, falling 23 percent from $600,000 to $462,000. This sleeve accounts for $138,000, or 91.4 percent, of your total $151,000 loss.

## AGGREGATE PORTFOLIO
## (AFTER MARKET DECLINE)

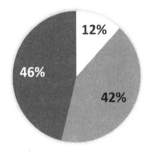

If circumstances permit, this could serve as a rebalancing opportunity due to the depressed price level of equities. Instead of a 56 percent stock / 34 percent bond split, we see equities under-weighted in your aggregate portfolio at 46 percent and bonds having grown to 42 percent. Selling shares in your bond funds and using these to purchase shares of equity mutual funds would realize the gain in bonds, buy stocks on the dip, and reset the overall asset allocation closer to what it was before the stock market decline.

**Appendix Summary**

New doctors have many years until the concepts presented in this appendix will be applicable. Nevertheless, it can be useful to glimpse into portfolio management as you approach and enter retirement. An aggregate view of your investments may not always give an accurate representation, particularly during stock market declines when the majority of your loss is concentrated in the last two-thirds of retirement years with little value lost in the first decade of planned withdrawals. Dividing your portfolio into sleeves and buckets can show which part protects against a stock market decline, while the other side serves as an inflation hedge with more equity exposure. Last, remember that your retirement may span almost as long as your career, so the management of your portfolio should not be static. It is just as important to rebalance your portfolio in retirement as it was during your accumulation years, the specifics of which should be outlined in your investment policy statement.

---

### Key Takeaways

Doctors entering or already in retirement see their portfolios pressured by *short-term and long-term risks* due to the immediacy of beginning withdrawals over a decades-long retirement.

Dividing your aggregate portfolio into *sleeves* (by asset allocation) and *buckets* (by retirement years) identifies how much of your money is earmarked for withdrawal throughout retirement, ranging from cash and bond buckets to majority-equity buckets.

Expect to have one or two economic recessions and significant stock market declines per decade. The majority of your portfolio's lost value will be attributed to your later buckets, giving you time to live off of cash and bond holdings and allowing your stock holdings to recover their value.

Periodic *rebalancing* can involve selling equity mutual funds to replenish your cash sleeve after a positive year in the stock market or using cash and bond proceeds to purchase additional shares in equity mutual funds after a poor year in the stock market.

---

# PROCEEDS TO CHARITY: WATER

All proceeds from the sale of this book are donated to charity: water, a nonprofit organization working to provide clean drinking water to people in developing nations. Since 2006, charity: water has funded over 28,000 water projects serving over eight million people with access to clean water.

# charity: water

## SUPPORTER

See their story at www.charitywater.org.

# ACKNOWLEDGMENTS

Bringing this book to life was not as easy or as quick as we initially thought. Its roots can be traced back to December 2014, when we decided to produce a simple yet comprehensive resource for doctors. Easier said than done, as the saying goes. Three and a half years later, we submitted our work to the publisher for review. We would like to thank several people whose contributions have helped make this book a reality.

We greatly appreciate those who reviewed earlier versions of our manuscript, including Julie Martin, Jim Pedroarena, Cary Weintraub, Peter Becker, Sarah Bonck, Aaron Bonck, and Anders Ramstad. This book is better because of you. We would also like to thank Zach Kill and Ian Hubbard for their time researching investment data. Evan White's work on the College Education Funding chapter helped shape that section. Corey Janoff, James Fox, Karl Rainer, Owen Chambers, and Jeff Pratt also contributed to various sections. We appreciate Don Pitsch and Ryan Kramer lending their tax expertise, particularly during the changing tax landscape of late 2017. Shawnee Smith helped with the arduous task of citing outside sources. Nathan Dasco did an excellent job designing the cover. Our team at Archway Publishing provided valuable insight and pushed this project through the finish line. Special thanks go to Virginia Morrel, Tim Fitch, and Nolan Estes for their unwavering support. Last but certainly not least, we would like to thank our clients and others in the medical community for their input. The content provided is largely a result of your feedback over the years.

# GLOSSARY

**#**

**529 College Savings Plans**—State-sponsored investment accounts used to save for higher education expenses.

**7 percent rule**—Helps differentiate between "good debts" below 7 percent and "bad debts" above 7 percent. Applies the concept of opportunity cost to advise we aggressively pay off debts with an interest rate above 7 percent before investing in the stock market, while debts below 7 percent should be balanced among other priorities in your financial plan.

**A**

**active share**—Measures how much of a portfolio's holdings overlap with the index. An active share of 0 percent indicates identical overlap with the benchmark, which is what we see in index funds. An active share of 100 percent indicates complete differentiation from the index with no overlap in holdings.

**actively managed mutual fund**—Mutual funds that aim to beat their benchmark on an absolute or risk-adjusted basis and have higher expenses than index funds.

**adjustable-rate mortgage (ARM)**—Mortgage structure with an interest rate that is fixed for an initial time period and then adjusts based on a measure that tracks interest rates.

**adjusted gross income (AGI)**—Gross income less adjustments (above-the-line deductions). It determines your eligibility for other tax deductions and is the income number used to calculate your monthly student loan payments under income-driven repayment methods.

**alternative minimum tax (AMT)**—An alternative tax system that ensures high earners with a large amount of deductions pay at least a minimum amount of tax.

**alternatives** (as an asset class)—Real estate, commodities, precious metals, and other asset classes that are not included within equity, fixed income, or cash equivalents.

**annuity**—Financial product sold by insurance companies with the option to structure for guaranteed income for life.

**appraiser**—Provides an assessment of the property's value when buying or refinancing a home.

**asset class**—A category of investments that shares distinct characteristics. The main asset classes are stocks (equities), bonds (fixed income), alternatives, and cash equivalents.

**asset location**—The strategy of considering both the tax characteristics of the account and the investment itself when deciding which securities to hold in each account to lower the amount of taxes and earn a higher after-tax return.

**auto insurance**—Insurance that covers a driver, their vehicle, and property damage that may occur in an accident. It also includes liability insurance for expenses arising out of injuries to passengers affected by an accident.

**B**

**behavioral finance**—A subfield of behavioral economics that studies why people make certain decisions regarding their finances, particularly with their investments.

**benchmark**—See index.

**beneficiary**—A person entitled to receive benefits from a life insurance policy, retirement account, or trust.

**bonds (fixed income)**—A debt security issued by a company or government entity.

> **corporate bonds**—Bonds issued by companies, rather than a government entity.
>
> **high-yield bonds**—Bonds issued by entities whose creditworthiness is below investment grade. High-yield bonds offer higher interest rates to compensate the investor for increased risk of default.
>
> **municipal bonds**—Bonds issued by states, counties, cities, and other municipalities. Their coupon payments receive preferential tax treatment and are received free of federal income tax.
>
> **treasury bonds**—Bonds issued by the US Treasury and backed by the full faith and credit of the US federal government. These bonds are seen as having virtually no credit risk and are therefore issued at lower interest rates.
>
> **taxable equivalent yield**—Interest rate a Treasury or corporate bond would need to provide for an investor to be indifferent between the taxable bond and municipal bond.
>
> **yield after tax**—Interest rate a municipal bond would need to provide for an investor to be indifferent between it and a taxable bond.

**bucket**—Concept of dividing a portfolio into groups of years when planning retirement withdrawals.

**business liability insurance**—Insurance that protects against claims not due to professional negligence but rather those resulting from an event on your business premises that causes bodily injury or property damage.

**buy-sell agreement**—Contracts between owners of a business that outline how a business will be operated and owned by the remaining parties in the event of a disability, death, retirement, or other change in circumstance of one of the owners.

## C

**capital gain**—The difference between an asset's basis (how much you paid to acquire it and any adjustments since then) and the amount you received when you disposed the asset.

**capital gain taxes**—Tax levied on the gain of a capital asset. Capital gain taxes are not assessed until a taxable event realizes the capital gain.

**CERTIFIED FINANCIAL PLANNER™ (CFP® professional)**—Advanced designation a financial advisor may obtain. Focuses on comprehensive financial planning.

**Chartered Financial Analyst® (CFA®) designation**—Advanced designation a financial advisor, financial analyst, or other investment professional may obtain. Focuses on investment analysis and portfolio management.

**Chartered Financial Consultant® (ChFC®)**—Advanced designation a financial advisor may obtain. Focuses on comprehensive financial planning.

**Chartered Life Underwriter® (CLU®)**—Advanced designation a financial advisor or insurance agent may obtain. Focuses on insurance planning.

**compound growth**—Earned on the principal balance as well as all appreciation from past periods and results in exponential growth.

**Consumer Price Index for All Urban Consumers (CPI-U)**—A common inflation measure. Tracks the change in price level over time.

**contingent beneficiary**—Beneficiary who is entitled to receive assets from a life insurance policy, retirement account, or trust only if all primary beneficiaries are deceased.

**contract** (by way of passing assets upon death)—Process by which life insurance proceeds and retirement accounts pass to designated beneficiaries when the insured or account owner dies. This happens outside of probate, but these amounts may be included in the deceased's estate.

**conventional mortgage**—Loans under $453,100 (in most regions) that conform to established guidelines. Conventional loans do not require as extensive underwriting as jumbo loans.

**correlation**—Specifies the degree to which the values of two variables fluctuate together.

**correlation coefficient**—Quantifies the similarity of values between two variables with a range of +1.0 (perfectly positive relationship) to 0 (no relationship) to -1.0 (perfectly negative relationship). Quantifies the level of diversification between asset classes.

**coupon payments**—Bond interest payments.

**Coverdell Education Savings Accounts (ESAs)**—Account used to save for educational expenses. Terms are more limited than 529 plans.

**credits** (tax)—Direct dollar-for-dollar reductions in taxes owed.

# D

**debt-to-income ratio (DTI)**—The ratio of monthly debt payments over monthly gross income. Lenders generally like to see a DTI under 43 percent to qualify for the best mortgage rates available.

**deductions (standard and itemized)**—Adjustments made to gross income and adjusted gross income that lower your taxable income and result in less taxes owed.

**deferment**—Deferring, or delaying, payments on your student loans until a later date because of additional training.

**defined benefit plans**—Employer retirement plans that define the benefit paid to an employee. A common example is a pension, which promises employees a stipend throughout retirement based on their length of service and income level.

**defined contribution plans**—Employer retirement plans that specify how much an employer or employee may contribute to the plan but do not define how much the final benefit will be.

**disability insurance**—Type of insurance that pays the insured a monthly benefit if unable to work.
> **short-term**—Disability insurance characterized by short waiting and benefit periods. Often begins paying a benefit immediately or after one to two weeks, but the benefit may only last a few months.
> **long-term**—Disability insurance that may pay a benefit for many years, such as to age sixty-five.

**Social Security**—Provided by the government. Contains restrictive contract language and is more difficult to qualify for a benefit compared to other sources of coverage.

**group**—Disability insurance provided by an employer or association.

**individual**—Disability insurance policy an individual owns outside of their employer or association.

**definition of disability**—The contract language within the policy that must be satisfied for the insured to qualify as being disabled.

**any occupation definition of disability**—You are only considered disabled if unable to perform any gainful occupation you may reasonably be suited to do based on your education, training, or experience.

**own occupation definition of disability**—You are considered disabled if you are unable to perform the material and substantial duties of your own occupation.

**residual disability**—Rider that provides a partial benefit if partially disabled. Benefit amount is often based on percentage of income lost from pre-disability earnings.

**future increase option (FIO)**—An additional benefit amount you can purchase to add to your base monthly benefit without having to repeat health screening. This allows you to increase your benefit periodically as your income rises over your career, even if you have had an adverse change in health.

**inflation protection (cost of living adjustment)**—Rider that increases your monthly benefit if disabled over multiple years.

**catastrophic benefit**—Rider that pays an extra monthly benefit if severely disabled.

**business overhead expense (BOE)**—Business form of disability insurance that pays a benefit to help cover operating expenses if the owner or another significant employee is unable to support the business due to a disability.

**key person**—Business form of disability insurance that is meant to replace the income lost from a disability to a key employee.

**discretionary income**—Adjusted gross income (AGI) minus 150 percent of the poverty level for your family size for all income-driven repayment methods.

**disposition effect**—A phenomenon in which investors prefer to sell stocks whose value has appreciated since they were purchased (winners) and continue holding stocks that have decreased in value (losers). Deemed to be a blunder due to its tax inefficiency of maximizing realized capital gains while not harvesting capital losses to offset them.

**dividend**—Payment of a company's excess profits to its shareholders.

# E

**earnest money**—A deposit of money made by the home buyer into an escrow account.

**escrow**—Escrow may refer to the neutral third party who holds the home buyer's down payment and other settlement costs before releasing these to the seller. The term escrow may also refer to the account used to hold this money, known as an escrow account.

**emergency reserve account**—Money set aside for unexpected costs that come up from time to time. Aim for three to six months' worth of fixed expenses.

**estate taxes**—Part of the unified transfer tax system, which taxes assets gifted while alive and those transferred upon death.

**exchange-traded funds (ETFs)**—Pooled investments that allow investors to buy into a diversified portfolio. They are structured differently than mutual funds, and this allows them to be more tax efficient, particularly during the process of selling, or redeeming, the ETF.

**exclusion on gain from the sale of primary residency**—If you have lived in your home as your primary residence for two out of the last five years, then you can exclude $250,000 of gain from the sale. Married taxpayers can each claim the exclusion, avoiding taxes on up to $500,000 of gain. Section 121 of the Internal Revenue Code.

**expense ratio**—The fee mutual funds and ETFs charge shareholders.

**extended reporting coverage**—See tail Insurance.

**F**

**FHA Loan**—Mortgages that are insured by the Federal Housing Administration.

**FICA tax**—A tax on income that funds Social Security. Named after the Federal Insurance Contributions Act.

**FICO score**—A commonly used measure to assess a borrower's creditworthiness. Ranges from 300 (poor credit) to 850 (best credit).

**fiduciary duty**—Acting in the interest of someone other than yourself.

**filing status** (tax)—Determines which set of tax brackets and deduction amounts apply to your tax return. Single, Married Filing Jointly, Married Filing Separately, and Head of Household are the four tax filing statuses.

**financial advisor**—A professional who works with individuals, families, and businesses to achieve their financial goals. May also recommend strategies or products to protect the client and their financial plan from unexpected developments.

**fixed-rate mortgage**—Mortgage whose interest rate does not change throughout the loan term.

**flexible spending account (FSA)**—Account used to save for health care costs on a tax-deductible basis. Amount contributed but not used by the end of the year is forfeited.

## G

**gifting assets**—A gift is made when money or an asset is transferred to someone else for less than the full value of consideration received by the giver, or donor.

> **annual gift tax exclusion**—Each donor is allowed a $15,000 annual gift tax exclusion per recipient.
>
> **charitable deduction**—Unlimited deductions for a gift made to a qualified charity.
>
> **marital deduction**—Unlimited deductions for a gift made to a spouse who is a US citizen. The gift is not a terminable interest (ends at a certain event).
>
> **taxable gift**—The amount of a gift that exceeds the annual exclusion and does not qualify for the unlimited marital or charitable deductions.

**global financial crisis of 2008**—Severe economic recession and significant decline in the stock market due to a housing and mortgage crisis, which caused a liquidity crisis in the financial system.

**good faith estimate (GFE)**—A legal disclosure lenders must provide you that lists a potential loan amount, interest rate, and all fees involved with the mortgage.

**grantor**—Creates a trust and gifts assets into it.

**gross income**—Total income earned throughout the year.

# H

**health professional shortage areas (HPSAs)**—Areas in which there is a shortage of health care professionals. Some HPSAs may have student loan repayment plans or other programs that incentivize doctors to practice in the area.

**health savings account (HSA)**—An account used to save for future health care costs with tax advantages.

**homeowners insurance**—Insurance that reimburses you for damage to your home, unless the loss is due to an excluded risk, such as an earthquake or flood.

# I

**income tax (ordinary)**—Tax on ordinary income earned.

**income in respect of a decedent (IRD)**—Certain assets that do not qualify for a step up in basis upon the owner's death. These include IRAs, qualified retirement plans, and annuities.

**income replacement ratio**—The gross (before tax) income received from Social Security divided by gross preretirement income.

**independent advisor**—An advisor is independent when neither they nor their registered investment advisor (the entity that directly oversees their investment activity and transactions) are directly or indirectly affiliated with an insurance carrier or investment company that manufactures financial products, underwrites securities, creates research, or engages in investment banking. In addition, an independent advisor is not an employee of an investment or insurance firm that creates their own financial products for distribution.

**index**—A formal grouping of similar stocks, bonds, or securities in another asset class that serves as a benchmark for how an investment category is performing.

> **Bloomberg Barclays U.S. Aggregate Bond Index**—Index that tracks the performance of the overall bond market in the United States.
>
> **Morgan Stanley Capital International Europe, Australasia and Far East (MSCI EAFE)**—Index that tracks the performance of stocks whose companies are based in developed nations outside of the United States.
>
> **Morgan Stanley Capital International Emerging Markets (MSCI EM)**—Index that tracks the performance of stocks whose companies are based in developing nations outside of the United States.
>
> **Russell 2000**—Index that tracks the performance of stocks of small and midsized companies based in the United States.
>
> **Standard and Poor's (S&P 500)**—Index that tracks the performance of stocks of about five hundred of the largest companies based in the United States.

**index fund**—Passively managed mutual funds whose underlying holdings and performance aim to mirror that of the index that the fund tracks.

**individual retirement account (IRA)**—Type of retirement account individuals can invest within that provides tax-deductible contributions, tax-deferred growth, and distributions are taxed as income.

> **inherited IRA**—IRA inherited from someone who has passed away. Special distribution rules apply based on the deceased's age and beneficiary's relationship to the deceased (spouse or non- spouse).

**inflation**—The increase in the cost of goods and services over time.

**inspector**—Performs a thorough evaluation of the property and will provide an assessment of the home's general condition during a home purchase.

**Internal Revenue Code**—The tax code. Rules and regulations that govern the taxation of income, capital gains, retirement accounts, estates, gifts, and everything else tax related.

**investing**—The act of putting out money in order to gain a profit.

## J

**jumbo mortgage**—Loans above $453,100 (in most regions).

## K

## L

**life insurance**—Insurance that pays a death benefit to a beneficiary or beneficiaries if the insured passes away.

> **term life insurance**—Temporary life insurance that provides protection for a certain period of time, after which the policy expires if the insured is still alive. If the insured dies during the term period, the death benefit is paid to the beneficiaries.
>
> **permanent life insurance**—Life insurance that is designed to last for one's entire life and pay a death benefit when the insured passes away. Cost of insurance is higher than term life insurance due to higher probability of a death benefit being paid.
>
> **cash value**—Reserve account in a permanent life insurance policy that holds the cash value, or extra amount paid above the cost of insurance. The cash value can earn interest, or gain or lose value, depending on the type of policy used, and can be accessed during the insured's lifetime with certain tax advantages.

**whole life insurance**—A form of permanent life insurance characterized by a fixed death benefit amount and fixed monthly premium.

**universal life insurance**—A form of permanent life insurance characterized by flexible death benefit and premium amounts.

**variable universal life insurance**—A form of permanent life insurance characterized by the ability to invest the cash value in subaccounts, which are similar to mutual funds.

**indexed universal life insurance**—A form of permanent life insurance whose cash value gains value based on the performance of an index (such as the S&P 500) with a cap and floor on the amount of interested credited within a single period.

**business uses**—Business uses of life insurance include as collateral for business loans, protection for key employees, executive compensation plans, and business succession planning.

**lifetime gift and estate tax exemption**—Each person is allowed a $11.2 million lifetime exemption in 2018 to offset taxable gifts and, upon death, the amount of the deceased's taxable estate. The amount of the lifetime exemption was recently increased by the Tax Cuts and Jobs Act of 2017 and may change again in the future.

**living will**—A type of medical directive that declares what medical treatment, if any, may be used in the case of terminal illness or other life-threatening conditions in which the patient becomes incapacitated or unconscious.

**loan officer**—An employee of a bank or other lending institution that assists you in securing a loan.

**loan underwriter**—An employee of a bank or other lending institution who assesses your creditworthiness and approves your loan.

**loan-to-value (LTV)**—The ratio of a home's mortgage balance (and any home equity debt) divided by the home's value.

**loss aversion**—Feeling more displeasure from a loss than happiness from an equivalent gain.

## M

**malpractice insurance**—Professional liability insurance that covers the costs of dealing with a claim. If the claim results in an indemnity payment, then malpractice insurance will pay the amount owed, up to the limit of the malpractice policy.

> **occurrence**—Covers claims that occur when the malpractice policy is in force, regardless of when the claim is filed.
> **claims-made**—Covers claims only if you are continuously covered by the same company when both the act happened and the claim is filed.

**market capitalization**—The metric of choice for calculating a company's size, arrived at by multiplying the number of shares of stock outstanding by the stock's current price.

**Monte Carlo analysis**—A statistical modeling technique that produces a range of how possible outcomes may be distributed based not only on multiple variables but also on the probability of those variables occurring at different values.

**monthly spending analysis**—A monthly cash flow statement that details income and expenses.

**mortgage broker**—An independent broker who has access to many lenders and can help you shop the loan market to obtain financing for a home purchase.

**mutual fund**—A collection of individual securities pooled together and managed as a portfolio by the portfolio manager and his or her team of analysts and traders.

# N

**net worth statement**—A document that lists your assets (what you own) and subtracts your liabilities (what you owe) to provide an idea of your financial standing at a point in time.

**nominal rate of return**—Absolute rate of return on investments, not adjusted for inflation.

**non-retirement account**—Type of investment account that does not provide the tax advantages of formal retirement accounts but also does not have any contributions or withdrawal limitations.

# O

**operation of law**—Way of passing assets to another party upon death without additional instructions needed. Avoids probate. An example is property held in joint tenancy with right of survivorship, which automatically passes to surviving joint tenants.

**opportunity cost**—Tradeoffs with limited resources, such as time or money. The cost of the most beneficial alternative that was not chosen because a different option is pursued.

# P

**pension**—Employer retirement plans usually structured as defined benefit plans that promise employees a stipend throughout retirement based on their length of service and income level.

**physician loan (doctor mortgage)**—Special mortgages structured for doctors that require less than a 20 percent down payment and do not have private mortgage insurance.

**points (discount points)**—One point is 1 percent of the mortgage value. Discount points refer to paying an additional amount upfront to lower the interest rate of the loan.

**portfolio rebalancing**—Adjusting your portfolio's asset allocation to be in line with its target allocation.

**post-tax retirement accounts**—Roth IRAs, Roth 401(k)s, and Roth 403(b)s. Contributions are made with money that has already been taxed, investments grow tax-deferred, and qualified withdrawals are tax-free.

**power of attorney**—Authorizes someone else to act on your behalf, often used if you are incapacitated and cannot make decisions on your own.

**preapproval**—The process of getting preapproved for a mortgage, in which your credit report is formally checked and income documents are reviewed. Results in a preapproval letter being issued by a lender.

**prepaid tuition plans**—Allow you to buy credits today to be applied to future tuition costs.

**prequalification**—Informal process done with a lender to receive an estimate of the mortgage you may be able to qualify for (amount and interest rate). Prequalification does not run your credit report and does not guarantee you will be approved for a loan with the characteristics in the estimate. This is an optional step in the mortgage process.

**pretax retirement accounts**—Traditional IRAs, 401(k)s, 403(b)s, and other non-Roth retirement accounts. Contributions are tax-deductible and made on a pretax basis, investments grow tax deferred, and withdrawals are taxed as income.

**price volatility**—Type of investment risk. Buying an investment and ending with less than you began with.

**principal, interest, taxes, and insurance (PITI)**—The components of a total monthly mortgage payment.

**private mortgage insurance (PMI)**—A form of insurance that reimburses the lender in the event the borrower defaults on their loan. Avoided with physician loans.

**probate**—The process of distributing the deceased's assets that fall within their probate estate. Includes assets passing by a will.

**prospect theory**—A theory for decision making that incorporates human tendencies and challenged the traditional economic decision model based on a rational agent.

**public service loan forgiveness (PSLF)**—Federal loan forgiveness program in which the balance of a borrower's federal Direct Loans are discharged tax-free after making 120 qualifying monthly payments.

# Q

# R

**rating agencies**—Moody's Investors Service and Standard & Poor's are the two major bond rating agencies. If a bond issuer's creditworthiness deteriorates enough, they will rate the entity below investment grade.

**real estate agent (Realtor)**—Represents you when buying or selling a home.

**renters insurance**—Reimburses you for the loss of property and can include a liability insurance component too.

**real rate of return (inflation-adjusted rate of return)**—Rate of return earned on investments above inflation.

**required minimum distributions (RMDs)**—Owners of pretax retirement accounts must begin taking required minimum distributions (RMDs) from their accounts by April 1 of the year following the year of their seventy and a half birthday.

**Roth IRA**—Type of post-tax retirement account. Contributions are made with after-tax money, investments grow tax deferred, and qualified withdrawals are tax-free. Contribution limits apply based on the owner's income.

# S

**security**—A tradeable financial asset, such as a stock, bond, or mutual fund.

**simple growth**—Earned on the principal balance only and results in linear growth.

**sleeve**—Concept of dividing a portfolio into groups by asset allocation when planning retirement withdrawals.

**Social Security**—A government program designed to supplement personal savings and act as a safety net if other income sources are depleted.

**SPIVA scorecard**—Short for S&P Indices Versus Active. A semiannual report analyzing the performance of actively managed funds against their respective benchmarks.

**step up in basis**—If a relative or friend were to pass away and leave a capital asset to you, its basis will be adjusted to fair market value at the date of death. Eliminates any unrealized gain that accrued before death.

**student loans**—Loans taken out to pay for educational costs.
　　**subsidized**—No interest is charged before a loan is in repayment.

**unsubsidized**—Interest accrues immediately, and capitalizes annually, adding to the original loan balance.

**standard ten-year**—Level payments calculated as a function of the loan balance, interest rate, and repayment term over 120 months.

**extended twenty-five-year**—Level payments calculated as a function of the loan balance, interest rate, and repayment term over three hundred months.

**graduated**—Payments begin low and gradually increase over a ten- to thirty-year period.

**refinancing**—Changing the interest rate on your student loans to a lower rate with a private lender.

**income-driven repayment (IDR)**—Student loan repayment methods in which the borrower's payments are based on their discretionary income, rather than their loan balance and interest rate.

**income-contingent repayment (ICR)**—IDR method in which payments are based on 20 percent of discretionary income. Qualifying repayment method for PSLF.

**income-based repayment (IBR)**—IDR method in which payments are based on 15 percent of discretionary income. Qualifying repayment method for PSLF.

**income-based repayment (IBR) for new borrowers**—IDR method in which payments are based on 10 percent of discretionary income. Qualifying repayment method for PSLF.

**Pay As You Earn (PAYE)**—IDR method in which payments are based on 10 percent of discretionary income. Qualifying repayment method for PSLF.

**Revised Pay As You Earn (REPAYE)**—IDR method in which payments are based on 10 percent of discretionary income. Qualifying repayment method for PSLF.

**National Institutes of Health Loan Repayment Program (NIH LRP)**—If you commit to at least two years of conducting qualified research funded by a domestic nonprofit organization or US federal, state, or local government entity, the NIH may repay up to $35,000 of your qualified student loan debt each year.

**stocks (equity)**—Shares of ownership in a company.
    **growth**—Growth stocks aim to provide shareholder value by pursuing more aggressive plans to grow their size and profitability. Instead of distributing their extra profits to shareholders, these companies reinvest their earnings to create new products through research and development, improve their manufacturing capabilities, or expand into a new market.
    **value**—Value stocks often pay a regular dividend to their shareholders, passing through the company's excess profits to their owners. They may also exhibit lower price valuations compared to growth stocks (as measured by the PE ratio, or other valuation metrics).

**systematic risk**—Risk that is found across all companies that operate in the same market. Cannot be eliminated by holding other stocks.

# T

**tail insurance**—Extends the period over which a claims-made malpractice insurance policy is in effect to cover prior acts once have moved on from an employer.

**target allocation**—The proportion of each asset class held in your portfolio. Largely determined by the investor's time horizon and risk tolerance.

**tax deductible contributions**—Allows an investor to deduct the amount contributed into a pretax retirement plan from his or her gross income for that year.

**tax-deferred growth**—Allows an investor to avoid paying taxes on dividends, interest, or realized capital gains on your investments throughout the year.

**taxable income**—Income that is applied to tax brackets to determine tax liability.

**time horizon**—The time from now until a point in the future when you need to sell your investments for cash to spend. Is a large driver of how your asset allocation should be structured.

**trust**—A separate legal entity that holds assets, manages them, and distributes them to beneficiaries according to instructions outlined within the trust document.

> **revocable**—Allows the grantor to revoke or change the trust document while alive. Becomes irrevocable at the grantor's death and is then managed by the trustee on behalf of the beneficiaries.
> **irrevocable**—Cannot be modified once established. Causes the grantor to permanently give up control of the trust document and property it holds.
> **living (inter vivos)**—Established while the grantor is alive. Trust assets avoid probate.
> **testamentary**—Created at the grantor's death through instructions listed in their will. Trust assets are subject to probate.
> **special needs**—A trust designed to provide care for a dependent with special needs.

**trustee**—Manages trust assets, pays taxes, and facilitates distributions to trust beneficiaries.

# U

**UGMAs (Uniform Gift to Minor Act) and UTMAs (Uniform Transfer to Minor Act)**—Custodial accounts that allow an adult to manage this investment account for the benefit of a minor. The minor assumes full control of the account upon reaching legal age of majority in their state (typically eighteen to twenty-one).

**umbrella liability insurance**—Personal liability insurance that pays a benefit in the event that the liability limits on the insured's underlying auto, homeowners, or renters insurance policies are exceeded.

**unsystematic risk**—Risk specific to a company. Can be diversified away by holding stocks of other companies.

# V

**VA Loan**—Special mortgages available to those who have served in the military.

# W

**will**—An estate planning document that conveys the wishes of the deceased with regard to how they would like their assets distributed upon death and care for minor children.

# X

# Y

**yield to maturity (YTM)**—The internal rate of return an investor will earn if they buy a bond at the current market price and hold it until maturity with all coupon and principal payments made on time.

# Z

# ENDNOTES

## Introduction

**Only 11.4 percent of the population**: "Educational Attainment in the United States: 2017," United States Census Bureau, last modified December 11, 2017, https://www.census.gov/data/tables/2017/demo/education-attainment/cps-detailed-tables.html.

**The average American who retires today at sixty-two**: Lisa Greenwald, Craig Copeland, and Jack VanDerhei, "The 2017 Retirement Confidence Survey—Many Workers Lack Retirement Confidence and Feel Stressed About Retirement Preparations," EBRI Issue Brief, no. 431 (Employee Benefit Research Institute, March 21, 2017).

**The average student loan balance of a doctor recently graduated from medical school is around $190,000**: "Medical Student Education: Debt, Costs, and Loan Repayment Fact Card," Association of American Medical Colleges (October 2017), https://members.aamc.org/iweb/upload/2017%20Debt%20Fact%20Card.pdf.

**Median doctor salaries of $217,000 (primary care) and $316,000 (specialists)**: "Medscape Physician Compensation Report, 2017," Medscape, accessed April 2, 2018, https://login.medscape.com/login/sso/getlogin?urlCache=aHR0cHM6Ly93d3cubWVkc2NhcGUuY29tL3NsaWRlc2hvdy9jb21wZW5zYXRpb24tMjAxNy1vdmVydmlldy02MDA4NTQ3&ac=401#2.

**Top 5 percent of households**: "Historical Income Tables: Households," United States Census Bureau, last modified August 10, 2017, https://www.census.gov/data/tables/time-series/demo/income-poverty/historical-income-households.html.

**Nearly four to six times the national average**: "2012–2016 American Community Survey 5-Year Estimates," American FactFinder, accessed April 2, 2018, https://factfinder.census.gov/faces/tableservices/jsf/pages/productview.xhtml?src=bkmk.

## Personal Finance Basics

**About $3 trillion of cash in the US economy, and the total amount of credit is estimated at $50 trillion**: Dalio, Ray. "How The Economic Machine Works." Economic Principles. https://www.economicprinciples.org/economic-principles/index.html (accessed April 4, 2017).

## Tax Basics

**Generally, you must report all income except income that is exempt from tax by law**: "1040 Instructions 2017," Department of the Treasury, Internal Revenue Service, 2017, https://www.irs.gov/pub/irs-pdf/i1040gi.pdf.

**Highest Historical Federal Income Tax Rate**: "Historical Individual Income Tax Parameters," Tax Policy Center, last modified October 30, 2017, http://www.taxpolicycenter.org/statistics/historical-individual-income-tax-parameters.

**Congressional Budget Office report**: Kevin Perese, "The distribution of Household Income and Federal Taxes, 2013," Congress of the United States Congressional Budget Office Publication 51361, Washington, DC, 2016.

**Highest Historical Long-Term Capital Gain Tax Rate**: "Historical Capital Gaines and Taxes," Tax Policy Center, last modified May 4, 2017, http://www.taxpolicycenter.org/statistics/historical-capital-gains-and-taxes.

**Highest Historical Long-Term Capital Gain Tax Rate**: "Historical Capital Gaines and Taxes," Tax Policy Center, last modified May 4, 2017, http://www.taxpolicycenter.org/taxfacts/displayafact.cfm?Docid=161.

## Debt Management

**The S&P 500 Index, has had an average annual return of 11.9 percent per year since 1937**: S&P Global. "S&P 500®." S&P Dow Jones Indices, LLC, accessed February 7, 2018, https://us.spindices.com/indices/equity/sp-500.

## Student Loans

**The average student loan balance of a doctor recently graduated from medical school is around $190,000**: "Medical Student Education: Debt, Costs, and Loan Repayment Fact Card," Association of American Medical Colleges (October 2017), https://members.aamc.org/iweb/upload/2017%20Debt%20Fact%20Card.pdf.

**Over $1.5 trillion of student loans outstanding**: "Student Loans Owned and Securitized, Outstanding (SLOAS)," Board of Governors of the Federal Reserve System (US), accessed July 2, 2018, https://fred.stlouisfed.org/series/SLOAS.

**Approximately 75 percent of doctors who graduated medical school in 2017 owed student loans**: "Medical Student Education: Debt, Costs, and Loan Repayment Fact Card," Association of American Medical Colleges (October 2017), https://members.aamc.org/iweb/upload/2017%20Debt%20Fact%20Card.pdf.

**Average tuition for a year of undergraduate education**: "Average Estimated Undergraduate Budgets, 2017–18," CollegeBoard, accessed March 19, 2018, https://trends.collegeboard.org/college-pricing/ figures-tables/average-estimated-undergraduate-budgets-2017-18.

**Average tuition for a year of medical education**: "Tuition and Student Fees," Association of American Medical Colleges, last modified October 2017, https://www.aamc.org/data/tuitionandstudentfees/.

**Room and board costs are estimated at another $10,000 to $15,000 per year**: "Average Estimated Undergraduate Budgets, 2017-18," CollegeBoard, accessed March 21, 2018, https://trends.collegeboard. org/college-pricing/figures-tables/average-estimated-undergraduat e-budgets-2017-18.

**Nearly half (46 percent) of recent medical school graduates were planning to enroll in one of the loan forgiveness programs**: "Medical Student Education: Debt, Costs, and Loan Repayment Fact Card," Association of American Medical Colleges (October 2017), https:// members.aamc.org/iweb/upload/2017%20Debt%20Fact%20Card.pdf.

**Michael's estimated monthly payment**: "Repayment Estimator," United States Department of Education, accessed March 21, 2018, https://studentloans.gov/myDirectLoan/mobile/repayment/ repaymentEstimator.action#view-repayment-plans.

**Defines an eligible employer**: "Public Service Loan Forgiveness: Employment Certification Form," United States Department of Education, accessed March 21, 2018, https://studentaid.ed.gov/sa/sites/ default/files/public-service-employment-certification-form.pdf.

**Montana Rural Physician Incentive Program**: "Montana Rural Physician Incentive Program," Montana University System, accessed March 21, 2018, http://mus.edu/Prepare/Pay/Loans/MRPIP.asp.

**AAMC website for loan repayment, forgiveness, and scholarship programs**: "Loan Repayment/Forgiveness and Scholarship Programs," Association of American Medical Colleges, accessed March 21, 2018, https://services.aamc.org/ fed_loan_pub/index.cfm?fuseaction=public.welcome&CFID=1&CFT OKEN=61A8BB1C-9880-FA01-0D9DBC2B43939F20.

## Professional Liability Insurance

A *New England Journal of Medicine* article: Anupam B. Jena, Seth Seabury, Darius Lakdawalla, and Amitabh Chandra, "Malpractice Risk According to Physician Specialty," *New England Journal of Medicine* 365 (2011): 629–636, doi:10.1056/NEJMsa1012370.

## Life insurance

**The online calculator at LifeHappens.org**: "Calculate Your Needs," Life Happens, accessed March 21, 2018, https://www.lifehappens.org/ insurance-overview/life-insurance/calculate-your-needs/.

**Dividend rates on whole life policies have generally been decreasing over the past few decades**: "Dividend Interest Rates for 2015," M Financial Group (July 2015), http://www.mbl-advisors.com/resources/ Dividend%20Interest%20Rates%20White%20Paper.pdf.

**Universal life interest crediting rates have decreased steadily over the past couple of decades**: Peter C. Katt, "History of Cash Value Life Insurance and Implications for Existing Policies," *Journal of Financial Planning*, accessed March 21, 2018, https://www.onefpa.org/journal/ Pages/AUG15-History-of-Cash-Value-Life-Insurance-and-Implicatio ns-for-Existing-Policies.aspx.

**Estate Planning**

**Accenture estimates**: "The 'Greater' Wealth Transfer: Capitalizing on the Intergenerational Shift in Wealth," Accenture (2015), https://www. accenture.com/t20160505T020205Z__w__/us-en/_acnmedia/PDF-16/ Accenture-CM-AWAMS-Wealth-Transfer-Final-June2012-Web-Version. pdf#zoom=50.

**College Saving**

**Average tuition and fees**: "Average Estimated Undergraduate Budgets, 2017–18," CollegeBoard, accessed March 7, 2018, https:// trends.collegeboard.org/college-pricing/figures-tables/average-estimate d-undergraduate-budgets-2017-18.

**Tuition and fees increase at an average annual rate**: Jennifer Ma, Sandy Baum, Matea Pender, and Meredith Welch, "Trends in College Pricing 2016," CollegeBoard (2016), https://trends.collegeboard.org/ sites/default/files/2016-trends-college-pricing-web_0.pdf.

**Inflation averaged 1.8 percent per year**: US Bureau of Labor Statistics. Databases, Tables & Calculators by Subject Consumer Price Index - All Urban Consumers, U.S. Bureau of Labor Statistics, accessed February 20, 2017, https://data.bls.gov/timeseries/ CUUR0000SA0?output_view=pct_12mths. Web. 20 Feb. 2017.

**Historically been higher than the increase in the general cost of living**: Ma et al., "Trends in College Pricing 2016."

**Averaging about $15,000 per year**: "Average Estimated Undergraduate Budgets, 2017-18," CollegeBoard, accessed March 7, 2018. https:// trends.collegeboard.org/college-pricing/figures-tables/average-estimate d-undergraduate-budgets-2017-18.

**Room and board costs have historically risen at lower rates than tuition inflation**: Ma et al., "Trends in College Pricing 2016."

**SavingForCollege.com's 529 institution eligibility search**: "Is your institution 529 eligible?" Savingforcollege.com, accessed March 7, 2018. http://www.savingforcollege.com/eligible_institutions/.

**Prepaid tuition plans have started to limit new enrollment or have even shut down**: "Prepaid Tuition Plans – Listed by State" Edvisords, accessed March 7, 2018, https://www.edvisors.com/plan-for-college/saving-for-college/prepaid-tuition-plans/state-list/.


**Playing Catch-Up**

**Studies estimate a 50 percent probability**: Charles D. Ellis, Alicia H. Munnell, and Andrew D. Eschtruth, *Falling Short: The Coming Retirement Crisis and What to Do About It* (New York, NY: Oxford University Press, 2014).

**Studies estimate a 50 percent probability**: Samantha M. Azzarello, Gabriela D. Santos, Alexander W. Dryden, David M. Lebovitz, Abigail D. Yoder, John C. Manley, Jordan K. Jackson, Tyler J. Voight, and David P. Kelly, "Guide to the Markets," J.P. Morgan Asset Management, accessed February 28, 2018, https://am.jpmorgan.com/us/en/asset-management/gim/adv/insights/guide-to-the-markets/viewer.

**Roughly 10,000 baby boomers will turn sixty-five each day**: Cohn, D'Vera and Paul Taylor, "Baby Boomers Approach 65 – Glumly," Pew Research Center (December 2010), http://www.pewsocialtrends.org/2010/12/20/baby-boomers-approach-65-glumly/.

**The S&P 500 declined 86 percent**: Azzarello et al., "Guide to the Markets."

**Unemployment reached a high of 25 percent**: Ellis et al., *Falling Short*.

**5.1 workers paying into the system**: Gayle L. Reznik, Dave Shoffner, and David A. Weaver, "Coping with the Demographic Challenge: Fewer Children and Living Longer," Social Security Administration, Vol 66, no 4 (2005/2006), https://www.ssa.gov/policy/docs/ssb/v66n4/v66n4p37.html.

**By 2014, the worker-to-beneficiary ratio had fallen to 2.8 and is projected to be 2.1 in 2034**: "Fast Facts & Figures About Social Security, 2015," Social Security Administration no 13-11785 (2015), https://www.ssa.gov/policy/docs/chartbooks/fast_facts/2015/fast_facts15.pdf.

**Maximum 2015 social security benefit**: "Workers with Maximum-Taxable Earnings," Social Security Administration, accessed March 21, 2018, https://www.ssa.gov/oact/cola/examplemax.html.

**Workers were covered by a pension plan**: Ellis et al., *Falling Short*.

**Employee 401(k) coverage increasing from 38 percent to 84 percent**: Ellis et al., *Falling Short*.

**Average retirement for males**: "Retirement Period of Males, 1962-2050," Center for Retirement Research at Boston College, March 2013, http://crr.bc.edu/wp-content/uploads/1012/01/figure-101.pdf.

**Americans had negative savings rates in 2005 and 2006**: "U.S. savings rate sinks to lowest since Great Depression – Business – International Herald Tribune," *New York Times*, 2007, http://www.nytimes.com/2007/02/01/business/worldbusiness/01iht-save.4436274.html.

**Estimates 50 percent of households may not have enough saved**: Alicia H. Munnell, Wenliang Hou, and Geoffrey T. Sanzenbacher, "Do Households Have A Good Sense of Their Retirement Preparedness?"

Center for Retirement Research at Boston College 17-4 (2017), http://crr.bc.edu/wp-content/uploads/2017/02/IB_17-4.pdf.

**The Employee Benefit Research Institute's 2017 Retirement Confidence Survey**: Lisa Greenwald, Craig Copeland, and Jack VanDerhei, "The 2017 Retirement Confidence Survey—Many Workers Lack Retirement Confidence and Feel Stressed About Retirement Preparations," EBRI Issue Brief, no. 431 (Employee Benefit Research Institute, March 21, 2017).

**Most workers expect to retire**: Greenwald et al., "The 2017 Retirement Confidence Survey."

**Social Security benefits are not intended to be your only source of income when you retire**: Berryhill, Nancy A. "Your Social Security Statement," Social Security Administration, accessed January 2, 2018, https://www.ssa.gov/myaccount/materials/pdfs/SSA-7005-SM-SI%20Wanda%20Worker%20Near%20retirement.pdf.

**Expected retirement age of sixty-five**: Greenwald et al., "The 2017 Retirement Confidence Survey."

**Median retirement age of retirees**: Greenwald et al., "The 2017 Retirement Confidence Survey."

**Of those who retired early**: Greenwald et al., "The 2017 Retirement Confidence Survey."

**A sixty-five-year-old in 2018**: "Life Expectancy," Social Security Administration, accessed March 21, 2018, https://www.ssa.gov/planners/lifeexpectancy.html.

**Inflation has ranged**: US Bureau of Labor Statistics. Databases, Tables & Calculators by Subject Consumer Price Index - All Urban Consumers, U.S. Bureau of Labor Statistics, accessed February 20, 2017, https://data.

bls.gov/timeseries/CUUR0000SA0?output_view=pct_12mths. Web. 20 Feb. 2017.

**Social Security benefits are not intended**: "Your Social Security Statement," Social Security Administration, accessed January 2, 2018, https://www.ssa.gov/myaccount/materials/pdfs/SSA-7005-SM-SI%20 Wanda%20Worker%20Near%20retirement.pdf.

**Required employers to increase their pension contributions by nearly three times**: Marric Buessing and Mauricio Soto, 2006, "The State of Private Pensions: Current 5500 Data," Issue in Brief 42. Chestnut Hill, MA: Center for Retirement Research at Boston College.

## Time Horizon Diversification

**3.3 year average stock market recovery**: Mark Hulbert, "Don't Fear the Bear." *The Wall Street Journal*. Dow Jones & Company, 7 Mar. 2014. Web. 20 Feb. 2017.

**Inflation has averaged between 2.1 percent to 4.1 percent per year**: US Bureau of Labor Statistics. Databases, Tables & Calculators by Subject Consumer Price Index - All Urban Consumers, U.S. Bureau of Labor Statistics, accessed February 20, 2017, https://data.bls.gov/ timeseries/CUUR0000SA0?output_view=pct_12mths. Web. 20 Feb. 2017.

## Tax Treatment Diversification

**Highest Historical Income and Long-Term Capital Gain Tax Rates**: "2015 Tax Brackets," Tax Foundation, last modified October 2014, https://taxfoundation.org/2015-tax-brackets.

**Highest Historical Income and Long-Term Capital Gain Tax Rates**: "Top Federal Income Tax Rates Since 1913," Citizens for Tax Justice, last modified November 2011, http://www.ctj.org/pdf/regcg.pdf.

**Highest Historical Income and Long-Term Capital Gain Tax Rates**: "Historical Individual Income Tax Parameters," Tax Policy Center, last modified October 2017. http://www.taxpolicycenter.org/statistics/historical-individual-income-tax-parameters.

**Highest Historical Income and Long-Term Capital Gain Tax Rates**: "Top Federal Income Tax Rates Since 1913," Citizens for Tax Justice, last modified November 2011, http://www.ctj.org/pdf/regcg.pdf.

**Dollar amounts adjusted for inflation**: "CPI Inflation Calculator," Bureau of Labor Statistics, accessed March 21, 2018, https://data.bls.gov/cgi-bin/cpicalc.pl?cost1=20&year1=198501&year2=201701.

**Asset Class Diversification**

**Down from 40 percent in 1960**: Mike Patton, "U.S. Role in Global Economy Declines Nearly 50%," *Forbes*, last modified February 29, 2016, https://www.forbes.com/sites/mikepatton/2016/02/29/u-s-role-in-global-economy-declines-nearly-50/#66d393985e9e.

**Accounts for about 25 percent of worldwide economic production**: "World Development Indicators," The World Bank, last modified March 1, 2018, https://datacatalog.worldbank.org/dataset/world-development-indicators.

**China's 1.4 billion people**: "World Population Prospects: The 2017 Revision," United Nations, last modified June 21, 2017, https://www.un.org/development/desa/publications/world-population-prospects-the-2017-revision.html.

**Middle class projected to reach 550 million consumers**: Kim Iskyan, "China's Middle Class is Exploding," *Business Insider*, last modified August 27, 2016, http://www.businessinsider.com/chinas-middle-class-is-exploding-2016-8.

**India, home to 1.3 billion**: "World Population Prospects: The 2017 Revision," United Nations, last modified June 21, 2017, https://www.un.org/development/desa/publications/world-population-prospects-the-2017-revision.html.

**Expected to surpass China as the world's most populous by 2024**: "World Population Prospects: The 2017 Revision," United Nations, last modified June 21, 2017, https://www.un.org/development/desa/publications/world-population-prospects-the-2017-revision.html.

**Home to over 85 percent of global population**: "IMF DataMapper - Population," International Monetary Fund, accessed March 21, 2018, http://www.imf.org/external/datamapper/LP@WEO/OEMDC/ADVEC/WEOWORLD.

**Only 40 percent of economic production**: "IMF DataMapper – GDP, current prices," International Monetary Fund, accessed March 21, 2018, http://www.imf.org/external/datamapper/LP@WEO/OEMDC/ADVEC/WEOWORLD.

**A commonly cited *Financial Analysts Journal* article**: Gary P. Brinson, L. Randolph Hood, and Gilbert L. Beebower, "Determinants of Portfolio Performance," *Financial Analysts Journal* 42, no. 4 (1986): 39–48.

**A commonly cited *Financial Analysts Journal* article**: Gary P. Brinson, Brian D. Singer, and Gilbert L. Beebower, "Determinants of Portfolio Performance II: An Update," *Financial Analysts Journal* 47, no. 3 (1991): 40–8.

**Subsequent studies**: Joseph H. Davis, Francis M. Kinniry Jr., Glenn Sheay, "The Asset Allocation Debate: Provacative Questions, Enduring Realities," Vanguard (2007), https://www.vanguard.com/pdf/icradd.pdf.

**Subsequent studies**: Roger G. Ibbotson and Paul D. Kaplan, "Does Asset Allocation Policy Explain 40, 90, or 100 Percent of Performance?" *Financial Analysts Journal* (2000) 56(1):26–33.

**As famed investor Warren Buffett acknowledges**: Warren Buffet, "Buy American. I Am." *New York Times*, 2008, http://www.nytimes.com/2008/10/17/opinion/17buffett.html.

**Not a single ideal strategy for rebalancing**: Colleen M. Jaconetti, Francis M. Kinniry Jr., and Yan Zilbering, "Best Practices for Portfolio Rebalancing," Vanguard (2010), https://www.vanguard.com/pdf/ISGPORE.pdf.

**The SPIVA scorecard**: Aye M. Soe, and Ryan Poirier, "SPIVA U.S. Year-End 2016 Scorecard," S&P Dow Jones Indices (2016), https://us.spindices.com/documents/spiva/spiva-us-year-end-2016.pdf.

**Vanguard's "Keys to improving the odds of active management success" study**: Daniel W. Wallick, Brian R. Wimmer, and James Balsamo, "Keys to improving the odds of active management success," Vanguard (2015), https://personal.vanguard.com/pdf/ISGKEY.pdf.

**Low cost has proven to be the most consistent and effective quantitative factor**: Wallick et al., "Keys to improving the odds of active management success."

**Growing consensus**: Antti Petajisto, "Active Share and Mutual Fund Performance," *Financial Analysts Journal* 69, no. 4 (2013) 73–93.

**Growing consensus**: Todd Schlanger, Christopher B. Philips, and Karin Peterson LaBarge, "The search for outperformance: Evaluating 'active share,'" Vanguard (2012), https://institutional.vanguard.com/iam/pdf/VIPS_outperformance.pdf.

**Studies have found low active share to be predictive of underperformance**: Petajisto, "Active Share and Mutual Fund Performance."

**Studies have found low active share to be predictive of underperformance**: Schlanger et al., "The search for outperformance: Evaluating 'active share.'"

**US equity mutual funds in the top active share quintile outperformed**: Petajisto, "Active Share and Mutual Fund Performance."

**Investor in the Mirror**

**Their 1979 landmark paper**: Daniel Kahneman and Amos Tversky, "Prospect Theory: An Analysis of Decision under Risk," *Econometrica* 47, no. 2 (1979): 263–291.

**Backed by research**: Terrance Odean, "Do investors trade too much?" *American Economic Review* 89 (1999): 1279–1298.

**One review**: Francis M. Kinniry Jr., Colleen M. Jaconetti, Michael A. DiJoseph, Yan Zilbering, and Donald G. Bennyhoff, "Putting a value on your value: Quantifying Vanguard Advisor's Alpha," Vanguard (2016), https://www.vanguard.com/pdf/ISGQVAA.pdf.

**A separate study**: Kinniry et al., "Putting a value on your value: Quantifying Vanguard Advisor's Alpha."

**One survey found 93 percent of American drivers polled consider their driving skills to be above average**: Ola Svenson, "Are we all less risky and more skillful than our fellow drivers?" *Acta Psychologica* 47 (1981): 143–148.

**Several studies**: Daniel Dorn and Gur Humberman, "Talk and action: what individual investors say and what they do," *Review of Finance* 9 (2005): 437–481.

**Several studies**: Markus Glaser and Martin Weber, "Overconfidence and trading volume," *Geneva Risk and Insurance Revue* 32 (2007): 1–36.

**Several studies**: Brad M. Barber and Terrance Odean, "Trading is hazardous to your wealth: The common stock investment performance of individual investors," *Journal of Finance* 55 (2000): 773–806.

**Several studies**: Brad M. Barber and Terrance Odean, "Boys will be boys: Gender, overconfidence, and common stock investment," *Quarterly Journal of Economics* 116 (2001): 261–292.

**Investors with an average level of trading trailed the market by 1.50 percent a year**: Brad M. Barber and Terrance Odean, "Trading is hazardous to your wealth: The common stock investment performance of individual investors," *Journal of Finance* 55 (2000): 773–806.

**Men, on average, were more overconfident**: Brad M. Barber and Terrance Odean, "Boys will be boys: Gender, overconfidence, and common stock investment," *Quarterly Journal of Economics* 116 (2001): 261–292.

Barber, Brad M. and Odean, Terrance, The Behavior of Individual Investors (September 7, 2011). Available at SSRN: https://ssrn.com/abstract=1872211 or http://dx.doi.org/10.2139/ssrn.1872211

# INDEX

# DISCLOSURES

Examples are hypothetical and for illustrative purposes only. Rates of return do not represent any actual investment and cannot be guaranteed. Any investment involves potential loss of principal. Cambridge does not provide tax, insurance, or legal advice. Please consult with your tax, insurance, or legal professional to discuss your unique circumstances.

Diversification and asset allocation strategies do not assure profit or protect against loss.

Investing regular amounts steadily over time (dollar-cost averaging) may lower your average per-share cost. Periodic investment programs cannot guarantee profit or protect against loss in a declining market. Dollar-cost averaging is a long-term strategy involving continuous investing, regardless of fluctuating price levels, and, as a result, you should consider your financial ability to continue to invest during periods of fluctuating price levels

Investors should carefully consider investment objectives, risks, charges, and expenses. This and other important information are contained in the fund prospectuses, summary prospectuses, and 529 Product Program Description, which can be obtained from a financial professional and should be read carefully before investing. Depending on your state of residence, there may be an in-state plan that offers tax and other benefits, which may include financial aid, scholarship funds, and protection from creditors. Before investing in any state's 529 plan, investors should consult a tax advisor. If withdrawals from 529 plans are used for purposes other than qualified education, the earnings will be subject to a 10 percent federal tax penalty in addition to federal and, if applicable, state income tax.

The Dow Jones Industrial Average (DJIA) is a price-weighted index composed of thirty widely traded blue-chip US common stocks. The S&P 500 is a market-cap weighted index composed of the common stocks of five hundred leading companies in leading industries of the US economy. The NASDAQ Composite Index is a market-value weighted index of all common stocks listed on the NASDAQ stock exchange. The Russell 2000 is a market-cap weighted index composed of two thousand US small-cap common stocks. The Global Dow is an equally weighted index of 150 widely traded blue-chip common stocks worldwide. Market indexes listed are unmanaged and are not available for direct investment.

# ABOUT THE AUTHORS

## Marshall Weintraub, CFP®

Marshall's practice focuses on the special planning challenges doctors and their families face. His areas of professional interest include student loan management, home buying, and investment portfolio design. In addition to this book, he has written personal finance articles for the American College of Cardiology. Marshall graduated from the University of Washington, where he endured an 0–12 football season. He remains a cautiously optimistic Huskies fan.

## Michael Merrill, CFP®, ChFC®, CLU®

Michael Merrill is a senior partner and financial advisor at Finity Group and one of the original founding members of Finity Group. He's directly involved in a wide scope of the firm's operations, most notably leading marketing efforts and setting a tone of integrity and diligence as the head of our compliance supervision department. Michael also maintains a personal financial planning practice, serving the needs of high net worth families by directly assisting in the development and maintenance of their financial plan strategies. His professional certifications include CERTIFIED FINANCIAL PLANNER™, Chartered Financial Consultant® (ChFC®), and Chartered Life Underwriter® (CLU®).

## Cole Kimball, CFA, AIF®

Cole serves as the Chief Investment Officer at Finity Group and as a financial advisor to his clients. After graduating from the University of Colorado Boulder, he started his career on the institutional side of finance working at different boutique broker-dealers before transitioning to the advisor role. In his free time, Cole enjoys being active and taking advantage of all the outdoor opportunities the Pacific Northwest has to offer. In the winter, there is a good chance you will bump into him on the mountains snowboarding, and in the summer, biking around town.